# THE MOTORIST'S INTERPRETER

2nd edition

Haynes

English Edition first published in Great Britain by
G T Foulis & Company Limited 1968
Reprinted 1970 and 1973 in Italy by AME-Stabilimento Grafico of Rome,
under ISBN 0 85429 087 7

This Second Edition 1975 is published by
Haynes Publishing Group
Sparkford Yeovil Somerset BA22 7JJ
England
Reprinted 1977, 1979

**ISBN 0 85696 278 3**

**A book in the HAYNES OWNERS HANDBOOK series**

INDEX

INDICE

INDEX

INHALTSVERZEICHNIS

INDICE

SADRZAJ

Index for Motorists Interpreter

ON THE ROAD

IN VIAGGIO

EN VOYAGE

AUF DER REISE

DE VIAJE

NA PUTU

| English | Italiano | Français |
|---|---|---|
| **FRONTIER POLICE** | **POLIZIA DI FRONTIERA** | **POLICE DE FRONTIERE** |
| Your passport / your identity card, please. | Prego, il suo passaporto / la sua carta d'identità. | Votre passeport / votre carte d'identité, s'il vous plaît. |
| Here is my passport. | Ecco il mio passaporto. | Voici mon passeport. |
| This passport is out of date. | Questo passaporto è scaduto. | Ce passeport est périmé. |
| Please look at the other pages. On one of them there is a renewal stamp. | Guardi per favore nelle pagine successive. C'è un timbro di rinnovo. | Veuillez regarder les pages suivantes: il y a un cachet de renouvellement. |
| Your passport is not valid for this country. | Il suo passaporto non è valido per questo paese. | Votre passeport n'est pas valable pour ce pays. |
| The extension of validity is on page. . . | L'estensione di validità è segnata alla pagina . . . | La prorogation de validité est à la page... |
| You have no visa for this country. | Non ha il « visto » per questo paese. | Vous n'avez pas le visa pour ce pays. |
| You can apply for one at the Consulate at . . . | Può richiederlo al Consolato a . . . | Vous pourrez le demander au Consulat à... |
| What are the names of your children and on which passport are they shown? | Come si chiamano i figli e su quale passaporto sono segnati? | Comment s'appellent vos enfants? Sur quel passeport figurent-ils? |
| On my wife's passport. | Sul passaporto di mia moglie. | Sur le passeport de ma femme. |
| Have you got vaccination certificates? | Ha i certificati di vaccinazione? | Avez-vous les certificats de vaccination? |
| You must be vaccinated, otherwise you cannot enter. | E' necessario fare le vaccinazioni, altrimenti lei non potrà entrare. | La vaccination est obligatoire, sinon vous ne pourrez pas entrer. |
| How long are you staying in this country? | Quanto tempo si tratterrà in questo paese? | Combien de temps pensez-vous séjourner dans ce pays? |
| How much money have you in foreign currency / in currency of this country / in traveller's cheques? | Quanto danaro ha in valuta estera / valuta di questo paese / in traveller's cheques? | Combien d'argent portez-vous en devises étrangères / en devises de ce pays / en traveller's chèques? |
| **I Passport and identity card** 1. validity 2. renewal 3. renewal stamp 4. stamp 5. prolongation of passport 6. photograph 7. husband 8. wife 9. children 10. visa 11. consulate 12. embassy. **II Vaccination certificates** 1. typhoid 2. smallpox 3. cholera 4. yellow fever. **III Currency** 1. coin 2. bank note 3. small denomination bank note 4. large denomination bank note. | **I Passaporto e carta d'identità** 1. validità 2. rinnovo 3. timbro di rinnovo 4. bollo 5. estensione del passaporto 6. fotografia 7. marito 8. moglie 9. figli 10. visto 11. consolato 12. ambasciata. **II Certificati di vaccinazione** 1. tifo 2. vaiolo 3. colera 4. febbre gialla. **III Valuta** 1. moneta 2. banconota 3. banconota di piccolo taglio 4. banconota di grosso taglio. | **I Passeport et carte d'identité** 1. validité 2. renouvellement 3. cachet de renouvellement 4. timbre 5. prorogation du passeport 6. photographie 7. mari 8. femme 9. enfants 10. visa 11. consulat 12. ambassade. **II Certificats de vaccination** 1. typhoïde 2. variole 3. choléra 4. fièvre jaune. **III Devises** 1. pièce de monnaie 2. billet 3. petite coupure 4. grosse coupure. |
| **CAR TRANSIT** | **TRANSITO DELLE VETTURE** | **PASSAGE DES VOITURES** |
| Your registration book, please. | Prego, il suo libretto di circolazione. | Votre carte grise, s'il vous plait. |
| Have you got a triptyque / green card? | Ha il trittico / la carta verde? | Avez-vous le tryptique / la carte verte? |
| Is my driving licence valid for this country? | La mia patente di guida è valida per questo paese? | Mon permis de conduire est-il valable dans ce pays? |
| I have an international driving licence. | Ho la patente internazionale | J'ai le permis international |

| Deutsch | Español | Srpsko-hrvatski |
|---|---|---|
| **GRENZPOLIZEI** | **POLICIA DE FRONTERA** | **PROGRANICNA MILICIJA** |
| Ihren Pass / Ihren Personalausweis bitte. | Por favor, su pasaporte / su carnet de circulación. | Molin vas pasoš / vašu ličnu kartu. |
| Hier ist mein Pass. | Aquí tiene mi pasaporte. | Evo mog pasoša. |
| Dieser Pass ist abgelaufen. | Su pasaporte ha caducado. | Ovom pasošu je istekla važnost. |
| Bitte sehen Sie auf den folgenden Seiten nach. Dort ist der Verlängerungsstempel. | Mire, por favor, en las páginas siguientes, donde está el timbre de renovación. | Pogledajte molim vas naredne stranice. Postoji pečat sa produženjem. |
| Ihr Pass ist für dieses Land nicht gültig. | Su pasaporte no es valedero para este país. | Vas pasoš ne važi za ovu zemlju. |
| Die Länder, für die der Pass gilt, sind auf Seite . . . angeführt. | La extensión de validez está indicada en la página... | Produženje važnosti je uneseno na strani . . . |
| Es fehlt der Sichtvermerk für dieses Land. | No tiene el « visado » para este país | Nemate vizu za ovu zemlju. |
| Wenden Sie sich an das Konsulat in . . . | Puede pedirlo al Consulado de... | Možete je zatražiti na Konzulatu u . . . |
| Wie ist der Name der Kinder und in welchem Pass sind sie eingetragen? | ¿Cuál es el nombre de los hijos que vienen con Vd. y en qué pasaporte están inscritos? | Kako se zovu djeca i na koji paso su unesena? |
| Im Pass meiner Frau. | Están inscritos en el pasaporte de mi mujer. | Na pasoš moje žene. |
| Haben Sie die Impfzeugnisse? | ¿Tiene el certificado de vacuna? | Imate li potvrdu o vakcinaciji? |
| Sie müssen sich impfen lassen, sonst können Sie nicht einreisen. | Tiene que vacunarse, de lo contrario no podrá obtener el visado de entrada. | Potrebno je izvršiti vakcinaciju, jer u protivnom nećete moći ući. |
| Wie lange werden Sie sich in diesem Land aufhalten? | ¿Cuánto tiempo se quedarà aquí? | Koliko vremena ćete se zadržati u ovoj zemlji? |
| Wieviel Geld haben Sie in ausländischer Valuta / in unserer Währung / in traveller's cheques? | ¿Cuánto dinero lleva en divisa extranjera / divisa de este país / en traveller's cheques? | Koliko novaca imate u stranoj valuti / u valuti ove zemlje / u traveller's čekovima? |
| **I. Pass und Personalausweis** 1. Gültigkeit 2. Verlängerung 3. Verlängerungsstempel 4. Stempel 5. Geltungsbereich 6. Foto 7. Mann 8. Ehefrau 9. Kinder 10. Sichtvermerk 11. Konsulat 12. Botschaft. **II. Impfzeugnisse** 1. Typhus 2. Pocken 3. Cholera 4. gelbes Fieber. **III. Valuta** 1. Münzen 2. Banknoten 3. kleine Banknoten 4. grosse Banknoten. | **I Pasaporte y carnet de identidad** 1. Validez 2. renovación 3. timbre de renovación 4. sello 5. extensión del pasaporte 6. fotografía 7. marido 8. mujer 9. hijos 10. visado 11. consulado 12. embajada. **II Certificados de vacuna** 1. tifus 2. viruela 3. cólera 4. fiebre amarilla. **III Divisas** 1. moneda 2. billetes de banco 3. billetes inferiores a . . . 4. billetes superiores a . . . | **I Pasoš i lična karta** 1. važnost 2. produženje 3. pečat sa produženjem 4. taksa 5. produženje pasoša 6. fotografija 7. muž 8. žena 9. djeca 10. viza 11. konzulat 12. ambasada. **II Potvrde o vakcinaciji** 1. tifus 2. velike boginje 3. kolera 4. žuta groznica. **III Valuta** 1 sitni novac 2. novčanica 3. sitna novčanica 4. krupna novčanica. |
| **FAHRZEUGKONTROLLE** | **TRANSITO DEL COCHE** | **PRIJELAZ VOZILA** |
| Ihren Fahrzeugschein bitte. | ¿Por favor, el permiso de circulación? | Molim vašu saobraćajnu knjižicu. |
| Haben Sie das Triptik / die grüne Karte? | ¿Tiene Vd. el tríptico / la carta verde? | Imate li triptik / zeleni list osiguranja? |
| Ist mein Führerschein in diesem Land gültig? | ¿Mi carnet de conducir, es valedero en este país? | Da li je moja vozačka dozvola važeća za ovu zemlju? |
| Ich habe den internationalen Führerschein. | Tengo el carnet internacional. | Imam internacionalnu vozačku dozvolu. |

| English | Italiano | Français |
| --- | --- | --- |
| Are you insured for third party risks? | E' assicurato per la responsabilità civile? | Etes-vous assuré pour la responsabilité civile? |
| How much does it cost to insure for a week / for a month? | Quanto costa assicurarsi per una settimana / per un mese? | Combien coûte l'assurance pour une semaine / pour un mois? |
| You can get this information at the Automobile Club frontier office. One of the staff there speaks your language. | Può informarsi presso l'ufficio di frontiera dell'Automobile Club. C'è un impiegato che parla la sua lingua. | Vous pourrez obtenir ces renseignements au bureau de l'Automobile Club de la frontière; il y a un employé qui parle votre langue. |
| How long can the car stay in this country? | Quanto tempo può restare l'auto in questo paese? | Combien de temps la voiture peut-elle rester dans ce pays? |
| You must cross the frontier again in a month / three months. | Deve ripassare la frontiera dopo un mese / tre mesi. | Il vous faut repasser la frontière dans un mois / trois mois. |
| How can I get a temporary import number plate? | Come si può ottenere la targa EE? | Comment peut-on obtenir la plaque d'immatriculation EE? |
| Is it possible to get petrol coupons? | E' possibile avere buoni benzina? | Puis-je avoir des bons d'essence? |
| How many litres of petrol are allowed? | Quanti litri di benzina vengono concessi? | A combien de litres d'essence a-t-on droit? |
| You can apply for further coupons at the Automobile Club headquarters in other towns. | Può richiedere altri buoni nella sede dell'Automobile Club in altre città. | Vous pourrez obtenir d'autres bons au siège de l'Automobile Club dans d'autres villes. |
| What is the number of octanes in the standard petrol? | Qual è il numero di ottano della benzina normale? | Quel est l'indice d'octane de l'essence normale? |
| **I Documents** 1. registration book 2. triptyque 3. driving licence 4. international driving licence 5. green card 6. compulsory insurance 7. third party insurance. **II Petrol coupons** 1. detachable coupons 2. maximum number of coupons 3. litres 4. standard / premium petrol 5. pre-payment 6. refund 7. validity 8. expiration 9. entries 10. car number 11. date when cashed. | **I Documenti** 1. libretto di circolazione 2. trittico 3. patente di guida 4. patente internazionale 5. carta verde 6. assicurazione obbligatoria 7. assicurazione per la responsabilità civile. **II Buoni benzina** 1. tagliandi 2. numero massimo dei tagliandi 3. litri 4. benzina normale / super 5. pagamento anticipato 6. rimborso 7. validità 8. scadenza 9. annotazioni 10. numero di targa 11. data dei rifornimenti. | **I Papiers** 1. carte grise 2. tryptique 3. permis de conduire 4. permis international 5. carte verte 6. assurance obligatoire 7. assurance pour la responsabilité civile. **II Bons d'essence** 1. coupons 2. nombre maximum de coupons 3. litres 4. essence normale / super 5. paiement d'avance 6. remboursement 7. validité 8. échéance 9. annotations 10. numéro de la plaque d'immatriculation 11. dates de ravitaillement. |

## CUSTOMS / DOGANA / DOUANE

| CUSTOMS | DOGANA | DOUANE |
| --- | --- | --- |
| Have you anything to declare? | Lei ha nulla da dichiarare? | Vous n'avez rien à déclarer? |
| Have you any cigarettes? How many? | Ha sigarette? Quante? | Avez-vous des cigarettes? Combien? |
| Only ten packets. | Solo dieci pacchetti. | Dix paquets seulement. |
| Have you any spirits / wines? | Ha liquori / vini? | Avez-vous des liqueurs / du vin? |
| Only one opened bottle / one unopened flask. | Solo una bottiglia aperta / un fiasco chiuso. | Seulement une bouteille entamée / une fiasque fermée. |
| You must declare your car radio / the spare wheel. | Deve dichiarare l'autoradio / la ruota di scorta. | Vous devez déclarer la radio de la voiture / la roue de secours. |
| Open the luggage boot, please. | Apra il portabagagli, per favore. | Veuillez ouvrir le coffre à bagages, s'il vous plaît. |
| Open this case / this package / this bag. | Apra questa valigia / questo pacco / questa borsa. | Veuillez ouvrir cette valise / ce paquet / ce sac. |

| Deutsch | Español | Srpsko-hrvatski |
| --- | --- | --- |
| Sind Sie haftpflichtversichert? | ¿Está asegurado contra la responsabilidad civil? | Da li ste osigurani za gradjansku odgovornost? |
| Wie hoch ist die Versicherungsprämie für eine Woche / für einen Monat? | ¿Cuál es el valor de la prima de seguro por una semana / por un mes? | Kolika je cijena osiguranja za jedan tjedan / za jedan mjesec? |
| Sie können sich bei der Grenzgeschäftsstelle des Automobil-Clubs erkundigen. Dort ist ein Beamter, der Ihre Sprache spricht. | Puede Vd. informarse en la oficina de frontera del Automóvil Club. Hay un empleado que habla su idioma. | Možete se informirati kod pograničnog ureda Auto kluba. Jedan namještenik govori vaš jezik. |
| Wie lange kann ich mich mit dem Wagen in diesem Land aufhalten? | ¿Cuánto tiempo puede quedar el coche en este país? | Koliko vremena može automobil ostati u ovoj zemlji? |
| Sie müssen nach einem Monat / nach drei Monaten wieder ausreisen. | Tendrá que pasar de nuevo la frontera después de un mes / tres meses. | Mora ponovno prijeći granicu nakon mjesec dana / tri mjeseca. |
| Wie bekommt man die Zoll-Nummer? | ¿Cómo se puede conseguir la matrícula EE? | Uz koje se uslove može dobiti registracija « RP »? |
| Kann man Benzin-Gutscheine bekommen? | ¿Es posible obtenere cupones de gasolina? | Da li je moguće dobiti bonove za benzin? |
| Wieviel Liter Benzin werden bewilligt? | ¿Cuántos litros de gasolina se conceden? | Koliko litara benzina su dozvoljeni? |
| Sie können bei den Geschäftsstellen des Automobil-Clubs in anderen Städten weitere Gutscheine beziehen. | Puede Vd. solicitar otros cupones en la oficina del Automóvil Club de otras ciudades. | Možete zatražiti bonove u sjedištu Auto kluba u drugim gradovima. |
| Wie hoch ist die Oktanzahl des Normalbenzins? | ¿Cuál es el número de octanos de la gasolina normal? | Koliki je oktanski broj normalnog benzina? |
| **I. Papiere** 1. Kraftfahrzeugschein 2. Triptik 3. Führerschein 4. internationaler Führerschein 5. grüne Karte 6. Pflichtversicherung 7. Haftpflichtversicherung **II. Benzin-Gutscheine** 1. Kupons 2. höchste Kuponzahl 3. Liter 4. Normalbenzin / Superbenzin 5. Vorauszahlung 6. Rückvergütung 7. Gültigkeit 8. Verfall 9. Eintragungen 10. Kennzeichen 11. Datum der Einlösung. | **I Documentos** 1. permiso de circulación 2. tríptico 3. carnet de conducir 4. carnet de conducir internacional 5. carta verde 6. seguro obligatorio 7. seguro contra la responsabilidad civil. **II Cupones de gasolina** 1. cupones 2. número máximo de cupones 3. litros 4. gasolina normal / super 5. Pago adelantado 6. reembolso 7. validez 8. vencimiento 9. observaciones 10. número de matrícula 11. Fecha de los abastecimientos. | **I Dokumenti** 1. saobraćajna knjižica 2. triptik 3. vozačka dozvola 4. internacionalna vozačka dozvola 5. zeleni list osiguranja 6. obavezno osiguranje 7. osiguranje za gradjansku odgovornost. **II Bonovi za benzin** 1. kuponi 2. maksimalni broj kupona 3. litre 4. normalni benzin / super 5. plaćanje unaprijed 6. naknada 7. važnost 8. istek 9. napomena 10. registarski broj 11. datum opskrbe. |

## ZOLL / ADUANA / CARINA

| ZOLL | ADUANA | CARINA |
| --- | --- | --- |
| Haben Sie etwas zu verzollen? | ¿Tiene Vd. algo que declarar? | Nemate ništa za deklarirati? |
| Haben Sie Zigaretten? Wieviel? | ¿Lleva cigarillos? ¿Qué cantidad? | Imate li cigarete? Koliko? |
| Nur zehn Schachteln. | Sólo diez paquetes. | Samo deset kutija? |
| Haben Sie Liköre / Weine? | ¿Trae licores / vinos? | Imate li žestokih pića / vina? |
| Nur eine offene Flasche / einen versiegelten Fiasco. | Sólo una botella descorchada / precintada. | Samo jednu otvorenu bocu / jednu zatvorenu pletenku. |
| Sie müssen das Autoradio / das Ersatzrad deklarieren. | Tiene que declarar el autoradio / la rueda de recambio. | Morate deklarirati autoradio / rezervni kotač. |
| Öffnen Sie den Gepäckraum bitte. | Abra por favor, el departamento de equipaje. | Molim, otvorite mi prtljažni prostor. |
| Öffnen Sie diesen Koffer / dieses Paket / diese Tasche. | Abra esta maleta / este paquete / esta cartera. | Otvorite ovaj kofer / ovaj paket / ovu torbu. |

| English | Italiano | Français |
|---|---|---|
| This case contains only personal belongings | Questa valigia contiene solo oggetti personali. | Cette valise ne contient que des effets personnels. |
| Here is the spare wheel / the tool bag. | Qui c'è la ruota di scorta / la borsa degli attrezzi. | Voici la roue de secours / la trousse à outils. |
| Have you got an export permit for this object? | Ha il permesso di esportazione per questo oggetto? | Avez-vous une licence d'exportation pour cet objet? |
| You will have to pay customs duties. | Lei dovrà pagare i diritti doganali. | Il vous faut acquitter les droits de douane. |
| How much must I pay? | Quanto devo pagare? | Combien dois-je payer? |
| If you fail to declare something beforehand, you'll have to pay a fine as well as customs duty. | In caso di mancata dichiarazione dovrà pagare una penalità oltre ai diritti di dogana. | En cas de non-déclaration, vous aurez une amende à payer, outre les droits de douane. |
| You would be committing an offence against the customs regulations. | Lei commetterebbe un reato contro la legge doganale. | Vous contreviendriez à la loi douanière. |
| **I Officials and rules** 1. customs inspector 2. excise officer 3. customs regulations 4. infringements of regulations 5. fine 6. customs declaration 7. import permit 8. export permit 9. import tax 10. export tax 11 customs duties. **II Objects to be declared** 1. cigarettes 2. cigars 3. tobacco 4. lighter 5. spirits 6. scent 7. camera 8. cinecamera 9. film 10. lens 11. filters 12. watch / clock 13. jewels 14. precious stones 15. diamonds 16. gold 17. chocolate 18. sweets 19. wool 20. silk 21. cotton 22. leather goods 23. medicines 24. painting 25 antique 26. car radio 27. transistor radio 28. portable television set 29. record player 30. spare wheel 31. tyres. | **I Funzionari e norme** 1. ispettore di dogana 2 guardia di finanza 3. leggi doganali 4. violazione delle norme 5. penalità 6. dichiarazione doganale 7. permesso di importazione 8. permesso di esportazione 9. tassa di importazione 10. tassa di esportazione 11. diritti doganali. **II Oggetti da dichiarare** 1. sigarette 2 sigari 3. tabacco 4. accendisigaro 5. liquori 6 profumi 7. macchina fotografica 8. cinepresa 9. pellicola 10. obiettivo 11. filtri 12. orologio 13. gioielli 14. pietre preziose 15. brillanti 16. oro 17. cioccolata 18. caramelle 19. lana 20. seta 21. cotone 22. oggetti in pelle 23. medicinali 24. quadro 25. oggetto d'antiquariato 26. autoradio 27. radio a transistor 28. televisore portatile 29. giradischi 30. ruota di scorta 31. gomme. | **I Fonctionnaires et règlements** 1. inspecteur de douane 2. garde de finance (douanier) 3. lois douanières 4. violation des règlements 5. amende 6. déclaration en douane 7. licence d'importation 8. licence d'exportation 9. taxe d'importation 10. taxe d'exportation 11 droits de douane. **II Objets à déclarer** 1. cigarettes 2. cigares 3. tabac 4. briquet 5. liqueurs 6. parfums 7. appareil photographique 8. caméra 9. pellicule 10. objectif 11. filtres 12. montre 13. bijoux 14. pierres précieuses 15. diamants 16. or 17. chocolat 18. bonbons 19. laine 20. soie 21. coton 22. objets de cuir 23. medicaments 24. tableau 25. antiquités 26. radio de voiture 27. radio à transistor 28. télévision portative 29. tourne-disques 30. roue de secours 31 pneus. |
| **MOTORWAY** | **AUTOSTRADA** | **AUTOROUTE** |
| Can you tell me please, where is the entry to the motorway for . . . ? | Per favore, dov'è l'ingresso dell'autostrada per . . . ? | Pouvez-vous m'indiquer l'entrée de l'autoroute pour . . . ? |
| How much is it as far as . . . ? | Quanto si paga per andare fino a . . . ? | Quel est le tarif jusqu'à ...? |
| The rates are fixed according to the horse power of the car. | Le tariffe sono fissate secondo la potenza delle vetture. | Le tarif est en fonction de la puissance des voitures. |
| Where must I branch off to go to . . . ? | Dove bisogna uscire per andare a . . . ? | Où faut-il sortir pour aller à ...? |
| You must leave the motorway at the . . . junction. | Dovrà uscire al casello di . . . | Vous devez sortir au poste de péage de ... |
| This motorway is open as far as . . . | Questa autostrada è in esercizio fino a . . . | Cette autoroute va jusqu'à ... |
| Don't lose this transit slip. If you do, you will have to pay the full rate when you leave the motorway. | Non smarrisca la scheda di passaggio. Altrimenti, uscendo, dovrà pagare l'intera tariffa. | Ne perdez pas votre ticket; sinon, à la sortie, il vous faudrait payer le tarif complet. |
| What is the maximum speed allowed on this motorway? | Qual è la velocità massima consentita su questa autostrada? | Quelle est la vitesse maximum autorisée sur cette autoroute? |

Dieser Koffer enthält nur Sachen für den persönlichen Gebrauch.

Esta maleta sólo contiene objetos personales.

Ovaj kofer sadrži samo predmete za ličnu upotrebu.

Hier ist das Ersatzrad / das Bordwerkzeug.

Aquí está la rueda de recambio / el saco con las herramientas.

Ovdje se nalazi rezervni kotač / torba sa alatom.

Haben Sie die Einfuhrerlaubnis für diesen Gegenstand?

¿Tiene Vd. el permiso de exportación para este objeto?

Imate li dozvolu izvoza za ovaj predmet?

Sie müssen Zoll zahlen.

Tendrá Vd. que pagar los derechos de aduana.

Morati ćete platiti carinske pristojbe

Wieviel muss ich zahlen?

¿Cuánto tengo que pagar?

Koliko moram platiti?

Wenn die Ware nicht deklariert wird, müssen Sie ausser dem Zollsatz eine Geldstrafe zahlen.

Si no declara antes lo que lleva, tendrá que pagar una multa, además de los derechos de aduana.

U slučaju neprijavljene robe, morati ćete platiti pored carinskih pristojbi još i kaznu.

Sie würden den Zollgesetzen zuwiderhandeln.

Vd. cometería una transgresión de la ley aduanera.

Vi bi učinili jedan akt, koji je u suprotnosti sa zakonom.

**I. Beamte und Bestimmungen** 1. Zollbeamter 2. Finanzer 3. Zollgesetz 4. Zuwiderhandlung gegen die Vorschriften 5. Geldstrafe 6. Zollerklärung 7. Einfuhrbewilligung 8. Ausfuhrbewilligung 9. Einfuhrzoll 10. Ausfuhrzoll 11. Zollsätze. **II. Deklarationspflichtige Gegenstände** 1. Zigaretten 2. Zigarren 3. Tabak 4. Feuerzeug 5. Spirituosen 6. Parfums 7. Fotoapparat 8. Filmapparat 9. Film 10. Objektiv 11. Filter 12. Uhr 13. Schmuck 14. Edelsteine 15. Brillanten 16. Gold 17. Schokolade 18. Fruchtbonbons 19. Wolle 20. Seide 21. Baumwolle 22. Lederwaren 23. Medikamente 24. Bild **25. Antiquitäten 26. Autoradio 27. Transistorengerät 28. Fernsehgerät 29. Plattenspieler 30. Ersatzrad 31. Reifen.**

**I Funcionarios y normas** 1. Inspector de aduanas 2. Guardia de Hacienda 3. leyes aduaneras 4. transgresión de las normas 5. multa 6. declaración aduanera 7. permiso de importación 8. permiso de exportación 9. derecho de importación 10. derecho de importación 11. derechos de aduana. **II Mercancias a declarar** 1. cigarrillos 2. cigarros puros 3. tabaco 4. encendedor 5. licores 6. perfumes 7. máquina fotográfica 8. filmadora 9. películas 10. objetivo 11. filtros 12. reloj 13. joyas 14. piedras preciosas 15. brillantes 16. oro 17. chocolate 18. caramelos 19. lana 20. seda 21. algodón **22. objetos de piel. 23 medicinas 24. cuadro 25. objetos de anticuariado 26. autoradio 27. radio de transistor 28. televisor portátil 29. tocadiscos 30. rueda de recambio 31. neumáticos.**

**I Funkcioneri i norme** 1. carinski inspektor 2. pogranična milicija 3. carinski zakoni 4. povreda normi 5. kažnjavanje 6. carinska deklaracija 7. dozvola uvoza 8. dozvola izvoza 9. uvozna taksa 10 izvozna taksa 11. carinsko pravo. **II Predmeti za deklaritati** 1. cigarete 2. cigare 3. duhan 4. upaljač za cigarete 5. žestoka pića 6. parfemi 7. fotografski aparat 8. kamera za snimaje 9. film 10. objektiv 11. filtri 12. sat 13. nakit 14. drago kamenje 15. briljanti 16. zlato 17. čokolada 18 bonboni 19. vuna 20. svila 21. pamuk 22. kožnati predmeti 23. lijekovi 24 slika 25. antikni predmeti 26. autoradio **27. tranzistorski radio 28. prjenosni televisor 29. gramofon 30. rezervni kotač 31. gume.**

## AUTOBAHN | AUTOPISTA | AUTOSTRADA

Bitte, wo ist die Autobahnzufahrt nach ...?

¿Dónde está, por favor, la entrada a la autopista para...?

Molim vas, gdje se nalazi ulaz na autostradu za ...?

Wie hoch sind die Gebühren bis ...?

¿Cuánto se paga para ir hasta...?

Koliko se plaća za vožnju do ...?

Der Betrag hängt von der Pferdestärke des Wagens ab.

La cantidad depende de la potencia de su coche.

Tarife su odredjene prema snazi vozila.

Wo ist die Ausfahrt nach ...?

¿Por dónde hay que salir para ir a...?

Gdje treba izaći da bi se stiglo u...?

Sie müssen bei der Sperre ... ausfahren.

Hay que salir por el puesto de...

Morati ćete izaći na izlaznoj stanici ...?

Diese Autobahn ist bis ... dem Verkehr übergeben.

Esta autopista llega hasta...

Ova autostrada vodi do ...

Verlieren Sie den Gebührenschein nicht, sonst müssen Sie bei der Ausfahrt den Gesamtbetrag, von der Ausgangsstation berechnet, bezahlen.

No pierda, por favor, el billete. De lo contrario, al salir, tendrá que pagar la cantidad total / el billette entero.

Nemojte izgubiti voznu karticu, jer ćete u protivnom morati platiti cijelu tarifu.

Wie hoch ist die auf dieser Autobahn erlaubte Höchstgeschwindigkeit?

¿Cuál es la velocidad máxima permitida en esta autopista?

Koja je maksimalna dozvoljena brzina na ovoj autostradi?

| English | Italiano | Français |
|---|---|---|
| There is no speed limit. | Non c'è alcun limite di velocità. | Il n'y a pas de limitation de vitesse |
| Signs along the road will give you the maximum speed. | Lungo il percorso troverà cartelli indicatori delle velocità consigliate. | Vous verrez le long du parcours des panneaux indiquant la vitesse maximum conseillée. |
| You must not exceed . . . kilometres an hour. | Non dovrà superare i . . . chilometri. | Vous ne devez pas dépasser . . . kilomètres. |
| Are there any icy stretches? | Vi sono dei tratti ghiacciati? | Y a-t-il des endroits verglacés? |
| Are there any road-works? | Vi sono lavori in corso? | Y a-t-il des travaux en cours? |
| There is a long stretch with single-lane traffic. | C'è un lungo tratto a corsia unica. | Il y a un long passage à voie unique. |
| There is a deviation from the . . . exit to the . . . exit. | C'è una deviazione dall'uscita di . . . all'uscita di . . . | Il y a une déviation depuis la sortie de ... jusqu'à celle de ... |
| It is forbidden to stop in the emergency lane except when the driver or one of the passengers feels unwell, or when the car has broken down. | Nella corsia di emergenza la sosta è vietata, salvo il caso di malessere del conducente o dei passeggeri, oppure di guasto alla vettura. | Il est interdit de stationner sur le couloir de secours, sauf en cas de panne, ou de malaise du conducteur ou de ses passagers. |
| Are there lay-bys? | Vi sono aree di parcheggio? | Il y a-t-il des plates-formes de parking? |
| Yes, every . . . kilometres. | Sì, ogni . . . chilometri. | Oui, tous les ... kilomètres. |
| Are there cafés and restaurants along the motorway? | Lungo l'autostrada vi sono bar e ristoranti? | Y a-t-il des bars et des restaurants le long de l'autoroute? |
| Yes, in all the service areas. | Sì, in tutte le aree di servizio. | Oui, dans toutes les stations de service. |
| You will find roadside cafes at . . . | Troverà degli autogrill nelle località di . . . | Vous trouverez des restauroutes à ... |
| How do I call the breakdown service, in case of need? | Come si fa, se necessario, a chiamare il soccorso stradale? | En cas de besoin, comment fait-on pour appeler le Secours Routier? |
| From the special telephone points, or by stopping a road police control car. | Dagli appositi posti telefonici, oppure fermando una pattuglia della polizia stradale. | Depuis les postes téléphoniques installés à cet effet, ou bien en arrêtant une patrouille de la police routière. |
| You only need to look out for signs with the letters SOS on them. | Basta osservare i cartelli con la scritta S.O.S. | Il suffit de repérer les panneaux portant la mention S.O.S. |
| If the car breaks down or someone is unwell, you only have to call the number shown at the telephone point. | In caso di guasto alla vettura o di malessere basta chiamare il numero indicato al posto telefonico. | En cas de panne ou de malaise du conducteur ou de ses passagers, il suffit d'appeler le numéro indiqué au poste téléphonique. |
| It is absolutely forbidden to cross the central reservation of the road. | E' assolutamente vietato attraversare l'aiuola spartitraffico. | Il est rigoureusement interdit de traverser l'accotement central. |
| How can I turn back? | Che cosa devo fare per invertire la marcia? | Que dois-je faire pour faire demi-tour? |
| You must leave the motorway at the next exit and re-enter by the opposite toll-point. | Deve uscire allo svincolo più vicino e rientrare al casello opposto | Il faut atteindre la sortie la plus proche et reprendre l'entrée opposée. |

| Deutsch | Español | Srpsko-hrvatski |
|---|---|---|
| Es besteht keine Geschwindigkeitsbegrenzung. | No hay límites de velocidad. | Ne postoji nikakovo ograničenje brzine. |
| Längs der Strecke stehen Schilder mit den empfohlenen Geschwindigkeiten. | A lo largo del recorrido, encontrará carteles indicadores de las velocidades aconsejadas. | Putem ćete naići na znakove sa preporučenom brzinom. |
| Sie dürfen . . . Kilometer nicht überschreiten. | No deberá superar los ... kilómetros. | Noćete smjeti prekoračiti . . . kilometara. |
| Gibt es vereiste Stellen? | ¿En esta autopista hay trechos helados? | Postoje li zaledjene dionice? |
| Gibt es Baustellen? | ¿Hay algún tramo en reparación? | Vrše li radovi na cesti? |
| Eine lange Strecke ist einspurig. | Hay un largo tramo de vía única. | Postoji jedna duga dionica sa jednosmejrnom stazom. |
| Von der Ausfahrt . . . bis zur Ausfahrt . . . finden Sie eine Umleitung. | Hay una desviación desde la salida de ... hasta la salida de ... | Postoji jedno skretanje od izlaza . . . do . . . |
| Auf dem befestigten Seitenstreifen ist das Halten untersagt, ausser im Fall des Unwohlseins des Fahrers oder der Insassen, oder im Fall einer Panne. | En la banda de emergencia está prohibido pararse, a no ser que el conductor se sienta mal o algunos de los pasajeros, o en caso de avería. | Na stazi za slučaj nužde zabranjeno je zaustavljanje, osim u slučaju ako se vozač ili putnici osjećaju loše, ili u slučaju kvara na vozilu. |
| Gibt es Parkplätze? | ¿Hay áreas para aparcar? | Postoje li parkirališta? |
| Ja, alle . . . Kilometer. | Sí, una cada ... kilómetros. | Da, svakih . . . kilometara. |
| Gibt es Bars und Restaurants längs der Autobahn? | ¿A lo largo de la autopista hay bares y restaurantes? | Postoje li putem uz autostradu restauracije? |
| Ja, in allen Service-Stationen. | Sí, se encuentran en todas las áreas de servicio. | Da, uz sva parkirališta. |
| Sie werden Autogrills bei . . . finden. | Encontrará autogrill en las localidades de . . . | Naići ćete na autorestauracije u slijedećim mjestima: . . |
| Wie ruft man im Notfall die Strassenhilfe? | Si es necesario, ¿qué hay que hacer para llamar al Socorro de carretera? | Sto je potrebno učiniti, da bi se u slučaju potrebe pozvala pomoć? |
| Über die Fernsprechstellen oder durch Anhalten einer Strassenpolizeistreife. | Llamar desde un teléfono público o parar a una patrulla de la Policía de carretera. | Nazvati sa odgovarajućih telefona ili zaustaviti milicijsku patrolu. |
| Beachten Sie die Schilder mit der Aufschrift S.O.S. | Basta con fijarse en los carteles con la inscripción S.O.S.. | Dovoljno je oučiti table sa natpisom S.O.S. |
| Im Fall einer Panne oder des Unwohlseins genügt es, die an den Notrufsäulen angeführte Nummer anzurufen. | En caso de avería o de malestar, basta con dirigirse al puesto telefónico y llamar al número indicado. | U slučaju kvara na vozilu ili bolesti dovolino je nazvati broj, označen uz telefon. |
| Es ist strengstens untersagt, den Grünstreifen zu überqueren | Está absolutamente prohibido cruzar la división de la autopista. | Apsolutno je zabranjeno prelaženje diobene površine autostrade |
| Wie kann ich wenden? | ¿Qué debo hacer para invertir el sentido de marcha? | Što je potrebno učiniti da bi se izmijenio smjer vožnje? |
| Sie müssen die Autobahn bei der nächsten Ausfahrt verlassen und über die entgegengesetzt liegende Zufahrt wieder einfahren. | Tiene que salir por la desvinculación más cercana y, por los empalmes, llegar a la entrada opuesta. | Morate izaći na prvoj izlaznoj stanici i ući na odgovarajućoj ulaznoj. |

**I Conditions and regulations** 1. smooth road surface 2. rough road surface 3. ice 4. snow 5. rain 6. mist 7. haze 8. toll road 9. toll 10. ticket 11. horse power of car 12. engine capacity 13. horse power 14. car 15. motor cycle 16. caravan 17. luggage / boat trailer 18. maximum speed 19. minimum speed 20. no parking. **II Equipment and services** 1. toll-point 2. entry 3. exit 4. lane 5. single lane 6. emergency stopping lane 7. central reservation 8. tunnel 9. viaduct 10. lay-by 11. service area 12. café 13. restaurant 14. snack-bar 15. breakdown service 16. breakdown vehicle 17. first aid 18. Red Cross 19. telephone point.

**I Condizioni e regolamenti** 1. fondo stradale liscio 2. fondo stradale accidentato 3. ghiaccio 4. neve 5. pioggia 6. nebbia 7. foschia 8. autostrada a pagamento 9. pedaggio 10. biglietto 11. potenza della vettura 12. cilindrata 13. cavalli vapore 14. autovettura 15. motocicletta 16. roulotte 17. rimorchio per bagagli / per barche 18. velocità massima 19. velocità minima 20. divieto di sosta. **II Attrezzatura e assistenza** 1. casello 2. entrata 3. uscita 4. corsia 5. corsia unica 6. corsia di emergenza 7. aiuola spartitraffico 8. tunnel 9. viadotto 10. area di parcheggio 11. area di servizio 12. bar 13. ristorante 14. tavola calda 15. soccorso stradale 16. carro attrezzi 17. pronto soccorso 18. croce rossa 19. posto telefonico.

**I Conditions et règlements** 1. Chaussée lisse 2. chaussée déformée 3. verglas 4. neige 5. pluie 6. brouillard 7. brume 8. autoroute à péage 9. péage 10. ticket 11. puissance de la voiture 12. cylindrée 13. chevaux vapeur 14. automobile 15. motocyclette 16. roulotte 17. remorque à bagages / remorque pour bateaux 18. vitesse maximum 19. vitesse minimum 20. interdiction de stationner. **II Equipement et assistance** 1. poste de péage 2. entrée 3. sortie 4. voie 5. voie unique 6. couloir de secours 7. accotement central 8. tunnel 9. viaduc 10. plate-forme de parking 11. station de service 12. bar. 13. restaurant 14. buffet chaud 15. secours routier 16. dépanneuse 17. secours d'urgence 18 croix rouge 19. poste téléphonique.

## SERVICE STATION

Please can you tell me where there's a filling station?

How far is the next service area?

Where can I find Esso / Shell / Mobil / Caltex / Gulf / BP / Total / Api / Agip petrol?

Good morning (afternoon), please fill up with normal / premium petrol.

Good evening, I'd like thirty litres, half normal and half premium.

How many octanes are there in the premium petrol?

How much is it a litre?

This engine runs on a mixture.

Put in two per cent of lubricating oil.

Be careful, the tank won't take more than ... litres.

Put in some anti-freeze / some running-in oil.

Check the water and oil, please.

The water is all right, but the oil is down to the minimum.

Please change the radiator cap

Clean the windscreen and headlamps.

Change the air cleaner.

## STAZIONE DI SERVIZIO

Per cortesia, dove posso trovare una stazione di rifornimento?

Quanto dista la più vicina area di servizio?

Dove si trova una stazione Esso / Shell / Mobil / Caltex / Gulf / BP / Total / Api / Agip?

Buon giorno, faccia il pieno di normale / super.

Buona sera, vorrei trenta litri, metà normale, metà super.

Qual è il numero di ottano della benzina super?

Quanto costa al litro?

Questo motore va a miscela.

Aggiunga il due per cento di olio lubrificante.

Faccia attenzione, nel serbatoio non entrano più di ... litri.

Aggiunga dell'anticongelante / dell'olio di rodaggio.

Controlli anche l'acqua e l'olio, per favore.

L'acqua è a posto, ma l'olio è al minimo.

Sostituisca, per favore, il tappo del radiatore.

Pulisca il parabrezza e i fari.

Mi cambi il filtro dell'aria.

## STATION DE SERVICE

Pourriez-vous me dire, s'il vous plaît, où je pourrais trouver un distributeur d'essence?

A quelle distance se trouve la station de service la plus proche?

Où y a-t-il une station Esso / Shell / Mobil / Caltex / Gulf / BP / Total / Api / Agip?

Bonjour, faites-moi le plein de normale / de super, s'il vous plaît.

Bonsoir, je voudrais trente litres, moitié normale, motié super.

Quel est l'indice d'octane du super?

Combien vaut le litre?

Ce moteur marche au mélange.

S'il vous plaît, ajoutez deux pour cent d'huile de graissage.

Attention, le réservoir ne contient pas plus de ... litres.

Ajoutez, s'il vous plaît, de l'antigel / de l'huile de rodage.

Pouvez-vous vérifier aussi le niveau d'eau et d'huile, s'il vous plaît.

L'eau va bien, mais l'huile est au minimum.

Voudriez-vous, je vous prie, changer le bouchon du radiateur.

S'il vous plaît, voulez-vous nettoyer le parebrise et les phares?

Il faudrait changer le filtre à air.

**I. Strassenverhältnisse und Vorschriften** 1. glatte Strassendecke 2. unebene Strassendecke 3. Glatteis 4. Schnee 5. Regen 6. Nebel 7. Dunst 8. gebührenpflichtige Autobahn 9. Gebühr 10. Gebührenschein 11. Motorleistung 12. Hubraum 13. Pferdestärke 14. Personenkraftwagen 15. Kraftrad 16. Wohnwagen 17. Gepäckanhänger / Bootanhänger 18. Höchstgeschwindigkeit 19. Mindestgeschwindigkeit 20. Halteverbot. **II. Einrichtungen und Dienstleistungen** 1. Sperre 2. Zufahrt 3. Abfahrt 4. Fahrbahn 5. einspurige Fahrbahn 6. befestigter Seitenstreifen 7. Grünstreifen 8. Tunnel 9. Viadukt 10. Parkplatz 11. Service-Station 12. Bar 13. Restaurant 14. Imbisstube 15. Strassenhilfe 16. Abschleppwagen 17. Erste Hilfe 18. Rotes Kreuz 19. Fernsprechstelle.

**I Condiciones y reglamentación** 1. firme liso de la carretera 2. firme accidentado 3. Hielo 4. nieve 5. lluvia 6. niebla 7. nieblina 8. autopista de pago 9. peaje 10. billete 11. potencia del coche 12. cilindrada 13. Caballos de vapor 14. coche 15. motocicleta 16. roulotte 17. remolque para equipajes / para lanchas 18. velocidad máxima 19. velocidad mínima 20. prohibición de aparcamiento. **II Instalaciones y asistencia** 1. puesto 2. entrada 3. salida 4. vía 5. vía única 6. banda de emergencia 7. división de la autopista 8. túnel 9. viaducto 10. área de aparcamiento 11. área de servicio 12. bar 13. restaurante 14. cafetería 15. socorro de carretera 16. coche-taller 17. puesto de socorro 18. cruz roja 19. puesto telefónico.

**I Uvjeti i pravila** 1. glatka površina ceste 2. uništena površina ceste 3. led 4. snijeg 5. kiša 6. magla 7. sumaglica 8. autostrada uz naplatu 9. cestarina 10. karta 11. snaga vozila 12. zapremnina 13. konjske snage 14. automobil 15. motocikl 16. prikolica za spavanje 17. prtljažna prikolica / za barku 18. maksimalna brzina 19. minimalna brzina 20. zabranjeno zaustavljanje. **II Oprema i usluge** 1. stanica 2. ulaz 3. izlaz 4. staza 5. jednosmjerna staza 6. staza za slučaj nužde 7. diobena površina autostrade 8. tunel 9. vijadukt 10. parkiralište 11. servisna stanica 12. ekspres restauracija 13. restauracija 14. toplo jelo 15. pomoć na cesti 16. pokretna radionica 17. hitna pomoć 18. crveni križ 19. telefonska govornica.

| SERVICE-STATION | AREA DE SERVICIO | SERVISNA STANICA |
|---|---|---|
| Bitte, wo kann ich eine Tankstelle finden? | Por favor, ¿dónde puedo encontrar un surtidor de gasolina? | Molim vas, gdje se nalazi pumpna stanica? |
| Wie weit ist es bis zur nächsten Service-Station? | ¿A qué distancia se encuentra el área de servicio más cercana? | Koliko je udaljena najbliža servisna stanica? |
| Gibt es hier eine Esso / Shell / Mobil / Caltex / Gulf / BP / Total / Api / Agip Tankstelle? | ¿Dónde puedo encontrar un surtidor de gasolina Esso / Shell / Mobil / Caltex / Gulf / BP / Total / Api / Agip? | Gdje se nalazi stanica Esso / Shell / Mobil / Caltex / Gulf / BP / Total / Api / Agip? |
| Guten Tag, füllen Sie den Tank mit Normal / Super bitte. | Buenos días, lléneme el depósito con gasolina normal / super. | Dobar dan, napunite mi normalni / super. |
| Guten Abend, ich möchte dreissig Liter, halb Normal / halb Super. | Buenas tardes, eche treinta litros, la mitad normal y la mitad super. | Dobar večer, želio bih trideset litara, pola normalnog, pola supera. |
| Wie hoch ist die Oktanzahl des Superbenzins? | ¿Cuál es el número de octanos de la gasolina super? | Koji je oktanski broj supera? |
| Wieviel kostet der Liter? | ¿Cuánto cuesta el litro? | Koliko košta po litri? |
| Dieser Motor läuft mit Mischung. | Este motor camina con mezcla. | Ovaj motor radi na mješavinu. |
| Setzen Sie bitte zwei Prozent Schmieröl zu. | Añada, por favor, el dos por ciento de aceite lubrificante. | Dodajte dva posto ulja za podmazivanje. |
| Geben Sie acht, der Tank fasst nicht mehr als . . . Liter. | Tenga cuidado, porque en el depósito no caben más que ... litros. | Budite oprezni, jer u rezervoar ne stanu više od . . . litara. |
| Setzen Sie bitte Frostschutzmittel / Einfahröl zu. | Añada, por favor, anticongelante / aceite de rodaje a la gasolina. | Dodajte sredstvo protiv zamrzavanja / ulje za uhodavanje. |
| Würden Sie bitte auch das Kühlwasser / den Ölstand nachprüfen? | No deje de comprobar también el agua y el aceite. | Molim, kontrolirajte takodjer vodu i ulje. |
| Das Wasser ist in Ordnung, aber das Öl steht an der untersten Grenze. | El agua está bien, pero el aceite está al mínimo nivel. | Voda je u redu, ali ulje je na minimumu. |
| Wechseln Sie bitte den Kühlerverschluss aus. | Cambie, por favor, el tapón del radiador. | Zamijenite mi molim vas poklopac hladnjaka. |
| Würden Sie bitte die Frontscheibe und die Scheinwerfer reinigen? | Limpie, por favor, el parabrisas y los faros. | Očistite mi prednje staklo i farove. |
| Wechseln Sie bitte den Luftfilter aus. | Cámbieme, por favor, el filtro del aire. | Promijenite mi filtar za zrak. |

| English | Italiano | Français |
|---|---|---|
| It would be a good idea to change the cartridge of the oil filter. | Sarà bene sostituire la cartuccia del filtro dell'olio. | Il faudrait changer la cartouche du filtre à huile. |
| The distilled water in the battery needs topping up. | Bisognerebbe rimboccare l'acqua distillata della batteria. | Il faudrait vérifier le niveau de l'eau distillée de la batterie. |
| The battery is flat. | La batteria è scarica. | La batterie est déchargée. |
| The windscreen-wiper motor isn't working. | Non funziona il motorino del tergicristallo | Le mécanisme de l'essuie-glace ne fonctionne pas. |
| This engine is losing oil / water. | Questo motore perde olio / acqua. | Ce moteur perd de l'huile / de l'eau. |
| The engine cuts out when idling. | Questo motore non regge il minimo. | Ce moteur ne tient pas le ralenti. |
| The sparking plugs are dirty. | Le candele sono sporche. | Les bougies sont encrassées. |
| The fan belt has snapped. | Si è rotta la cinghia del ventilatore. | La courroie du ventilateur est cassée |
| A bulb has fused. | Si è fulminata una lampadina. | L'ampoule a sauté. |
| Check the tyres, please. | Controlli le gomme, per favore. | Voudriez-vous vérifier les pneus, s'il vous plaît. |
| The front / rear tyre pressure should be . . . | La pressione delle gomme anteriori / posteriori deve essere di . . . | La pression des pneus avant / arrière doit être de . . . |
| The spare tyre, too, should be inflated to | Anche la ruota di scorta va gonfiata a . . . | La roue de secours doit aussi être gonflée à . . . |
| There's a puncture in the spare tyre. | La ruota di scorta è bucata. | La roue de secours est crevée. |
| Have you got an inner tube the right size? | Ha una camera d'aria a misura? | Auriez-vous une chambre à air de la bonne dimension? |
| Can you put on / take off the chains? | Potrebbe montare / smontare le catene? | Pourriez-vous, s'il vous plaît, monter / démonter les chaînes? |
| The bearings of the front wheels should be greased. | Si dovrebbero ingrassare i cuscinetti delle ruote anteriori. | Je vous rappelle de graisser les roulements des roues avant. |
| I think you'll have to add some oil to the dampers. | Credo che dovrà aggiungere olio agli ammortizzatori. | Je crois qu'il faudrait ajouter de l'huile aux amortisseurs. |
| Check the brake fluid. | Controlli l'olio dei freni. | Voudriez-vous contrôler l'huile des freins, je vous prie? |
| Can you wash and grease the car while I'm in the restaurant? | Può lavare e ingrassare la vettura mentre sono al ristorante? | Pourriez-vous laver et graisser cette voiture pendant que je suis au restaurant? |
| Where can I find a recognised garage? | Dove posso trovare un'officina abilitata? | Où puis-je trouver un atelier autorisé? |
| Have you got a road map / map of the town? | Ha una carta stradale / una piantina della città? | Auriez-vous une carte routière / un plan de la ville, s'il vous plaît? |
| How much is there to pay in all? | Quanto pago in tutto? | Combien vous dois-je en tout? |
| Keep the change. | Tenga pure il resto. | Gardez la monnaie. |
| Goodbye and thank you. | Arrivederci e grazie. | Au revoir et merci. |

| Deutsch | Español | Srpsko-hrvatski |
|---|---|---|
| Es wird gut sein, die Ölfilterpatrone auszuwechseln. | Sará bien cambiar el cartucho del filtro del aceite. | Bilo bi dobro zamijeniti uložak uljnog filtra. |
| Das destillierte Wasser der Batterie müsste aufgefüllt werden. | Sería necesario añadir agua destilada a la batería. | Trebalo bi nadoliti destiliranu vodu u akumulator. |
| Die Batterie ist entladen. | La batería está descargada. | Akumulator je ispražnjen. |
| Der Scheibenwischermotor funktioniert nicht. | El motor del limpiaparabrisas no funciona. | Ne funkcionira motor brisača stakla. |
| Dieser Motor hat einen Ölverlust / Wasserverlust. | Este motor pierde aceite / agua. | Ovaj motor gubi ulje / vodu. |
| Der Motor setzt im Leerlauf aus. | El motor no gira al ralentí. | Motor ne održava minimalni broj okretaja. |
| Die Zündkerzen sind verschmutzt. | Las bujías están sucias. | Svjećice su zaprljane. |
| Der Ventilatorriemen ist gebrochen. | Se ha roto la correa del ventilador. | Prekinuo se klinasti remen ventilatora. |
| Eine Birne ist ausgebrannt. | Se ha quemado una bombilla. | Pregorjela je žaruljica. |
| Würden Sie bitte den Reifendruck kontrollieren? | Controle, por favor, la presión de los neumáticos. | Ispitajte gume. |
| Der Druck der Vorderräder / Hinterräder muss ... sein. | La presión de las ruedas delanteras / posteriores debe ser de ... | Pritisak prednjih guma / stražnjih guma mora biti ... |
| Auch der Ersatzreifen muss auf ... gefüllt werden. | También la rueda de recambio debe estar a la presión de... | Takodjer rezervni kotač mora biti napumpan na ... |
| Der Ersatzreifen hat ein Loch. | La rueda de recambio está pinchada. | Rezervni kotač je probušen. |
| Haben Sie einen passenden Schlauch? | ¿Tiene una cámara de aire de este tamaño? | Imate li odgovarajuću zračnicu? |
| Würden Sie die Schneeketten aufziehen / abnehmen? | ¿Podría montar / desmontar las cadenas? | Možete li mi montirati / odmontirati lance? |
| Die Vorderradlager müssten geschmiert werden. | Se deberían engrasar los cojinetes de las ruedas delanteras. | Protebno bi bilo podmazati ležajeve prednjih kotača. |
| Ich glaube, Sie müssen etwas Stossdämpfer-Öl zusetzen | Creo que habrá que engrasar los amortiguadores. | Mislim da ćete morati nadodati ulje u amortizere. |
| Bitte kontrollieren Sie den Stand der Bremsflüssigkeit. | Controle el aceite de los frenos. | Pregledajte ulje za kočenje. |
| Könnten Sie den Wagen waschen und abschmieren während ich im Restaurant bin? | ¿Puede lavar y engrasar el coche mientras voy al restaurante? | Možete li mi oprati i podmazati kola za vrijeme dok se nalazim u restauraciji? |
| Wo kann ich eine Vertragswerkstatt finden? | ¿Dónde puedo encontrar un taller mecánico autorizado? | Gdje mogu naći jednu stručnu radionicu? |
| Haben Sie eine Strassenkarte / einen Stadtplan? | ¿Tiene un mapa de carreteras / un crokis de la ciudad? | Imate li jednu autokartu / plan grada? |
| Was bin ich schuldig? | ¿Cuánto pago por todo? | Koliko plaćam ukupno? |
| Der Rest ist für Sie. | Quédese con la vuelta. | Zadržite ostatak. |
| Auf Wiedersehen. Danke. | Adiós y muchas gracias. | Dovidjenja i hvala. |

| English | Italiano | Français |
|---|---|---|
| Is there a telephone, please? | Per cortesia c'è un telefono? | S'il vous plaît, avez-vous le téléphone? |
| Where is the cloakroom? | Dov'è la toilette? | Où sont les toilettes? |
| **I Replenishments** 1. normal / premium petrol 2. number of octanes 3. anti-knock 4. mixture 5. price per litre 6. petrol coupons 7. reserve 8. antifreeze 9. running-in oil 10. thin / thick oil 11. winter / summer oil 12. multigrade oil 13. oil level 14. water 15. water level 16. radiator 17. liquid to clean windscreen **II Various needs** 1. air cleaner 2. cartridge 3. gearbox oil / final drive oil / steering box oil / brake fluid / damper oil 4. oil filter 5. oil cap / oil outlet cap 6. dipstick 7. radiator cap 8. battery 9. distilled water 10. terminals 11. electrolyte 12. windscheen-wiper motor 13. windscreen-wiper blades 14. fan belt 15. tyres 16. spare wheel 17. tyre pressure 18. inner tube 19. tyre repair 20. wash 21. greasing. | **I Rifornimenti** 1. benzina normale/ super 2. numero di ottano 3. antidetonante 4. miscela 5. prezzo per litro 6. buoni benzina 7. riserva 8. anticongelante 9. olio di rodaggio 10. olio fluido / denso 11. olio invernale / estivo 12. olio multigrade 13. livello dell'olio 14. acqua 15. livello dell'acqua 16. serbatoio dell'acqua 17. liquido per pulire i vetri. **II Assistenza varia** 1. filtro dell'aria 2. cartuccia 3. olio del cambio / del differenziale / della scatola guida / dei freni / degli ammortizzatori 4. filtro dell'olio 5. tappo dell'olio / tappo di scarico 6. asticina di misurazione dell'olio 7. tappo del radiatore 8. batteria 9. acqua distillata 10. morsetti 11. elettrolito 12. motorino del tergicristallo 13. spazzole del tergicristallo 14. cinghia del ventilatore 15. pneumatici 16. ruota di scorta 17. pressione delle gomme 18. camera d'aria 19. vulcanizzazione 20. lavaggio 21. ingrassaggio. | **I Ravitaillement** 1. essence normale / super 2. indice d'octane 3. additif antidétonnant 4. mélange 5. prix au litre 6. bons d'essence 7. réserve 8. antigel 9. huile de rodage 10. huile fluide / dense 11. huile pour l'hiver / l'été 12. huile multigrade 13. niveau de l'huile 14. eau 15. niveau de l'eau 16. réservoir d'eau 17. liquide pour le nettoyage des vitres. **II Assistance en général** 1. filtre à air 2. cartouche 3. huile de la boîte de vitesse / du différentiel / du boîtier de direction / des freins / des amortisseurs 4. filtre à huile 5. bouchon de l'huile / purge 6. jauge d'huile 7. bouchon du radiateur 8. batterie 9. eau distillée 10. goupilles 11. électrolyte 12. petit moteur actionnant l'essuie-glace 13. balais de l'essuie-glace 14. courroie du ventilateur 15. pneus 16. roue de secours 17. pression des pneus 18. chambre à air 19. vulcanisation 20. lavage 21. graissage. |

| ROADSIDE CAFE AND RESTAURANT | AUTOGRILL E RISTORANTE | RESTAUROUTE ET RESTAURANT |
|---|---|---|
| Can I park the car here? | Posso parcheggiare quì la vettura? | Puis-je garer la voiture ici? |
| Is the restaurant open? | Il ristorante è aperto? | Le restaurant est-il ouvert? |
| Where is the cloakroom / the telephone. | Dov'è il guardaroba / il telefono? | Pourriez-vous m'indiquer le vestiaire / le téléphone? |
| I want to wash my hands. | Vorrei lavarmi le mani. | Je voudrais me laver les mains. |
| What would the gentleman / the lady like? | Che cosa desidera il signore / la signora? | Monsieur / Madame désire? |
| What would the gentlemen like? | Che cosa desiderano i signori? | Ces Messieurs désirent? |
| Is it possible to have a fixed-price meal? | E' possibile consumare un pasto a prezzo fisso? | Avez-vous un menu à prix fixe? |
| Have you a tourist menu? | Avete un menu turistico? | Avez-vous un menu touristique? |
| Would you like an aperitif? | Desidera un aperitivo? | Désirez-vous un apéritif? |
| Yes, I should like a non-alcoholic aperitif. | Sì, vorrei un aperitivo analcolico. | Oui, je voudrais un apéritif sans alcool. |
| Bring me the menu / the wine list. | Mi porti la lista delle vivande / dei vini. | Voulez-vous me donner la carte / la carte des vins, je vous prie. |
| What is your speciality? | Qual è la vostra specialità? | Quelle est votre spécialité? |
| Please serve me at once. I must leave as soon as possible. | La prego di farmi mangiare subito. Devo ripartire al più presto. | Auriez-vous l'amabilité de me servir tout de suite, je dois repartir immédiatement. |
| I should like something very light. | Vorrei mangiare qualcosa di molto leggero. | Je voudrais manger très légèrement. |

| Deutsch | Español | Srpsko-hrvatski |
|---|---|---|
| Haben Sie Telefon bitte? | Por favor, ¿hay un teléfono? | Molim, postoji li telefon? |
| Wo ist die Toilette? | ¿Dónde están los retretes? | Gdje se nalazi toaleta? |
| **I. Tanken** 1. Normalbenzin / Superbenzin 2. Oktanzahl 3. klopffest 4. Mischung 5. Literpreis 6. Benzin-Gutscheine 7. Reserve 8. Frostschutzmittel 9. Einfahröl 10. dünnflüssiges / dickflüssiges Öl 11. Winteröl / Sommeröl 12. Mehrbereichsöl 13. Ölstand 14. Wasser 15. Wasserstand 16. Kühler 17. Flüssigkeit zum Fensterreinigen. **II. Verschiedene Dienstleistungen** 1. Luftfilter 2. Patrone 3. Getriebeöl / Differentialöl / Lenkgehäuseöl / Bremsflüssigkeit / Stossdämpferöl 4. Ölfilter 5. Öleinfüllschraube / Ölablasschraube 6. Ölmesstab 7. Kühlerverschlussdeckel 8. Batterie 9. destilliertes Wasser 10. Klemmen 11. Elektrolyt 12. Scheibenwischermotor 13. Scheibenwischer 14. Ventilatorriemen 15. Reifen 16. Ersatzrad 17. Reifendruck 18. Schlauch 19. Vulkanisierung 20. Waschen 21. Schmieren. | **I Surtidores** 1. gasolina normal / super 2. número de octanos 3. antidetonante 4. mezcla 5. precio por litro 6. cupones de gasolina 7. reserva 8. anticongelante 9. aceite de rodaje 10. aceite flúido / denso 11. aceite para el invierno / para el verano 12. multigrado 13. nivel del aceite 14. agua 15. nivel del agua 16. depósito del agua 17. líquido para desengrasar los vidrios. **II Asistencias diversas** 1. filtro del aire 2. cartucho 3. aceite del cambio / del diferencial / del carter de guia / de los frenos / de los amortiguadores 4. filtro del aceite 5. tapón del aceite 6. tapón de descarga 6. asta para medir el aceite 7. tapón del radiador 8. batería 9. agua destilada 10. bornes 11. electrolito 12. motor del limpia parabrisas 13. escobillas del limpiaparabrisas 14. correa del ventilador 15. neumáticos 16. rueda de recambio 17. presión de los neumáticos 18. cámara de aire 19. vulcanización 20. lavado 21. engrasado. | **I Snabdjevanje** 1. normalni benzin / super 2. oktanski broj 3. antidetonirajući 4. mješavina 5. cijena po litri 6. bonovi za benzin 7. rezerva 8. sredstvo protiv zamrzavanja 9. ulje za uhodavanje 10. ulje rijetko / gusto 11. ulje zimsko / ljetno 12. ulje multigrade 13. razina ulja 14. voda 15. razina vode 16. rezervoar za vodu 17. tekućina za čišćenje stakala. **II Razne usluge** 1. filtar za zrak 2. uožak 3. ulje za mjenjač / za diferencijal / za upravljačku kutiju / za kočnice / za amortizere 4. filtar za ulje 5. čep za ulje / čep za ispust 6. šipka za mjerenje razine ulja 7. poklopac hladnjaka 8. akumulator 9. destilirana voda 10. priključni polovi 11. elektrolit 12. motor brisača stakala 13. četke brisača 14. klinasti remen ventilatora 15. gume 16. rezervni kotač 17. pritisak guma 18. zračnica 19. vulkanizacija 20. pranje 21. podmazivanje. |
| **AUTOGRILL UND RESTAURANT** | **AUTOGRILL Y RESTAURANTE** | **AUTO-RESTAURACIJA** |
| Kann ich den Wagen hier parken? | ¿Puedo aparcar aquí el coche? | Mogu li parkirati kola? |
| Ist das Restaurant offen? | ¿Está abierto el restaurante? | Da li je otvorena restauracija? |
| Wo ist die Kleiderablage / das Telefon? | ¿Dónde está el guardarropas / el teléfono? | Gdje je garderoba / telefon? |
| Ich möchte mir die Hände waschen. | Quisiera lavarme las manos. | Želio bih oprati ruke. |
| Was wünscht der Herr / die Damen? | ¿Qué desea el señor / la señora? | Što želi gospodin / gospodja? |
| Was wünschen die Herrschaften? | ¿Qué desean los señores? | Što žele gospoda? |
| Haben Sie ein Menü zu festem Preis? | ¿Es posible comer a precio fijo? | Mogu li dobiti jedan meni? |
| Gibt es das Touristen-Menü? | ¿Existe el menú turístico? | Imate li turistički meni? |
| Wünschen Sie einen Aperitif? | ¿Desea un aperitivo? | Želite li jedan aperitiv? |
| Ja, ich möchte einen alkoholfreien Aperitif. | Sí, quisiera un aperitivo no alcohólico | Da, želio bih jedan bezalkoholni aperitiv |
| Bringen Sie mir bitte die Speisekarte / die Weinkarte. | ¿Puede enseñarme la carta / la lista de los vinos? | Donesite mi jelovnik / vinsku kartu. Koji je vaš specijalitet? |
| Was ist die Spezialität des Hauses? | ¿Cuál es la especialidad de la casa? | Molim da mi jelo pripremite odmah. |
| Ich möchte so rasch als möglich essen. Ich muss sofort weiterfahren. | Le ruego que me sirva enseguida. Tengo que marcharme enseguida. | Moram otputovati što je moguće prije. |
| Ich möchte etwas sehr Leichtes essen. | Quisiera comer algo muy ligero. | Želio bih jesti nešto vrlo lagano. |

| English | Italiano | Français |
|---|---|---|
| I should like to begin with a mixed hors d'oeuvre. | Vorrei cominciare con un antipasto misto. | Je voudrais un hors d'oeuvre varié pour commencer. |
| I should like a consommé / vegetable soup. | Desidero un consommé / una minestra di verdura. | Je voudrais un consommé / un potage de légumes. |
| I should like some roast meat with potatoes. | Vorrei della carne arrosto con patate. | Je voudrais du rôti et des pommes de terre. |
| The roast veal is finished. There is some excellent roast beef. | L'arrosto di vitella è terminato. C'è dell'ottimo roast-beef. | Le rôti de veau est terminé mais il y a de l'excellent rosbif. |
| Bring me a rare / well-done beef steak. | Mi dia una bistecca al sangue / molto cotta. | Donnez-moi un steak saignant / très cuit. |
| If you want the escalopes, it will take fifteen minutes. | Se desidera le scaloppine dovrà attendere quindici minuti. | Pour les escalopes, il faut attendre un quart d'heure. |
| I can't eat fried food or meat sauce. | Non posso mangiare fritto o sughi di carne. | Je ne mange pas de friture / de sauces. |
| Is there any boiled chicken or boiled fish? | C'è del pollo lesso o pesce bollito? | Avez-vous du poulet bouilli / du poisson bouilli? |
| I should like some salad with an oil and lemon dressing. | Vorrei dell'insalata condita con olio e limone. | Je voudrais de la salade assaisonnée à l'huile et au citron. |
| I'll have a mixed salad without tomatoes. | Desidero dell'insalata mista senza pomodoro | Je voudrais une salade variée sans tomates. |
| Have you any cooked green vegetables. | Ha della verdura cotta? | Avez-vous des légumes cuits? |
| Bring me some lemon. | Mi porti del limone. | Pourriez-vous m'apporter du citron? |
| This knife doesn't cut | Questo coltello non taglia. | Ce couteau ne coupe pas. |
| Can you bring me another glass, please. | Può portarmi un altro bicchiere, per favore? | Voulez-vous me donner un autre verre, s'il vous plaît? |
| Bring me some not too gassy / very cool / not too iced mineral water. | Mi porti dell'acqua minerale / poco gassata / fredda / non troppo ghiacciata. | Donnez-moi de l'eau minérale / peu gazeuse / fraîche / qui ne soit pas trop glacée. |
| Could I have a little ice? | Potrei avere un po' di ghiaccio? | Pourrais-je avoir un peu de glace? |
| I should like some white / red / dry / sweet wine. | Vorrei del vino bianco / rosso / secco / dolce. | Je voudrais du vin blanc / rouge / sec / doux. |
| Would you like some bottled / named wine? | Vuole vino in bottiglia / di marca? | Voulez-vous du vin en bouteille / d'appellation contrôlée? |
| No, bring me half a litre of local wine. | No, mi porti mezzo litro di vino locale. | Non, donnez-moi un demi-litre de vin du pays. |
| Have you got any foreign wines? | Avete vini esteri? | Avez-vous des vins étrangers? |
| This wine is too sweet / warm / tastes of cork. | Questo vino è troppo dolce / caldo / sa di tappo | Ce vin est trop sucré / chaud / sent le bouchon. |
| I should like a pale ale / brown ale / small beer / large beer. | Vorrei una birra chiara / scura / piccola / grande. | Je voudrais une bière blonde / brune / petite / grande. |
| I should like two boiled / fried / scrambled eggs. | Vorrei due uova à la coque / all'occhio di bue / strapazzate. | Je voudrais deux oeufs à la coque / au plat / brouillés. |

| Deutsch | Español | Srpsko-hrvatski |
|---|---|---|
| Als erstes hätte ich gern etwas Hors d'oeuvre. | Quiero empezar con entremeses variados. | Želio bih početi sa jednim mješanim predjelom. |
| Ich möchte eine Fleischbrühe / eine Gemüsesuppe. | Deseo un consommé / una sopa de verduras. | Želim jednu čistu juhu / juhu od povrća. |
| Ich möchte einen Braten mit Kartoffeln | Quisiera carne asada con patatas. | Želio bih pečeno meso sa krumpirom. |
| Kalbsbraten haben wir nicht mehr. Es gibt ein sehr gutes Roastbeef. | El asado de ternera se ha terminado. Tenemos roas-beef excelente. | Telećeg pečenja više nema Imamo odličan roast-beef. |
| Bringen Sie mir ein / rasch durchbratenes / gut durchbratenes Beefsteak. | Sírvame una chuleta / poco pasada / muy pasada. | Dajte mi jedan biftek / krvav / jako pržen |
| Wenn Sie Escalopes wünschen, müssen Sie fünfzehn Minuten warten. | Si desea unas rajitas de ternera asada, tendrá que esperar quince minutos. | Ako želite prženi odrezak, morati ćete pričekati petnaest minuta. |
| Ich vertrage weder Gebackenes noch Fleischsossen | No puedo comer fritos o salsas de carne. | Ne mogu da jedem prženo ili umake od mesa |
| Haben Sie gesottenes Huhn oder blau gekochten Fisch? | ¿Tiene Vd pollo o pescado cocido? | Imamo kuhano pile ili kuhanu ribu. |
| Ich möchte mit Öl und Zitrone angemachten Salat. | Desearía ensalada con aceite y limón. | Želio bih salatu začinjenu uljem i limunom |
| Ich hätte gern gemischten Salat ohne Tomaten. | Deseo ensalada mixta sin tomates. | Želim mješanu salatu bez paradajza. |
| Haben Sie gekochtes Gemüse? | ¿Tiene Vd. verdura cocida? | Imate li kuhanog povrća? |
| Bringen Sie mir etwas Zitrone bitte. | Tráigame limón. | Donesite mi limuna. |
| Dieses Messer schneidet nicht. | Este cuchillo no corta. | Ovaj nož ne reže. |
| Würden Sie mir bitte ein anderes Glas bringen? | ¿Puede traerme otro vaso, por favor? | Možete li mi donijeti jednu drugu čašu? |
| Bringen Sie mir bitte ein / kohlensäurearmes / kaltes / nicht zu kaltes Mineralwasser. | Tráigame agua mineral / poco gaseosa / fría / no demasiado helada. | Donesite mi mineralnu vodu / slabo plinovitu / hladnu / ne previše ledenu. |
| Könnte ich etwas Eis haben? | ¿Puede darme un poco de hielo? | Da li bih mogao dobiti malo leda? |
| Ich möchte trockenen / süssen Weisswein / Rotwein. | Quisiera vino blanco / tinto / seco / dulce. | Želio bih vino bijelo / crno / oporo / slatko. |
| Wünschen Sie Flaschenwein / Markenwein? | ¿Lo desea en botella / de marca? | Želite li flaširano vino / sortno vino. |
| Nein, bringen Sie mir einen halben Liter hiesigen Wein. | No, tráigame medio litro de vino local. | Ne, donesite mi pola litre ovdašnjeg vina. |
| Haben Sie ausländische Weine? | ¿Hay vinos extranjeros? | Imate li uvozna vina? |
| Dieser Wein ist zu süss / zu warm / schmeckt nach Kork. | Este vino es demasiado dulce / caliente / sabe al tapón. | Ovo vino je preslatko / toplo / ima okus po čepu. |
| Ich möchte ein helles / dunkles / kleines / grosses Bier. | Quisiera una cerveza clara / negra / pequeña / grande. | Želio bih jedno pivo svijetlo /crno / malo / veliko. |
| Ich möchte zwei Eier à la coque / Spiegeleier / Rühreier. | Quisiera dos huevos a la coque / estrellados / revueltos. | Želio bih dva jaja srednje kuhana / na oko / kajganu. |

| English | Italiano | Français |
|---|---|---|
| I'll have an omelette. | Desidero un'omelette. | Je voudrais une omelette. |
| How would you like it? With cheese / ham / mushrooms? | Come la vuole? Al formaggio / al prosciutto / ai funghi? | Comment la désirez-vous? Au fromage / au jambon / aux champignons? |
| What cheese have you got? | Che formaggi ha? | Quels fromages avez-vous? |
| I should like a strong / mild / fresh / fermented cheese. | Vorrei un formaggio piccante / dolce / fresco / fermentato. | Je voudrais un fromage fort / doux / frais / fermenté. |
| Give me a portion of this cheese. | Mi dia una porzione di questo formaggio. | Donnez-moi une portion de ce fromage. |
| Bring me some bread / grissini / biscuits. | Mi porti del pane / dei grissini / dei cracker. | Je voudrais du pain / des gressins / des crackers. |
| I should like some fresh / cooked fruit. | Vorrei della frutta fresca / cotta | Je voudrais des fruits frais / cuits. |
| Bring me an orange squash. | Mi porti una spremuta d'arancia | Apportez-moi un jus d'orange, s'il vous plaît. |
| What sweets have you? | Quali dolci ci sono? | Quels desserts avez-vous? |
| There is a chocolate sweet / sweet without liqueur. | C'è un dolce al cioccolato / senza liquore. | Nous avons du gâteau au chocolat / sans liqueur. |
| Give me a piece of cake | Mi dia una porzione di torta. | Donnez-moi une part de tarte |
| An espresso coffee / white coffee, please | Per favore un caffè espresso / un cappuccino. | Un café « espresso » / un « cappuccino », s'il vout plaît. |
| I should like a caffeine-free coffee. | Vorrei un caffè decaffeinato. | Je voudrais un café décaféiné. |
| Bring me some sugar, please. | Mi porti dello zucchero, per cortesia | Donnez-moi du sucre, s'il vous plaît. |
| Waiter, the bill please. | Cameriere, il conto per favore. | Garçon, l'addition, s'il vous plaît. |
| Is service included? | Il servizio è incluso? | Le service est-il compris? |
| Do I pay at the cash-desk? | Devo pagare alla cassa? | Dois-je payer à la caisse? |
| Thank you, goodbye. | Grazie, arrivederci. | Merci, au revoir. |

**I Service** 1. waiter 2. waitress 3. cloakroom 4. cloakroom attendant 5. bill. 6. change 7. tip 8. cash-desk 9. cashier. **II Table appointments** 1. chair 2. tablecloth 3. napkin 4. plate 5. knife 6. fork 7. spoon 8. teaspoon 9. glass 10. bottle 11. carafe 12. cup 13. salt cellar 14. salt 15. oil 16. vinegar 17. pepper 18. French mustard 19. English mustard 20. bread 21. breadsticks 22. biscuits. **III Aperitif** 1. alcoholic 2. non-alcoholic 3. bitter 4. dry / sweet / white / red vermouth. **IV Hors d'oeuvre** 1. cooked / raw ham 2. olives 3. pickles 4. anchovies 5. sardines 6. tunny fish 7. smoked salmon 8. mushrooms 9. peppers 10. butter. **V Soups** 1. chicken broth 2. vegetable soup 3. rice in broth 4. fish soup 5. spaghetti with butter / tomato sauce / meat sauce 6. baked pasta 7. rice with butter and cheese / with sauce. **VI Meat** 1. beef 2. veal 3. pork 4. chicken 5. sweetbreads 6. brain 7. liver 8. stew 9. braised meat 10. boiled meat 11. beefsteak 12. fillet 13. rib steak 14. pork chop 15. ragout 16. Milanese cutlet 17. tongue 18. leg 19. breast 20. turkey

**I Servizio** 1. cameriere 2. cameriera 3. guardaroba 4. guardarobiera 5. conto 6. resto 7. mancia 8. cassa 9. cassiera. **II Tavola apparecchiata** 1. sedia 2. tovaglia 3. tovagliolo 4. piatto 5. coltello 6. forchetta 7. cucchiaio 8. cucchiaino 9. bicchiere 10. bottiglia 11. caraffa 12. tazza 13. saliera 14. sale 15. olio 16. aceto 17. pepe 18. senape 19. mostarda 20. pane 21. grissini 22. cracker. **III Aperitivo** 1. alcolico 2. analcolico 3. amaro 4. vermouth secco / dolce / bianco / rosso. **IV Antipasti** 1. prosciutto / cotto / crudo 2. olive 3. sottaceti 4. acciughe 5. sardine 6. tonno 7. salmone affumicato 8. funghi 9. peperoni 10. burro. **V Minestre** 1. brodo di pollo 2. minestra di verdura 3. riso in brodo 4. zuppa di pesce 5. spaghetti al burro / al pomodoro / al sugo di carne 6. pasta al forno 7. risotto in bianco / al sugo. **VI Carne** 1. manzo 2. vitella 3. maiale 4. pollo 5. animelle 6. cervello 7. fegato 8. stufato 9. brasato 10. bollito 11. bistecca 12. filetto 13. costata 14. braciola di maiale 15. spezzatino 16. cotoletta alla milanese

**I Service** 1. garçon 2. serveuse 3. vestiaire 4. préposée au vestiaire 5. addition 6. monnaie 7. pourboire 8. caisse 9. caissière. **II Table mise** 1. chaise 2. nappe 3. serviette 4. assiette 5. couteau 6. fourchette 7. cuiller 8. petite cuiller 9. verre 10. bouteille 11. carafe 12. tasse 13. salière 14. sel 15. huile 16. vinaigre 17. poivre 18. moutarde 19. condiment 20. pain 21. gressins 22. crackers. **III Apéritif** 1. alcoolisé 2. sans alcool 3. amer 4. vermouth sec / doux / blanc / rouge. **IV Hors d'oeuvre** 1. jambon cuit / cru 2. olives 3. pickles 4. anchois 5. sardines 6. thon 7. saumon fumé 8. champignons 9. poivrons 10. beurre. **V Entrées** 1. consommé de poulet 2. potage de légumes 3. consommé au riz 4. soupe de poisson 5. pâtes au beurre / à la sauce tomate / au jus de viande 6. gratin de pâtes 7. riz au beurre / à la sauce tomate. **VI Viandes** 1. boeuf 2. veau 3. porc 4. poulet 5. ris de veau 6. cervelle 7. foie 8. viande à l'étouffée 9. viande braisée 10. pot-au-feu 11. steak 12. filet 13. entrecôte 14. côte de porc 15. ragoût

| Deutsch | Español | Srpsko-hrvatski |
|---|---|---|
| Ich hätte gern ein Omelett. | Deseo una tortilla. | Želim jedan omlet. |
| Wie wünschen sie es? Mit Käse / Schinken / Champignons? | ¿Cómo la desea? ¿Con queso / con jamon / con setas? | Kako ga želite? Sa sirom / sa pršu tom / sa gljivama? |
| Was haben Sie für Käse? | ¿Qué calidad de quesos tiene? | Kakav sir imate? |
| Ich möchte einen pikanten / süssen / frischen Käse / Schimmelkäse. | Quisiera un queso picante / dulce / fresco / fermentado. | Želio bih jedan sir pikantni / slatki / svježi / fermentirani. |
| Geben Sie mir eine Portion von diesem Käse. | Sírvame por favor una ración de este queso. | Dajte mi jednu porciju ovoga sira |
| Bitte bringen Sie mir etwas Brot / Brotstangen / Cracker. | Tráigame pan / grisines / cracker. | Donesite mi kruh / grisine / slane kekse. |
| Ich möchte frisches / gekochtes Obst. | Quisiera fruta del tiempo / cocida. | Želio bih svježe voće / kuhano |
| Einen Orangensaft bitte. | Tráigame un poco de zumo de naranja. | Donesite mi prirodni narančin sok |
| Was für Mehlspeisen gibt es? | ¿Qué dulces tiene? | Što imate od slatkoga? |
| Wir haben eine Schokoladentorte / Kuchen ohne Likör. | Hay dulce de chocolate / sin licor. | Imamo kolač sa čokoladom / bez likera. |
| Eine Portion Torte bitte. | Deme una ración de torta. | Dajte mi jednu porciju torte. |
| Bitte einen Kaffee Espresso / einen Kapuziner. | Por favor, un café expreso / un café cortado. | Molim jednu ekspres kavu / kapuciner. |
| Ich möchte einen koffeinfreien Kaffe. | Quisiera un café descafeínado. | Želim jednu kavu bez kofeina. |
| Bringen Sie mir etwas Zucker bitte. | Tráigame un poco de azúcar, por favor. | Donesite mi šećer, molim vas. |
| Herr Ober, bitte zahlen. | Camarero, la cuenta por favor. | Konobar, donesite mi račun, molim. |
| Ist die Bedienung inbegriffen? | ¿Está incluído el servicio? | Da li je uračunat servis? |
| Muss ich an der Kasse zahlen? | ¿Tengo que pagar en la caja? | Moram li platiti na kasi? |
| Danke, auf Wiedersehen. | Gracias, hasta la vista. | Hvala, dovidjenja. |

**I. Bedienung** 1. Kellner 2. Kellnerin 3. Garderobe 4. Garderobenfrau 5. Rechnung 6. Rest 7. Trinkgeld 8. Kasse 9. Kassierin. **II. Gedeckter Tisch** 1. Stuhl 2. Tischtuch 3. Serviette 4. Teller 5. Messer 6. Gabel 7. Löffel 8. Kaffeelöffel 9. Glas 10. Flasche 11. Karaffe 12. Tasse 13. Salzfass 14. Salz 15. Öl 16. Essig 17. Pfeffer 18. Senf 19. Mostrich 20. Brot 21 Brot in dünnen Stangen 22. Cracker. **III. Aperitif** 1. alkoholhältig 2. alkoholfrei 3 bitter 4. Vermouth trocken / süss / weiss / rot. **IV. Hors d'oeuvre** 1. gekochter / roher Schinken 2. Oliven 3. Mixed-Pickles 4. Sardellen 5. Sardinen 6. Thunfisch 7. Raucherlachs 8. Champignons 9. Paprika 10. Butter. **V. Erster Gang** 1. Hühnerbrühe 2. Gemüsesuppe 3. Reissuppe 4. Fischsuppe 5. Spaghetti mit Butter / mit Tomatensosse / mit Fleischsosse 6. gratinierte Nudeln 7. Risotto ohne / mit Sosse. **VI. Fleischgerichte** 1. Rindfleisch 2. Kalbfleisch 3. Schweinefleisch 4. Huhn 5. Bries 6. Hirn 7. Leber 8. gedünstetes Fleisch 9. gedämpftes Fleisch 10. gesottenes Fleisch 11. Beefsteak 12. Filet 13. Rip-

**I Servicio** 1. camarero 2. camarera 3. guardarropa 4. guardarropera 5. cuenta 6. vuelta 7. propina 8. caja 9. cajera. **II Mesa puesta** 1. silla 2. mantel 3. servilleta 4. plato 5. cuchillo 6. tenedor 7. cuchara 8. cucharilla 9. vaso 10. botella 11. jarra 12. taza 13. salero 14. sal 15. aceite 16. vinagre 17. pimienta 18. jenabe 19. mostaza 20. pan 21. grisines 22. cracker. **III Aperitivos** 1. alcohólico 2. no alcohólico 3. amargo 4. vermouth seco / dulce / blanco / tinto. **IV Entremeses** 1. jamón cocido / crudo 2. aceitunas 3. hortalizas en vinagre 4. boquerones 5. sardinas 6. bonito 7. salmón ahumado 8. setas 9. pimentón 10. mantequilla. **V Sopas** 1. sopicaldo de pollo 2. sopa de verduras 3. sopa de arroz 4. sopa de pescado 5. macarrones con mantequilla / con jugo de tomate / con salsa de carne 6. macarrones al horno 7. arroz con mantequilla / al jugo. **VI Platos de carne** 1. carne de vaca 2. ternera 3. cerdo 4. pollo 5. lechecillas 6. sesos 7. hígado 8. estofado 9. estofado de vaca 10. carne de cocido 11. bisteo 12. solomillo 13. chuleta 14. chuleta de

**I Posluga** 1. konobar 2. konobarica 3. garderoba 4. garderoberka 5. račun 6. ostatak 7. napojnica 8. blagajna (kasa) 9. blagajnica. **II Postavljen stol** 1. stolac 2. stolnjak 3. ubrus 4. tanjur 5. nož 6. vilica 7. žlica 8. žličica 9. čaša 10. flaša 11. vrč 12. poslužavnik 13. soljenka 14. sol 15. ulje 16. ocat 17. papar 18. senf 19. muštarda 20. kruh 21. grisini 22. slani keksi. **III Aperitiv** 1. alkoholni 2. bezalkoholni 3. gorak 4. vermut trpki / slatki / bijeli / crveni. **IV Predjela** 1. pršut kuhani / sušeni 2. masline 3. u octu 4. sardele 5. sardine 6. tuna 7. dimljeni losos 8. gljive 9. feferoni 10. putar. **V Čorbe** 1. pileća juha 2. juha od povrća 3. riža u juhi 4. riblja juha 5. špageti na putru / sa paradajzom / sa mesnim umakom 6. pečeno tjesto 7. riža bez začina / sa umakom. **VI Meso** 1. govedina 2. teletina 3. svinjetina 4. piletina 5. žljezdasto meso 6 mozak 7. jetra 8. pirjano 9. dinstano 10. kuhano 11. biftek 12. odrezak 13. rebra 14. svinjski kotlet 15. usitnjeno meso 16. bečki odrezak 17. jezik 18. butina 19. prsa 20. puran 21. patka 22. golub 23. fazan

**English**

21. duck 22. pigeon 23. pheasant 24. wild boar 25. venison 26. deer 27 lamb. **VII Fish** 1. tunny fish 2. cod 3. dried salt cod 4. sole 5. mullet 6. trout 7. sea bream 8. bass 9. sea perch 10. dogfish 11. red mullet 12. lobster 13. shrimps 14 prawns 15. corn cockles 16. octopus 17. squid 18. mixed fried fish 19. oysters. **VIII Side dishes** 1. potatoes 2. purée 3. buttered potatoes 4. roast potatoes 5. green salad 6. carrots 7. broad beans 8. runner beans 9. peas 10. cabbage 11. Savoy cabbage 12. cauliflower 13. Brussels sprouts 14. tomato 15. asparagus 16. artichokes 17. aubergines 18. peppers 19. shallots 20. spinach. **IX Eggs** 1. sucking eggs 2. hard-boiled egg 3. fried egg 4. scrambled eggs 5. omelette. **X Cheese** 1. parmesan 2. gruyère 3. packet cheese. **XI Sweets** 1. vanilla / nougat / pistachio / chocolate ice 2. trifle 3. tart 4. chocolate cake 5. fruit pie 6. cream caramel. **XII Fruit** 1. apple 2. pear 3. orange 4. tangerine 5. white / black grapes 6. cherries 7. apricots 8. plums 9. fresh / dried figs 10. banana 11. dates 12. walnuts 13. grapefruit 14. strawberries 15. raspberries 16. melon 17. water melon. **XIII Drinks** 1. water 2. mineral water 3. beer 4. wine 5. a quarter of a litre 6. half a litre 7. three-quarters of a litre 8. a litre 9. spirits 10. brandy 11. cider 12. orangeade 13. lemonade 14. orange squash 15. lemon squash 16. black coffee 17. espresso coffee 18. white coffee 19. coffee with cream 20. iced coffee 21. milk 22. chocolate 23. camomile tea.

**Italiano**

17. lingua 18. cosciotto 19. petto 20. tacchino 21. anitra 22. piccione 23. fagiano 24. cinghiale 25. capriolo 26. cervo 27. agnello. **VII Pesce** 1. tonno 2. merluzzo 3. baccalà 4. sogliola 5. cefalo 6. trota 7. orata 8. spigola 9. cernia 10. palombo 11. triglia 12. aragosta 13. gamberi 14. scampi 15. mazzancolle 16. polpi 17. calamari 18. fritto misto 19. ostriche. **VIII Contorni** 1. patate 2. purea di patate 3. patate al burro 4. patate arrosto 5. insalata verde 6. carote 7. fagioli 8. fagiolini 9. piselli 10. cavolo 11. verza 12. cavolfiore 13. cavoli di Bruxelles 14. pomodoro 15. asparagi 16. carciofi 17. melanzane 18. peperoni 19. scalogni 20. spinaci. **IX Uova** 1. uova da bere 2. uovo sodo 3. uovo all'occhio di bue 4. uova strapazzate 5. frittata. **X Formaggio** 1. parmigiano 2. groviera 3. formaggini. **XI Dolci** 1. gelato di vaniglia / torrone / pistacchio / cioccolata 2. zuppa inglese 3. crostata 4. torta di cioccolata 5. torta di frutta 6. creme caramelle. **XII Frutta** 1. mela 2. pera 3. arancia 4. mandarino 5. uva bianca / nera 6. ciliege 7. albicocche 8. prugne 9. fichi freschi / secchi 10. banana 11. datteri 12. noci 13. pompelmo 14. fragole 15. lamponi 16. melone 17. cocomero. **XIII Bevande** 1. acqua 2. acqua minerale 3. birra 4. vino 5. un quarto di litro 6. mezzo litro 7. tre quarti di litro 8. un litro 9. liquori 10. acquavite 11. sidro 12. aranciata 13. limonata 14. spremuta di arancia 15. spremuta di limone 16. caffè 17. caffè espresso 18. cappuccino 19. caffè con panna 20. caffè freddo 21. latte 22. cioccolata 23. camomilla.

**Français**

16. escalope panée 17. langue 18. cuisseau 19. blanc 20. dinde 21. canard 22. pigeon 23. faisan 24. sanglier 25. cabri 26. cerf 27. agneau. **VII Poissons** 1. thon 2. merlan 3. morue 4. sole 5. mulet 6. truite 7. daurade 8. loup 9. mérou 10. chien de mer 11. rouget 12. langouste 13. crevettes 14. langoustines 15. crevettes bouquet 16. poulpes 17. calamars 18. friture variée 19. huîtres. **VIII Légumes** 1. pommes de terre 2. purée de pommes de terre 3. pommes de terre au beurre 4. pommes de terre rôties 5. salade verte 6. carottes 7. haricots blancs 8. haricots verts 9. petits pois 10. chou 11. chou frisé 12. chou-fleur 13. choux de Bruxelles 14. tomate 15. asperges 16. artichauts 17. aubergines 18. poivrons 19. échalotes 20. épinards. **IX Oeufs** 1. oeuf à la coque 2. oeuf dur 3. oeuf au plat 4. oeufs brouillés 5. omelette. **X Fromages** 1. parmesan 2. gruyère 3. crèmes de fromage en portions individuelles. **XI Desserts** 1. glace à la vanille / au nougat / à la pistache / au chocolat 2. « soupe » anglaise 3. tarte 4. gâteau au chocolat 5. tourte aux fruits 6. crème renversée. **XII Fruits** 1. pomme 2. poire 3. orange 4. mandarine 5. raisin blanc / noir 6. cerises 7. abricots 8. prunes 9. figues fraîches / sèches 10. banane 11. dattes 12. noix 13. pamplemousse 14. fraises 15. framboises 16. melon 17. pastèque. **XIII Boissons** 1. eau 2. eau minérale 3. bière. 4. vin 5. un quart de litre 6. un demi-litre 7. trois quarts de litre 8. un litre 9. liqueurs 10. eau de vie 11. cidre 12. orangeade 13. limonade 4. orange pressée 15. citron pressé 16. café 17. café « espresso » 18. « cappuccino » 19. café avec crème 20. café froid 21. lait 22. chocolat 23. camomille.

| MOTEL AND HOTEL | MOTEL E ALBERGO | MOTEL ET HOTEL |
|---|---|---|
| Good evening, I should like a single-bedded / two-bedded / three-bedded room for tonight / for two days / for a week. | Buona sera, desidero una stanza a un letto / a due / tre letti per questa notte / per due giorni / per una settimana. | Bonsoir, je voudrais une chambre à un lit / deux / trois lits pour cette nuit / pour deux jours / pour une semaine. |
| I should like a double-bedded room with bath / without bath / with shower. | Vorrei una camera matrimoniale con / senza bagno / con doccia. | Je voudrais une chambre pour deux personnes avec / sans salle de bains / avec douche. |
| I am sorry, we have no rooms free. | Mi dispiace non abbiamo stanze libere. | Je regrette, nous n'avons plus de chambres libres. |
| Can I telephone to another hotel? | Posso telefonare a un altro albergo? | Puis-je téléphoner à un autre hôtel? |
| How much is this room? | Qual è il prezzo di questa camera? | Quel est le prix de cette chambre? |
| Is heating / service / visitors' tax included? | E' compreso il riscaldamento / il servizio / la tassa di soggiorno? | Le chauffage / le service / la taxe de séjour est-il (elle) compris (e)? |
| I should like full pension / half pension. | Vorrei la pensione completa / mezza pensione. | Je voudrais la pension complète / la demi-pension. |
| Is it possible to eat here? | C'è la possibilità di mangiare qui? | Est-il possible de prendre un repas ici? |
| The restaurant is already closed. | Il ristorante è già chiuso. | Le restaurant est déjà fermé. |
| Can you wake me at . . . tomorrow morning? | Può svegliarmi alle. . domattina? | Pourriez-vous me réveiller à ... heures demain matin? |

penstück 14. Schweinskotelett 15. Ragout 16. Wiener Schnitzel 17. Zunge 18. Keule 19. Brust 20. Truthahn 21. Ente 22. Taube 23. Fasan 24. Wildschwein 25. Reh 26 Hirsch 27. Lamm. **VII. Fischgerichte** 1. Thunfisch 2. Kabeljau 3. Stockfisch 4 Seezunge 5. Meeräsche 6. Forelle 7. Goldbrasse 8. Wolfsbarsch 9. Seebarsch 10. Hundshai 11. Rotbarbe 12. Languste 13. Garnele 14. Scampi 15. Heuschreckenkrebs 16. Kraken 17. Tintenfisch 18. Backfische 19. Austern. **VIII. Beilagen** 1. Kartoffeln 2. Kartoffelpüree 3. Butterkartoffeln 4. Bratkartoffeln 5. grüner Salat 6. Möhren / Karotten 7. Bohnen 8. Zwergbohnen 9. Erbsen 10. Kohl 11. Wirsing 12. Blumenkohl 13. Rosenkohl 14. Tomaten 15. Spargel 16. Artischocken 17. Eierfrüchte 18. Paprikaschoten 19. Schalotte 20. Spinat. **IX. Eier** 1. Trinkeier 2. hartes Ei 3. Spiegelei 4. Rühreier 5. Omelett. **X. Käse** 1. Parmesan 2 Emmentaler 3. Streichkäschen. **XI. Dessert** 1. Vanilleeis / Nugateis / Pistazieneis / Schokoladeneis 2. eisgekühlte Biskuitcremetorte 3. Mürbteigkuchen 4 Schokoladentorte 5. Obstkuchen 6 Karamelcreme. **XII. Obst** 1. Apfel 2. Birne 3. Orange 4. Mandarine 5. weisse / blaue Trauben 6. Kirschen 7. Aprikosen 8. Pflaumen 9. frische / getrocknete Feigen 10. Banane 11. Datteln 12. Nüsse 13. Pampelmuse 14. Erdbeeren 15. Himbeeren 16. Melone 17. Wassermelone. **XIII. Getränke** 1. Wasser 2. Mineralwasser 3. Bier 4. Wein 5. ein viertel Liter 6. ein halber Liter 7. dreiviertel Liter 8. ein Liter 9. Liköre 10. Branntwein 11. Apfelwein 12. Orangeade 13. Limonade 14. Orangensaft 15. Zitronensaft 16. Kaffee 17. Espresso 18. Kapuziner 19. Kaffee mit Sahne 20. kalter Kaffee 21. Milch 22. Schokolade 23. Kamillentee.

cerdo 15. trozos de carne estofada 16. chuleta a la milanesa 17. lengua 18. pernil 19. pecho 20. pavo 21. pato 22. pichón 23. faisán 24. jabalí 25. cabrito 26. ciervo 27. cordero. **VII Pescado** 1. bonito 2. merluza 3. bacalao 4. lenguado 5. róbalo 6. trucha 7. dorada 8. lubina 9. cherna 10. cazón 11. salmonete 12. langosta 13. gambas 14. cangrejos 15. cigalas 16. pulpos 17. calamares 18. fritura de pescado 19. ostras. **VIII Verduras y hortalizas** 1 patatas 2. puré de patatas 3. patatas con mantequilla 4. patatas asadas 5. ensalada verde 6. zanahoria 7 alubias 8. judías verdes 9. guisantes 10. coles 11. berzas 12. coliflor 13. coles de Bruselas 14. tomate 15. espárragos 16. alcachofas 17. berenjenas 18. pimiento 19. chalote 20. espinacas. **IX Huevos** 1. huevos de aldea 2. huevo cocido 3. huevo estrellado 4. huevos revueltos 5. tortilla. **X Quesos** 1. parmesano 2. gruyera 3. quesitos. **XI Dulces** 1 helado de vainilla / turrón / alfónsigo / chocolate 2. sopa inglesa 3. pastel glaseado 4. tarta de chocolate 5. tarta de fruta 6. creme caramelle. **XII Fruta** 1. manzana 2. pera 3. naranja 4. mandarinas 5. uva blanca / negra 6. cerezas 7. albaricoques 8. ciruelas 9. higos frescos / pasos 10. plátanos 11. dátiles 12. nueces 13. pomelo 14. fresas 15. frambuesas 16. melón 17. sandía. **XIII Bebidas** 1. agua 2. agua mineral 3. cerveza 4. vino 5. un cuarto 6. medio litro 7. tres cuartos 8. un litro 9. licores 10. aguardiente 11. sidra 12. naranjada 13. limonada 14. zumo de naranja 15. zumo de limón 16. café 17. café expreso 18. café cortado 19. café suizo 20. café frío 21. leche 22. chocolate 23. manzanilla

24. vepar 25. srndać 26. jelen 27. janje **VII Riba** 1. tuna 2. oslić 3. bakalar 4. obični list 5 cipal 6. pastrva 7. ovrata 8. brancin 9. kirnja 10. palombo 11. barbun 12. jastog 13. rakovi 14. škampi 15. mazzancolle 16. hobotnice 17. lignji 18. pržena miješana riba 19. ostrige. **VIII Dodatak** 1. krumpir 2. piré krumpir 3. krumpir na putru 4. pečeni krumpir 5. zelena salata 6. mrkva 7. grah 8. mahune 9. zeleni grašak 10. zelje 11. kelj 12. cvjetača 13. briselsko zelje 14. paradajz 15. špargla 16. artičoki 17. patlidžani 18 feferoni 19. ljutika 20 špinat. **IX Jaja** 1. jaja za popiti 2. tvrdo kuhano jaje 3. jaje na oko 4. kajgana 5. pržena jaja **X Sirevi** 1. parmezan 2. gruvier 3. mali sirevi. **XI Slatko** 1. sladoled od vanilije / mandule / pistacchio / čokolada 2. engleska juha 3. pita od jabuka 4. čokoladna torta 5. voćna torta 6. karamel krema. **XII Voće** 1. jabuka 2. kruška 3. naranča 4. mandarina 5. grozdje bijelo / crno 6. trešnje 7. marelice 8. šljive 9. smokve svježe / sušene 10. banane 11. datulje 12. orasi 13. grape fruit 14. jagode 15. maline 16. dinje 17. lubenice. **XIII Pića** 1. voda 2. mineralna voda 3. pivo 4. vino 5. četvrt litre 6. pola litre 7. tričetvrt litre 9. jedna litra 10. rakija 11. jabukovača 12. sok od naranči 13. limonada 14. prirodni narančin sok 15. prirodni limunov sok 16. kava 17. ekspres kava 18. kapuciner 19. kava sa šlagom 20. hladna kava 21. mlijeko 22 čokolada 23. kamilica.

| Deutsch | Español | Srpsko-hrvatski |
|---|---|---|
| Guten Abend, ich möchte ein Einbettzimmer / ein Doppelbettzimmer / ein Zimmer mit drei Betten für heute Nacht / für zwei Tage / für eine Woche. | Buenas noches, deseo una habitación de una cama / de dos / de tres camas para esta noche / por dos días / por una semana. | Dobar večer, želim sobu sa jednim krevetom / sa dva / tri kreveta za ovu noć / za dva dana / za jedan tjedan. |
| Ich möchte ein Doppelbettzimmer mit / ohne Bad / mit Dusche. | Desearía una habitación matrimonial con / sin baño / con ducha. | Želio bih jednu sobu sa bračnim krevetom sa / bez kupaone / sa tušem. |
| Es tut mir leid, wir haben keine Zimmer frei. | Lo siento mucho pero no tenemos habitaciones libres. | Žalim, ali nemano slobodnih soba. |
| Könnte ich ein anderes Hotel anrufen? | ¿Puedo llamar desde aquí a otro hotel? | Mogu li telefonirati u jedan drugi hotel? |
| Was kostet das Zimmer? | ¿Cuánto cuesta esta habitación? | Kolika je cijena ove sobe? |
| Ist die Heizung / die Bedienung / die Kurtaxe inbegriffen? | ¿Están incluídos la calefacción / el servicio / el impuesto de estancia? | Da li je uračunato grijante / servis / boravišna taksa? |
| Ich möchte Vollpension / Halbpension. | Desearía estar a pensión completa / a media pensión. | Želio bih kompletan pansion / polupansion. |
| Kann man hier essen? | ¿Es posible comer aquí? | Postoji li mogućnost, da jedem ovdje? |
| Das Restaurant ist schon geschlossen. | El restaurante está cerrado. | Restauracija je već zatvorena. |
| Würden Sie mich morgen um . . . Uhr wecken? | ¿Puede despertarme mañana a las . . . ? | Možete li me probuditi ujutro u . . . sati? |

| English | Italiano | Français |
|---|---|---|
| I should like breakfast for two in the bedroom. | Vorrei la colazione per due in camera. | Je voudrais un petit déjeuner pour deux dans la chambre, s'il vous plaît. |
| Here is the key | Ecco la chiave. | Voici la clef. |
| Can I park the car in front of the hotel? | Posso parcheggiare la vettura davanti all'albergo? | Peut-on garer la voiture devant l'hôtel? |
| Is there a garage? | C'è un garage? | Avez-vous un garage? |
| Is it possible to have the car washed and greased before nine tomorrow? | E' possibile far lavare e ingrassare la vettura prima delle nove di domani? | Est-il possible de laver et graisser la voiture pour demain matin à neuf heures? |
| Please send me the maid. | Per cortesia, mandi la cameriera. | Voudriez-vous m'envoyer la femme de chambre, je vous prie. |
| I'd like some hangers / some towels. | Potrei avere delle stampelle / degli asciugamani? | Pourrais-je avoir des cintres / des serviettes? |
| I have some laundry to be washed / some clothes to be pressed. | Ho della biancheria da lavare / dei vestiti da stirare. | J'ai du linge à faire laver / des vêtements à repasser. |
| Can it be ready tomorrow morning / tomorrow evening / the day after tomorrow? | Può essere pronta domattina / domani sera / dopodomani? | Peut-il est prêt demain matin demain soir / après-demain? |
| The heating isn't working. | Il riscaldamento non funziona. | Le chauffage ne fonctionne pas. |
| There isn't any hot water. | Nón c'è acqua calda. | Il n'y a pas d'eau chaude. |
| The cold tap doesn't turn off. | Il rubinetto dell'acqua fredda non chiude. | Le robinet de l'eau froide ne se ferme pas. |
| The wash-basin is blocked. | Il lavandino è otturato. | Le lavabo est bouché. |
| A bulb has fused. Can you change it please? | Si è fulminata la lampadina. La può cambiare per favore? | L'ampoule est grillée, seriez-vous assez gentil pour me la changer? |
| What is the voltage here? | Qual è il voltaggio qui? | Quel voltage avez-vous ici? |
| Where is the bathroom? | Dov'è il bagno? | Où est la salle de bains? |
| It's on the floor above / below. | E' al piano di sopra / di sotto. | A l'étage au-dessus / au-dessous |
| Please send the porter with / for the luggage. | Per cortesia, mandi il facchino con / per i bagagli. | Pourriez-vous m'envoyer le porteur avec / pour les bagages? |
| Have you got a telephone directory? | Ha un elenco telefonico? | Avez-vous un annuaire du téléphone? |
| Can you call this number at . . . for me? | Può chiamarmi questo numero a . . . ? | Voudriez-vous m'appeler ce numéro à ..., s'il vous plaît? |
| You will have to wait. The number is engaged. | Deve attendere. Il numero è occupato. | Le numéro est occupé, il vous faut attendre. |
| How much does it cost to call . . .? | Quanto costa una conversazione con . . .? | Quel est le prix d'une conversation avec ...? |
| How many minutes did I speak? | Quanti minuti ho parlato? | Pendant combien de minutes ai-je parlé? |
| How much do I owe for this conversation? | Quanto devo per questa comunicazione? | Combien vous dois-je pour cette communication? |

| Deutsch | Español | Srpsko-hrvatski |
|---|---|---|
| Könnten Sie das Frühstück für zwei auf das Zimmer bringen lassen? | Quisiera dos desayunos en la habitación. | Želim u sobu doručak za dvoje. |
| Hier ist der Schlüssel. | Aquí tiene la llave. | Izvolite ključ. |
| Kann ich den Wagen vor dem Hotel parken? | ¿Podemos aparcar el coche delante del hotel? | Mogu li dobiti vješalice / ručnike? |
| Haben Sie eine Garage? | ¿Hay un garaje? | Postoji li garaža? |
| Wäre es möglich, den Wagen bis morgen früh um neun Uhr zu waschen und zu schmieren? | ¿Es posible lavar y engrasar el coche antes de las 9 de mañana. | Da li je moguće do ujutro do devet sati oprati i podmazati kola? |
| Bitte schicken Sie mir das Zimmermädchen. | Por favor, mande la camarera. | Molim da mi pošaljete sobaricu. |
| Bitte bringen Sie mir Kleiderbügel / Handtücher. | ¿Puede traerme algunas perchas / toallas. | Mogu li dobiti vješalice / ručnike? |
| Ich habe Wäsche zu waschen / Kleider zu bügeln. | Tengo ropa para lavar / vestidos para planchar. | Iman rublje za pranje / odijela za peglanje. |
| Kann ich sie morgen vormittag / morgen abend / übermorgen zurückbekommen? | ¿Podrá estar lista para mañana por la mañana / mañana por la tarde / pasado mañana? | Može li biti gotovo ujutro / sutra uveče / preksutra? |
| Die Heizung funktioniert nicht. | La calefacción no funciona. | Grijanje ne funkcionira. |
| Es rinnt kein warmes Wasser. | No hay agua caliente. | Nema tople vode. |
| Der Kaltwasserhahn schliesst nicht. | El grifo del agua fría no cierra bien. | Ventil za hladnu vodu ne zatvara. |
| Das Waschbecken ist verstopft. | El lavabo está obstruído. | Umivaonik je začepljen. |
| Die Birne ist ausgebrannt. Würden Sie sie bitte auswechseln? | Se ha fundido una bombilla. ¿Puede cambiarla por favor? | Pregorjela je žarulja. Možete li je izmijeniti? |
| Was für eine Stromspannung haben Sie hier? | ¿Qué voltaje tienen aquí? | Koliki je ovdje napon struje? |
| Wo ist das Bad? | ¿Dónde está el baño? | Gdje je kupaona? |
| Im oberen / unteren Stock. | En el piso de arriba / de abajo. | Nalazi se na katu iznad / ispod. |
| Bitte schicken Sie den Hausdiener mit dem / um das Gepäck. | Por favor, envie al mozo con / a por los equipajes. | Molim da mi pošaljete nosača / za prtljagu. |
| Haben Sie ein Telefonbuch? | ¿Tiene la lista de teléfonos? | Imate li telefonski imenik? |
| Könnten Sie mich mit dieser Nummer in . . . verbinden? | ¿Puede llamar Vd. a este número de . . .? | Možete li mi nazvati ovaj broj iz . . .? |
| Sie müssen warten. Die Nummer ist besetzt. | Tiene que esperar. Están comunicando. | Morate sačekati. Broj je zauzet. |
| Wieviel kostet ein Gespräch mit . . .? | ¿Cuánto cuesta una conversación con . . .? | Koliko košta jedan razgovor sa . . .? |
| Wie viele Minuten habe ich gesprochen? | ¿Cuántos minutos ha hablado? | Koliko minuta sam govorio? |
| Was bin ich für dieses Gespräch schuldig? | ¿Cuánto pago por esta comunicación? | Koliko sam dužan za ovaj razgovor? |

| English | Italiano | Français |
|---|---|---|
| Please give me a counter for the telephone. | Mi dia per favore un gettone telefonico. | Je voudrais un jeton de téléphone, s'il vous plaît. |
| How much is a counter? | Quanto costa un gettone? | Combien coûte un jeton? |
| What is the number of the exchange? | Qual è il numero del centralino? | Quel est le numéro du standard? |
| You can call direct. This is the prefix. | Lei può parlare in teleselezione. Questo è il prefisso. | Vous pouvez parler sur l'automatique; voici le préfixe. |
| I am leaving tomorrow morning early. Can you prepare my bill, please? | Parto domani mattina presto. Mi può preparare il conto per favore? | Je voudrais partir demain matin de bonne heure. Pourriez-vous me préparer ma note? |
| I should like to pay the bill. | Vorrei pagare il conto. | Je voudrais payer ma note. |
| Do you take cheques? | Accetta assegni? | Acceptez-vous les chèques? |
| Can I pay in traveller's cheques? | Posso pagare con traveller's cheques? | Puis-je payer en traveller's chèques? |

**I Bedroom and services** 1. single room 2. two-bedded room 3. child's bed 4. bathroom 5. shower 6. price 7. room with breakfast 8. full pension 9. half pension 10. heating 11. visitors' tax 12. overnight stay 13. stay 14. lift 15. first / second / third floor 16. hall porter 17. waiter 18. waitress / maid 19. porter 20. telephone 21. switchboard 22. telephone number 23. room service 24. bill 25. cheque 26. foreign currency 27. cash 28. tip 29. garage 30. wash 31. greasing. **II Breakfast** 1. black coffee 2. white coffee 3. chocolate 4. tea 5. milk 6. lemon 7. orange squash 8. grapefruit 9. bread 10. butter 11. jam 12. honey 13. breadsticks 14. biscuits 15. toast. **III Furnishings and fittings** 1. bed 2. mattress 3. sheet 4. blanket 5. eiderdown 6. quilt 7. pillow 8. pillow-case 9. bedside table 10. lamp 11. bulb 12. bell 13. ashtray 14. cupboard 15. hanger 16. key 17. door 18. bathroom 19. bath 20. wash-basin 21. tap 22. hot / cold water 23. electric point 24. voltage 25. towel 26. soft towel 27. soap 28. toothpaste 29. toothbrush 30. razor blade 31. shaving cream 32. shaving brush 33. brush 34. needle 35. white / black / grey thread 36. button 37. safety pin. **IV Clothes** 1. laundry 2. socks 3. shirt 4. pants 5. handkerchiefs 6. pyjamas 7. nightdress 8. blouse 9. skirt 10. trousers 11. jacket 12. man's suit 13. dress 14. to wash 15. to press 16. to remove stains 17. to dry-clean.

**I Camera e servizi** 1. camera a un letto 2. camera a due letti 3. letto per bambini 4. bagno 5. doccia 6. prezzo 7. camera con prima colazione 8. pensione completa 9. mezza pensione 10. riscaldamento 11. tassa di soggiorno 12. pernottamento 13. soggiorno 14. ascensore 15. primo / secondo / terzo piano 16. portiere 17. cameriere 18. cameriera 19. facchino 20. telefono 21. centralino 22. numero del telefono 23. servizio in camera 24. conto 25. assegno 26. valuta estera 27. danaro in contanti 28. mancia 29. garage 30. lavaggio 31. ingrassaggio. **II Prima colazione** 1. caffè 2. caffellatte 3. cioccolata 4. tè 5. latte 6. limone 7. spremuta di arancia 8. pompelmo 9. pane 10. burro 11. marmellata 12. miele 13. grissini 14. biscotti 15. fette tostate. **III Arredamento e oggetti vari** 1. letto 2. materasso 3. lenzuola 4. coperta 5. piumino 6. imbottita 7. cuscino 8. federa 9. comodino 10. lume 11. lampadina 12. campanello 13. portacenere 14. armadio 15. stampelle 16. chiave 17. porta 18. bagno 19. vasca da bagno 20. lavandino 21. rubinetto 22. acqua calda / fredda 23. presa 24. voltaggio 25. asciugamano 26. asciugamano di spugna 27. sapone 28. dentifricio 29. spazzolino da denti 30. lamette 31. sapone da barba 32. pennello da barba 33. spazzola 34. ago 35 filo bianco / nero / grigio 36. bottone 37. spilla di sicurezza. **IV Indumenti** 1. biancheria 2. calzini 3. camicia 4. mutande 5. fazzoletti 6. pigiama 7. camicia da notte 8. camicetta 9. gonna 10. pantaloni 11. giacca 12. vestito da uomo 13. vestito da donna 14. lavare 15. stirare 16. smacchiare 17. pulire a secco.

**I Chambre et services** 1. chambre à un lit 2. chambre à deux lits 3. lit d'enfant 4. salle de bains 5. douche 6. prix 7. chambre avec petit déjeuner 8. pension complète 9. demi-pension 10. chauffage 11. taxe de séjour 12. séjour d'une nuit 13. séjour 14. ascenseur 15. premier / deuxième / troisième étage 16. concierge 17. valet de chambre 18. femme de chambre 19. porteur 20 téléphone 21. standard 22. numéro de téléphone 23. service dans la chambre 24. note 25. chèque 26. devises étrangères 27. espèces 28. pourboire 29. garage 30. lavage 31. graissage. **II Petit déjeuner** 1.café 2. café au lait 3. chocolat 4. thé 5. lait 6. citron 7. orange pressée 8. pamplemousse 9. pain 10. beurre 11. confiture 12. miel 13. gressins 14. biscuits 15. pain grillé. **III Ameublement et objets variés** 1. lit 2. matelas 3. draps 4. couverture 5. édredon 6. courtepointe 7. oreiller 8. taie d'oreiller 9. table de chevet 10. lampe 11. ampoule 12. sonnette 13. cendrier 14. armoire 15. cintres 16. clef 17. porte 18. salle de bains 19. baignoire 20. lavabo 21. robinet 22. eau chaude / froide 23. prise 24. voltage 25. serviette 26. serviette éponge 27. savon 28. dentifrice 29. brosse à dents 30. lames de rasoir 31. savon à barbe 32. blaireau 33. brosse 34. aiguille 35. fil blanc / noir / gris 36. bouton 37. épingle de sûreté. **IV Vêtements** 1. linge 2. chaussettes 3. chemise 4. slip 5. mouchoirs 6. pyjama 7. chemise de nuit 8. chemisier 9. jupe 10. pantalon 11. veste 12. complet d'homme 13. robe 14. laver 15. repasser 16. détacher 17. nettoyer à sec.

| CAMPING | CAMPEGGIO | CAMPING |
|---|---|---|
| Can you please tell me if camping is unrestricted in this area? | Per cortesia, sa se in questa zona si può campeggiare liberamente? | S'il vous plaît, pouvez-vous me dire si l'on peut camper librement dans cet endroit? |
| Is there a camping site hereabouts? | C'è nelle vicinanze un campeggio? | Y a-t-il un camping dans les parages? |

| Deutsch | Español | Srpsko-hrvatski |
|---|---|---|
| Eine Telefonmünze bitte. | ¿Me da por favor una ficha telefónica? | Dajte mi molin jedan žeton za telefon. |
| Wieviel kostet eine Münze? | ¿Cuánto pago por una ficha? | Koliko košta jedan žeton? |
| Wie ist die Nummer der Telefonzentrale? | ¿Cuál es el número de la central? | Koji je broj centrale? |
| Sie können durchwählen. Dies ist die Vorwahlnummer. | Vd. puede hablar por teleselección. El prefijo es . . . | Možete razgovarati automatski. Ovo je prefiks. |
| Ich fahre morgen sehr früh ab. Würden Sie bitte die Rechnung vorbereiten? | Salgo mañana a primera hora. ¿Me puede preparar la cuenta? | Putujem sutra ujutro rano. Možete li mi pripraviti račun? |
| Ich möchte die Rechnung bezahlen. | Quisiera pagar mi cuenta. | Želio bih platiti račun. |
| Nehmen Sie Schecks an? | ¿Acepta Vd. cheques? | Primate li čekove? |
| Kann ich mit traveller's cheques bezahlen? | ¿Puedo pagar en traveller's cheques? | Mogu li platiti sa traveller's čekovima? |

**I. Zimmer und Bedienung** 1. Einbettzimmer 2. Doppelbettzimmer 3. Kinderbett 4. Bad 5. Dusche 6. Preis 7. Zimmer mit Frühstück 8. Vollpension 9. Halbpension 10. Heizung 11. Kurtaxe 12. Übernachtung 13. Aufenthalt 14. Aufzug 15. erster / zweiter / dritter Stock 16. Portier 17. Kellner 18. Zimmermädchen 19. Hausdiener 20. Telefon 21. Telefonzentrale 22. Telefonnummer 23. Zimmerservice 24. Rechnung 25. Scheck 26. ausländische Valuta 27. Bargeld 28. Trinkgeld 29. Garage 30. Waschen 31. Schmieren. **II. Frühstück** 1. Kaffee 2. Milchkaffee 3. Schokolade 4. Tee 5. Milch 6. Zitrone 7. Orangensaft 8. Pampelmuse 9. Brot 10. Butter 11. Marmelade 12. Honig 13. Brot in dünnen Stangen 14. Keks 15. Toast. **III. Einrichtung und verschiedene Gegenstände** 1. Bett 2. Matraze 3. Leintuch 4. Decke 5. Federbett 6. Steppdecke 7. Kissen 8. Kissenbezug 9. Nachttisch 10. Lampe 11. elektrische Birne 12. Klingel 13. Aschenbecher 14. Schrank 15. Kleiderbügel 16. Schlüssel 17. Türe 18. Bad 19. Badewanne 20. Waschbecken 21. Wasserhahn 22. warmes / kaltes Wasser 23. Steckdose 24. Stromspannung 25. Handtuch 26. Frottiertuch 27. Seife 28. Zahnpaste 29. Zahnbürste 30. Rasierklinge 31. Rasierseife 32. Rasierpinsel 33. Bürste 34. Nadel 35. weisser / schwarzer / grauer Faden 36. Knopf 37. Sicherheitsnadel. **IV. Kleidungsstücke** 1. Wäsche 2. Socken 3. Hemd 4. Unterhosen 5. Taschentücher 6. Pyjama 7. Nachthemd 8. Bluse 9. Rock 10. Hose 11. Jacke 12. Anzug 13. Kleid 14. waschen 15. bügeln 16. entflecken 17. chemisch reinigen.

**I Habitación y servicios** 1. habitación de una cama 2. habitación de dos camas 3. cama para niños 4. baño 5. ducha 6. precio 7. habitación y desayuno 8. pensión completa 9. media pensión. 10. calefacción 11. impuesto de estancia 12. pasar la noche 13. estancia 14. ascensor 15. primer / segundo / tercer piso 16. portero 17. camarero 18. camarera 19. mozo 20. teléfono 21. central 22. número de teléfono 23. servicio en la habitación 24. cuenta 25. cheque 26 divisa extranjera 27. dinero al contado 28. propina 29 garaje 30. lavado 31. engrasado. **II Desayuno** 1. café 2. café con leche 3. chocolate 4. té 5. leche 6. limón 7. zumo de naranja 8. pomelo 9. pan 10. mantequilla 11. mermelada 12. miel 13. grisines 14. bizcochos 15. tostadas de pan. **III Muebles y objetos diversos** 1. cama 2. colchón 3. sábana 4. manta 5. edredón 6. manta acolchada 7. almohada 8. funda de la almohada 9. mesita de noche 10. luz de mesa 11. bombilla 12. timbre 13. cenicero 14. armario 15. perchas 16. llave 17. puerta 18. baño 19. bañera 20. lavabo 21. grifo 22 agua caliente / fría 23. toma de corriente 24. voltaje 25. toalla 26. toalla de felpa 27. jabón 28. pasta de dientes 29. cepillo de dientes 30. cuchillas de afeitar 31. jabón de afeitar 32. brocha de afeitar 33. cepillo 34. aguja 35. hilo / blanco / negro / gris 36. botón 37. imperdible. **IV Indumentos** 1. ropa interior 2. calcetines 3. camisa 4. calzoncillos 5. pañuelos 6. pijama 7. camisa de noche 8. camiseta 9. falda 10. pantalones 11. chaqueta 12. traje de caballero 13. vestido de señora 14. lavar 15. planchar 16. limpiar 17. limpiar en seco.

**I Soba i posluga** 1. jednokrevetna soba 2. dvokrevetna soba 3. krevet za djecu 4. kupaona 5. tuš 6. cijena 7. soba sa doručkom 8. kompletni pansion 9. polupansion 10. grijanje 11. boravišna taksa 12. noćenje 13. boravak 14. dizalo 15. prvi / drugi / treći kat 16. portir 17. sobar 18. sobarica 19. nosač 20. telefon 21. centrala 22. broj telefona 23. posluga u sobu 24. račun 25. ček 26. strana valuta 27. gotovina 28. napojnica 29. garaža 30. pranje 31. podmazivanie. **II Doručak** 1. kava 2. bijela kava 3. čokolada 4. čaj 5. mlijeko 6. limun 7. prirodni narančin sok 8. grape fruit 9. kruh 10. putar 11. marmelada 12. med 13. grisini 14. keksi 15. prženi kruh. **III Namještaj i razni predmeti** 1. krevet 2. madrac 3. plahta 4. pokrivač 5. perjanica 6. vatirani pokrivač 7. jastuk 8. jastučnica 9. noćni ormarić 10. svjetiljka 11. žarulja 12. zvonce 13. pepeljara 14. ormar 15. vješalice 16. ključ 17. vrata 18. kupaonica 19. kada za kupanje 20. umivaonik 21. ventil 22 voda topla / hladna 23. utikačka kutija 24. napon struje 25. ručnik 26. frotir ručnik 27. sapun 28. zubna pasta 29. četka za zube 30. nožići za brijanje 31. sapun za brijanje 32. četka za brijanje 33. četka 34. igla 35. konac bijeli / crni / sivi 36. dugme 37. sigurnosna igla. **IV Odjeća** 1. rublje 2. čarape 3. košulja 4. gaće 5. maramice 6. pidžama 7. noćna košulja 8. ženska bluza 9. suknja 10. hlače 11. kratki kaput 12. muško odijelo 13. haljina 14. prati 15. peglati 16. očistiti mrlje 17. očistiti na suho.

| CAMPING | CAMPING | KAMPIRANJE |
|---|---|---|
| Können Sie mir bitte sagen, ob man in dieser Zone frei zelten kann? | ¿Tiene la amabilidad de decirme si en esta zona se puede levantar una tienda libremente? | Molim vas, da li znate ako se u ovoj zoni smije slobodno kampirati? |
| Ist ein Campingplatz hier in der Nähe? | ¿Hay por estos alrededores un campamento? | Postoji li u blizini camping? |

| English | Italiano | Français |
|---|---|---|
| Is it by the sea? | Si trova sul mare? | Se trouve-t-il au bord de la mer? |
| I think so. There's a signpost a little further on. | Credo di sì. Poco più avanti c'è un cartello indicatore. | Je crois que oui. Un peu plus loin, il doit y avoir un panneau indicateur. |
| At this time of the year is the camping site on the hill open? | In questa stagione è ancora aperto il campeggio in collina? | Le camping sur la colline est-il encore ouvert en cette saison? |
| Good morning (afternoon) / good evening, is there still room for two tents? | Buon giorno / buona sera, c'è ancora posto per due tende? | Bonjour / bonsoir, avez-vous encore de la place pour deux tentes? |
| Yes, you will find room beyond that copse on the right. Come along at your leisure to pay. | Sì, lo troverà oltre quel boschetto sulla destra. Per il pagamento venga pure con comodo. | Oui, vous trouverez l'endroit après le petit bois sur votre droite. Pour le règlement, venez quand vous voudrez. |
| How much is it a day for a car and two tents? | Quanto si paga al giorno per una macchina e due tende? | Combien doit-on payer par jour pour une voiture et deux tentes? |
| How much for a caravan? | Quanto si paga per una roulotte? | Combien doit-on payer pour une roulotte? |
| The showers and WCs are that way. | Le docce e la toilette sono da quella parte. | Les douches et sanitaires sont de ce côté. |
| The shop is open all day long, until . . . | Lo spaccio è aperto tutto il giorno, fino alle . . . | Le magasin est ouvert toute la journée, jusqu'à . . . |
| Is it drinking water? | L'acqua è potabile? | L'eau est-elle potable? |
| Only from the tap where it says so. | Solo quella del rubinetto dove c'è l'apposita indicazione. | Seulement celle du robinet qui en porte l'indication. |
| What food can we buy? | Che cosa si può comperare da mangiare? | Que peut-on acheter pour manger? |
| Milk, eggs, tinned food, jam, sauces, oil. In short, there's a little of everything. | Latte, uova, conserve, marmellata, salse, olio. Insomma c'è un po' di tutto. | Du lait, des oeufs, des conserves, de la confiture, des sauces, de l'huile: un peu de tout, en somme. |
| Do you sell cigarettes and tobacco too? | Avete anche tabacchi? | Avez-vous aussi un tabac? |
| Yes, in the other shop. If you need them, you'll find newspapers and camping equipment there. | Sì, nell'altro negozio. Là, se le occorrono, troverà anche giornali e attrezzi da campeggio. | Oui, dans l'autre magasin il y a un débit de tabac. Au besoin vous y trouverez aussi des journaux et du matériel de camping. |
| Even aluminium tent pegs? | Anche i picchetti di alluminio? | Même des piquets d'aluminium? |
| Yes, the normal ones at any rate. Perhaps not the ones for sand. | Sì, per lo meno quelli normali. Forse non ci sono quelli da sabbia. | Oui, du moins le modèle courant; peut-être pas le modèle pour le sable. |
| I also need a rubber mattress. | Avrei anche bisogno di un materassino pneumatico. | J'ai besoin d'un matelas pneumatique. |
| How late can the radio be kept on in the evening? | Fino a che ora, la sera, si può ascoltare la radio? | Jusqu'à quelle heure peut-on écouter la radio, le soir? |
| Until . . . Afterwards it's absolutely forbidden to disturb other campers. | Fino alle . . . Dopo è assolutamente vietato disturbare gli altri campeggiatori. | Jusqu'à . . . Après, il est rigoureusement interdit de déranger les autres campeurs. |
| **I Tent** 1. tent canvas 2. lean-to 3. tent pole 4. peg 5. elastic guy rope 6. rope. **II Other equipment** 1. hammer 2. mat- | **I Tenda** 1. telo da tenda 2. veranda 3. paletto 4. picchetto 5. tirante elastico 6. corda. **II Altri attrezzi** 1. mar- | **I Tentes** 1. toile de tente 2. auvent 3. pieu 4. piquet 5. tendeur en caoutchouc 6. corde. **II Autre équipement** 1. marteau |

| Deutsch | Español | Srpsko-hrvatski |
|---|---|---|
| Liegt er am Meer? | ¿Está cerca del mar? | Da li se nalazi na moru? |
| Ich glaube ja. Weiter vorn steht ein Schild. | Creo que sí. Un poco más adelante hay un cartel indicador. | Vjerujem da. Malo dalje se nalazi jedna tabla sa upozorenjem. |
| Ist in dieser Jahreszeit der Zeltplatz auf dem Hügel noch offen? | ¿En esta época funciona todavía el campamento de montaña? | Da li je u ovo vrijeme još otvoren camping u brdima? |
| Guten Tag / guten Abend, haben Sie noch Platz für zwei Zelte? | Buenos días / buenas tardes ¿hay sitio para dos tiendas? | Dobar, dan / dobar večer, ima li još mjesta za dva šatora? |
| Ja, rechts nach dem Wäldchen. Sie können später zum Zahlen kommen. | Sí, lo encontrará más allá de aquel bosquecillo, a la derecha. Para efectuar el pago no tenga prisa. | Da, naći ćete ga iza one šumice na desno. Za uplatu možete doći i naknadno. |
| Wie hoch ist die Tagesgebühr für einen Wagen und zwei Zelte? | ¿Cuánto se paga al día por un coche y dos tiendas? | Koliko se plaća dnevno za jedna kola i dva šatora? |
| Wie hoch ist die Gebühr für einen Wohnwagen? | ¿Cuánto se paga por una roulotte? | Koliko se plaća za jednu prikolicu za spavanje? |
| Die Duschen und die Toilette sind dort drüben. | Las duchas y los servicios higiénicos están en aquella parte. | Tuševi i toaleta su na onoj strani. |
| Der Laden ist ganztägig bis . . . Uhr geöffnet. | El despacho está abierto todo el día, hasta las... | Prodavaonica je otvorena cijeli dan do . . . sati. |
| Ist dies Trinkwasser? | ¿El agua es potable? | Da li je voda pitka? |
| Nur jenes aus dem Hahn mit der Trinkwasserüberschrift. | Sólo la del grifo indicado con el correspondiente letrero. | Samo ona iz slavine označene znakom. |
| Was kann man Essbares kaufen? | ¿Qué es lo que se puede comparar de comer? | Što se može kupiti za jelo? |
| Milch, Eier, Konserven, Marmelade, Sossen, Öl. Es gibt so ziemlich alles. | Leche, huevos, conservas, setas, aceite. En una palabra hay de todo un poco. | Mlijeko, jaja, konzerve, marmelada, sosovi, ulje. Uglavnom ima svega pomalo? |
| Haben Sie auch Tabakwaren? | ¿Se vende también tabaco? | Imate li i trafiku? |
| Ja, im anderen Laden. Dort werden Sie auch Zeitungen und Campinggeräte finden, sollten Sie etwas brauchen. | Sí, en otro despacho. Allí, si los necesita, encontrará tambien periódicos y utensilios para campamento. | Da, nalazi se u drugom dućanu. Ako vam zatreba, tamo ćete naći novine i pribor za kampiranje. |
| Auch Aluminium-Heringe? | ¿Hay también jalones de aluminio? | Takodjer i aluminijske kočiće? |
| Ja, zumindest die herkömmlichen. Vielleicht gibt es die für Sand nicht. | Sí, por lo menos los normales. Quizás no haya los de playa. | Da, barem one normalne. Možda nećete naći one za pijesak. |
| Ich bräuchte auch eine Luftmatraze. | Necesito un colchón neumático. | Trebao bih takodjer jedan zračni madrac. |
| Wie lange kann man abends Radio hören? | ¿Hasta qué hora, por la noche, se puede escuchar la radio? | Do koliko sati uvečer se može slušati radio? |
| Bis . . . Uhr. Nachher ist es strengstens verboten, die anderen Campinggäste zu stören. | Hasta las... Después está absolumente prohíbido molestar a los demás acampados. | Do . . . sati. Poslije je apsolutno zabranjeno unznemiravati ostale goste. |

**I. Zelt** 1. Zeltbahn 2. Veranda 3. Stock 4. Hering 5. Spannschnur 6. Seil. **II. Andere Geräte** 1. Hammer 2. kleine Hacke

**I Tienda** 1. tela para tienda de campaña 2. porche 3. palos 4. jalones 5. tirante elástico 6. cuerda. **II Otros uten-**

**I Šator** 1. šatorsko krilo 2. veranda 3. stup 4. kočić 5. elastični zatezač 6. konopac. **II Ostali pribor** 1. čekić 2. mo-

| English | Italiano | Français |
|---|---|---|
| tock 3. axe 4. sleeping bag 5. camp bed 6. mosquito net 7. electric lamp 8. oil lamp 9. gas lamp 10. water bucket 11. pedal pump shower 12. pocket torch 13. petrol stove 14. gas (cylinder) stove 15. oil stove 16. table 17. chair 18. hammock 19. saucepan 20. frying pan 21. plate 22. glass 23. cutlery. | tello 2. zappetta 3. scure 4. sacco-letto 5. branda 6. zanzariera 7. lanterna elettrica 8. lanterna a petrolio 9. lanterna a bombola di gas 10. recipiente per l'acqua 11. doccia con pompa a pedale 12. lampadina tascabile 13. fornello a benzina 14. fornello a bombola di gas 15. fornello a petrolio 16. tavolo 17. sedia 18. amaca 19. pentola 20. padella 21. piatto 22. bicchiere 23. posate. | 2. petite bêche 3. hache 4. sac de couchage 5. lit de camp 6. moustiquaire 7. lampe électrique 8. lampe à pétrole 9. lampe à butane 10. récipient pour l'eau 11. douche avec pompe à pédale 12. lampe de poche 13. réchaud à essence 14. réchaud à butane 15. réchaud à pétrole 16. table 17. chaise 18. hamac 19. casserole 20. poêle 21. assiette 22. verre 23. couverts. |

| ACCIDENTS | INCIDENTI | ACCIDENTS |
|---|---|---|
| Please let this person know about the accident I've had. This is the telephone number. | Per favore, avverta questa persona dell'incidente che mi è accaduto. Qui c'è il suo numero di telefono. | Veuillez avoir l'amabilité d'avertir cette personne de l'accident qui m'est arrivé. Voici son numéro de téléphone. |
| This man is injured. He must be taken to hospital. | Quest'uomo è ferito. Bisogna portarlo all'ospedale. | Cet homme est blessé, il faut le transporter à l'hôpital. |
| It would be dangerous to move this woman. | Questa donna non può essere mossa da noi, sarebbe pericoloso. | Nous ne pouvons pas déplacer cette femme, ce serait dangereux. |
| The car might catch fire. Let's try to get the occupants out. | La vettura può incendiarsi. Cerchiamo di liberare gli occupanti. | La voiture peut brûler. Essayons de dégager les occupants. |
| Have you got a fire extinguisher? | Avete un estintore? | Avez-vous un extincteur? |
| Be careful! The petrol tank is leaking. There's oil on the road. | Attenzione! Si è rotto il serbatoio della benzina. C'è dell'olio sulla strada. | Attention! Le réservoir d'essence perd. Il y a de l'huile sur la route. |
| Let's put a warning triangle before the bend. | Mettiamo il triangolo rosso prima della curva. | Il faut mettre le triangle rouge avant le virage. |
| Have you got a first-aid chest? | Avete una cassetta di pronto soccorso? | Avez-vous une trousse de premiers soins? |
| Call a doctor. | Chiami un medico. | Appelez un médecin. |
| Let's stop a car. | Fermiamo una vettura. | Arrêtons une voiture. |
| Where is the telephone to call for help? | Dov'è il telefono per il soccorso stradale? | Où se trouve le téléphone pour appeler le secours routier? |
| Let's call the ambulance. | Chiamiamo l'autoambulanza. | Appelons une ambulance. |
| I cannot move my right / left arm. | Non posso muovere il braccio destro / sinistro. | Je ne peux pas remuer le bras droit / gauche. |
| I have a sharp pain in my right / left leg. | Ho un forte dolore alla gamba destra / sinistra. | Ma jambe droite / gauche me fait très mal. |
| We need something to immobilize the leg / the arm. | Occorre qualche cosa per immobilizzare la gamba / il braccio. | Il faudrait quelque chose pour immobiliser la jambe / le bras. |
| I cannot walk. | Non riesco a camminare. | Je ne peux pas marcher. |
| My right / left hand is bleeding. | Mi sanguina la mano destra / sinistra. | Ma main droite / gauche saigne. |
| We need something round and a handkerchief to stop the bleeding. | Occorre un oggetto tondo e un fazzoletto per fermare il sangue. | Il me faudrait un objet rond et un mouchoir pour arrêter le sang. |

| Deutsch | Español | Srpsko-hrvatski |
|---|---|---|
| 3. Beil 4. Schlafsack 5. Feldbett 6. Moskitonetz 7. Handscheinwerfer 8. Petroleumlampe 9. Gaslampe 10. Wasserbehälter 11. Dusche mit Pedalpumpe 12. Taschenlampe 13. Benzinkocher 14. Gaskocher 15. Petroleumkocher 16. Tisch 17. Stuhl 18. Hängematte 19. Kochtopf 20. Pfanne 21. Teller 22. Glas 23. Besteck. | **silios** 1. martillo 2. azadilla 3. hacha 4. bolsacama 5. catre 6. mosquitero 7 linterna eléctrica 8. linterna de petróleo 9. linterna de gas 10. recipiente para el agua 11. ducha con bomba de pedal 12. linterna de bolsillo 13. hornillo de gasolina 14. hornillo de gas 15. hornillo de petróleo 16. mesa 17. silla 18. hamaca 19. olla 20. sartén 21. plato 22. vaso 23. cubiertos. | tika 3. sjekira 4. vreća za spavanje 5. poljski krevet 6. mreža protiv insekata 7. električna svjetiljka 8. petrolejska lampa 9. svjetiljka na bocu sa plinom 10. posuda za vodu 11. tuš sa pumpom na pedalu 12. džepna svjetiljka 13. benzinsko kuhalo 14. kuhalo na plin iz boce 15. petrolejsko kuhalo 16. stol 17. stolac 18. mreža za ležanje 19. šerpa 20. tava 21. tanjur 22. čaša 23. pribor za jelo. |

| UNFÄLLE | ACCIDENTES | NESREĆE |
|---|---|---|
| Bitte verständigen Sie diese Person von meinem Unfall. Hier ist die Telefonnummer. | Por favor, avise a esta persona del accidente que me ha ocurrido. Aquí está su número de teléfono. | Molin obavijestite ovu osobu o nesreći koja mi se dogodila. Tu je njen telefonski broj. |
| Dieser Mann ist verletzt. Er muss ins Krankenhaus gebracht werden. | Esta persona está herida. Hay que llevarla al hospital. | Ovaj čovjek je ranjen. Potrebno ga je prevesti u bolnicu. |
| Diese Frau darf nicht bewegt werden: es wäre gefährlich. | No conviene mover a esta señora, sería peligroso. | Ovu ženu mi ne smijemo pomicati, jer bi moglo biti opasno. |
| Der Wagen könnte in Brand geraten. Versuchen wir, die Insassen zu befreien. | El coche puede incendiarse. Tratemos de salvar a los ocupantes. | Kola se mogu upaliti. Gledajmo da oslobodimo putnike. |
| Haben Sie einen Feuerlöscher? | ¿Tiene un estintor? | Imate li aparat za gašenje požara? |
| Achtung, der Benzintank ist gebrochen! Es ist Öl auf der Strasse! | ¡Cuidado! que se ha roto el tanque de la gasolina. Que hay aceite en la carretera. | Oprez! Probušen je rezervoar za benzin. Ima ulja na cesti. |
| Stellen wir das Warndreieck vor der Kurve auf. | Coloquemos una señal con luz roja antes de la curva. | Stavimo signalni trokut prije zavoja. |
| Haben Sie eine Kassette für Erste Hilfe? | ¿Tiene un botiquín? | Imate li sanduk sa prvom pomoći? |
| Rufen Sie einen Arzt. | Llame a un médico. | Pozovite jednog liječnika. |
| Halten wir einen Wagen an. | Paremos un coche. | Zaustavimo jedna kola. |
| Wo ist die Notrufsäule für die Strassenhilfe? | ¿Dónde hay un teléfono para el socorro de carretera? | Gdje je telefon za zvanje pomoći? |
| Rufen wir einen Krankenwagen. | Llamemos una ambulancia. | Pozovimo kola hitne pomoći. |
| Ich kann meinen rechten / linken Arm nicht bewegen. | No consigo mover el brazo derecho / izquierdo. | Ne mogu micati ruku desnu / lijevu. |
| Ich spüre einen starken Schmerz im rechten / linken Bein. | Me duele mucho la pierna derecha / izquierda. | Osjećam jaku bol u nozi desnoj / lijevoj. |
| Es braucht etwas, um das Bein / den Arm zu schienen. | Se necesita algo para inmovilizar la pierna / el brazo. | Potrebno je nešto za ukočiti nogu / ruku. |
| Ich kann nicht gehen. | No puedo caminar. | Ne mogu hodati. |
| Meine rechte / linke Hand blutet. | Sangro por la mano derecha / izquierda. | Krvari mi ruka desna / lijeva. |
| Es braucht einen runden Gegenstand und ein Taschentuch, um das Blut zu stillen. | Se necesita un objeto redondo y un pañuelo para detener la sangre. | Potreban je jedan okrugli predmet i maramica za zaustaviti krvarenje. |

| English | Italiano | Français |
|---|---|---|
| When I breathe, my chest hurts. | Quando respiro avverto dolore al petto. | J'ai mal à la poitrine quand je respire. |
| Don't move. | Non si muova. | Ne bougez pas. |
| Does your head hurt? | Le duole la testa? | Avez-vous mal à la tête? |
| Have them bring a stretcher. | Faccia venire una barella. | Faites venir un brancard. |
| Let the police know. | Avvertano la polizia. | Il faudrait avertir la police. |
| The road police are coming to take particulars. | Sta arrivando la polizia stradale per i rilievi. | La police routière arrive pour faire le constat. |
| Your name and address, please. | Le sue generalità, per favore. | Votre identité, s'il vous plaît. |
| Your driving licence and registration book, please. | Favorisca la sua patente e il libretto di circolazione. | Voulez-vous me donner votre permis de conduire et votre carte grise. |
| What is the number of your car? | Qual è il numero di targa della sua vettura? | Quel est le numéro d'immatriculation de votre voiture? |
| Who was driving the car? | Chi era alla guida della vettura? | Qui était au volant de la voiture? |
| Here is my name and address. | Ecco il mio nome e il mio indirizzo. | Voici mon nom et mon adresse. |
| Give me the name and address of your insurance company. | Mi dia il nome e l'indirizzo della sua società assicuratrice. | Veuillez me donner le nom et l'adresse de votre compagnie d'assurances. |
| Are you insured for third party risks? | Lei è assicurato per la responsabilità civile? | Etes-vous assuré pour la responsabilité civile? |
| Would you please act as a witness to the accident. | La prego di testimoniare sull'incidente. | Je vous prie de bien vouloir témoigner sur l'accident. |
| You will have seen that this car did not observe the give-way / halt sign. | Avrà notato che questa vettura non ha rispettato il segnale di precedenza / di stop. | Vous avez certainement remarqué que cette voiture n'a pas respecté le signal de priorité / le stop. |
| Did you see that the other car swung over to its left while I was overtaking it? | Lei ha visto che l'altra vettura si è spostata sulla sua sinistra mentre la stavo sorpassando? | Avez-vous vu l'autre voiture se déplacer sur sa gauche tandis que je la doublais? |
| Did you notice that the other vehicle came round the bend well over on the wrong side? | Si è accorto che l'altra vettura è uscita dalla curva tenendosi tutta sulla sinístra? | Avez-vous remarqué que l'autre voiture est sortie du virage complètement sur la gauche? |
| You came out of the side road too fast. | Lei è uscito a velocità eccessiva dalla strada laterale. | Vous êtes sortis du chemin vicinal à trop grande vitesse. |
| Look at the braking marks. | Guardi il segno della frenata. | Regardez les traces du coup de frein. |
| Notice the position of the cars. | Noti la posizione delle vetture. | Observez la position des voitures. |
| Please remember the distance of the car from the centre / from the verge of the road. | La prego di ricordare la distanza della vettura dal centro / dal ciglio della strada. | Veuillez vous rappeler de la distance des voitures par rapport à l'axe / au bord de la route. |
| As you see, the car's trafficators don't work well. | La vettura, come vede, ha gli indicatori di direzione che non funzionano bene. | Je vous prie de noter que les indicateurs de direction de la voiture ne fonctionnent pas bien. |

| Deutsch | Español | Srpsko-hrvatski |
|---|---|---|
| Beim Atmen spüre ich einen Schmerz in der Brust. | Al respirar siento un dolor en el pecho. | Kada dišem, osjećam bol u grudima. |
| Bewegen Sie sich nicht. | No se mueva. | Nemojte se micati. |
| Schmerzt Sie der Kopf? | ¿Le duele la cabeza? | Boli li vas glava? |
| Lassen Sie eine Tragbare kommen. | Busque una camilla. | Potražite jedna nosila. |
| Benachrichtigen Sie die Polizei. | Avisen a la policía. | Obavijestite miliciju. |
| Es kommt die Strassenpolizei zu den Erhebungen. | Está llegando la policía de carretera para instruir las diligencias. | Dolazi saobraćajna milicija da bi izvršila uvidjaj. |
| Ihre Personalangaben bitte. | Sus datos de identificación, por favor. | Molim vaše podatke. |
| Ihren Führerschein und den Zulassungsschein bitte. | Su carnet de conducir y el permiso de circulación. | Pokažite mi vašu vozačku dozvolu i saobraćajnu knjižicu. |
| Wie ist die Kennummer Ihres Wagens? | ¿Qué número de matrícula tiene su coche? | Koji je registarski broj vaših kola? |
| Wer war am Steuer des Wagens? | ¿Quién conducía el coche? | Tko je bio za upravljačem kola? |
| Dies ist mein Name und meine Anschrift. | Aquí tiene Vd. mi nombre y dirección. | Izvolite moje ime i moju adresu. |
| Den Namen und die Anschrift Ihrer Versicherungsgesellschaft bitte. | Tenga la bondad de facilitarme el nombre y la dirección de su Casa de Seguros. | Dajte mi naziv i adresu vašeg Osiguravajućeg društva. |
| Sind Sie haftpflichtversichert? | ¿Está Vd. asegurado contra la responsabilidad civil? | Da li ste osigurani za gradjansku odgovornost? |
| Würden Sie bitte über den Unfall zeugen? | Le ruego que haga de testigo del accidente. | Molim vas da svjedočite u vezi sa nesrećom. |
| Sie werden beobachtet haben, dass dieser Wagen das Vorfahrtzeichen / das Stopzeichen nicht beachtet hat. | Se habrá dado cuenta que este coche no ha respetado la señal de prioridad / de stop. | Primijetili ste da ova kola nisu poštovala znak prednosti / znak stop. |
| Haben Sie gesehen, dass der andere Wagen, während ich ihn überholte, nach links ausscherte? | ¿Ha visto Vd. que el otro coche se ha desplazado hacia la izquierda mientras estaba en fase de adelantamiento? | Vi ste zapazili, da su se druga kola pomaknula na svoju lijevu stranu, dok sam ih pretjecao? |
| Haben Sie bemerkt, dass der andere Wagen vollkommen links aus der Kurve fuhr? | ¿Se ha dado cuenta que el otro coche ha terminado la curva completamente desplazado hacia la izquierda? | Da, točno je da su druga kola izašla iz zavoja, držeći se potpuno lijevo. |
| Sie sind mit übermässiger Geschwindigkeit aus der Seitenstrasse gefahren. | Vd. ha salido de la carretera lateral con excesiva velocidad. | Vi ste izašli prevelikom brzinom iz sporedne ceste. |
| Sehen Sie sich die Bremsspur an. | Mire Vd. las huellas dejadas por los neumáticos. | Pogledajte tragove kočenja. |
| Beobachten Sie die Stellung der Wagen. | Note la posición de los coches. | Primjećujete li pložaj kola? |
| Erinnern Sie sich bitte an den Abstand des Wagens von der Strassenmitte / vom Strassenrand. | Recuerde, por favor, la distancia del coche, de la división / del borde de la carretera. | Molim da zapamtite udaljenost kola od središta / od ruba ceste. |
| Wie Sie sehen, funktionieren die Winker nicht richtig. | Come ve, las luces indicadoras de dirección no funcionan bien. | Kao što se vidi, kola imaju neispravne pokazivače smjera. |

**English**

The driver of the other car didn't use his direction indicator in time.

On this car the red tail-lights aren't working / the side-lights are out / the tyres are quite smooth.

The car skidded a long way before it stopped.

You were driving in the fog / in the dark with your headlamps switched off.

This car overtook a car that was already overtaking another.

This lorry overtook just before a ridge.

This motor-cycle overtook me on the bend.

This trailer-truck swerved into my lane without warning, and I had to brake suddenly.

This car came across the central reservation.

I was dazzled by the headlamps of a vehicle.

To stop more quickly, I had to change down into second and ruined the gearbox.

The cyclist swerved without warning while I was overtaking him.

The bicycle couldn't be seen in the dark because it has no red reflectors / tail-light / phosphorent strips on the pedals.

This pedestrian wasn't crossing the road on the pedestrian crossing.

The pedestrian crossed the road without warning.

**I Consequences** 1. injuries to persons 2. damage to things 3. fire 4. car 5. three-wheeler van 6. van 7. lorry 8. trailer-truck 9. trailer 10. coach. **II Assistance** 1. ambulance 2. doctor 3. stretcher 4. injured person 5. man 6. woman 7. child 8. driver 9. passenger 10. injury 11. serious injury 12. internal injury 13. concussion 14. fracture 15. skull 16. arm 17. legs 18. hand 19. face 20. chest 21. kiss of life. **III Enquiries and responsibility** 1. road police 2. driving licence 3. registration book 4. Christian name 5. surname 6. address 7. number of car 8. running into the back of another car

**Italiano**

Il conducente dell'altra vettura non ha messo in tempo la freccia.

Questa vettura ha i segnali di stop che non funzionano / le luci di posizione spente / le gomme completamente lisce.

La vettura ha sbandato a lungo prima di fermarsi.

Lei procedeva nella nebbia / nel buio a fari spenti.

Questa vettura ha sorpassato in terza posizione.

L'autocarro ha superato in prossimità di un dosso.

La motocicletta mi ha superato in curva.

L'autotreno ha occupato improvvisamente la mia corsia, obbligandomi a frenare bruscamente.

La vettura ha superato lo spartitraffico.

Sono stato abbagliato dai fari di un automezzo.

Per fermare al più presto ho dovuto passare in seconda e ho rovinato il cambio.

Il ciclista ha sbandato improvvisamente mentre lo stavo sorpassando.

La bicicletta non era visibile nel buio perché non ha i catarifrangenti / la luce posteriore / le strisce fosforescenti sui pedali.

Questo pedone non attraversava la strada sulle strisce bianche.

Il pedone ha attraversato improvvisamente la strada.

**I Conseguenze** 1. danni alle persone 2. danni alle cose 3. incendio 4. autovettura 5. motofurgone 6. furgone 7. autocarro 8. autotreno 9. rimorchio 10. autocorriera. **II Soccorsi** 1. autoambulanza 2. medico 3. barella 4. ferito 5. uomo 6. donna 7. bambino 8. guidatore 9. passeggero 10. ferita 11. ferita grave 12. lesione interna 13. commozione cerebrale 14. frattura 15. cranio 16. braccia 17. gambe 18. mano 19. viso 20. torace 21. respirazione bocca a bocca. **III Rilievi e responsabilità** 1. polizia stradale 2. patente 3. libretto di circolazione 4. nome 5 cognome 6. indi-

**Français**

Le conducteur de l'autre voiture a mis la flèche trop tard.

Cette voiture a des signaux de stop qui ne marchent pas / les feux de position éteints / les bandes de roulement des pneus complètement lisses.

La voiture a dérapé longtemps avant de s'arrêter.

Vous marchiez dans le brouillard / dans l'obscurité tous phares éteints.

Cette voiture a doublé en troisième position.

Le camion a doublé à proximité d'un dos d'âne.

La motocyclette m'a doublé dans le virage.

Le train routier s'est trouvé tout d'un coup dans mon couloir, m'obligeant à freiner brusquement.

La voiture a franchi le talus central.

J'ai été ébloui par les phares d'un véhicule venant en sens inverse.

Pour m'arrêter au plus vite, j'ai dû mettre la seconde et j'ai abîmé mon changement de vitesse

Ce cycliste s'est déporté à l'improviste pendant que j'étais en train de le dépasser.

La bicyclette ne se voyait pas dans le noir parce qu'elle n'a pas de cataphotes / de feu arrière / de bandes phosphorescentes sur les pédales.

Ce piéton ne traversait pas la chaussée sur le passage réservé aux piétons.

Le piéton a traversé brusquement la route.

**I Conséquences** 1. dommages physiques 2. dégâts matériels 3. incendie 4. automobile 5. motofourgonnette 6. fourgon 7. camion 8. train routier 9. remorque 10. autocar. **II Secours** 1. ambulance 2. médecin 3. brancard 4. blessé 5. homme 6. femme 7. enfant 8. conducteur 9. passager 10. blessure 11. blessure grave 12. lésion interne 13. commotion cérébrale 14. fracture 15. crâne 16. bras 17. jambes 18. main 19. visage 20. thorax 21. respiration bouche à bouche. **III Constats et responsabilités** 1. police routière 2. permis de conduire 3. carte grise 4. prénom 5. nom de fa-

**Deutsch**

Der Fahrer des anderen Wagens hat den Winker nicht rechtzeitig betätigt.

Dieser Wagen hat Stoplichter, die nicht funktionieren / die Standlichter nicht eingeschaltet / völlig glatte Reifen.

Dieser Wagen kam ins Schleudern bevor er anhielt.

Sie fuhren bei Nebel / bei Dunkelheit ohne Licht.

Dieser Wagen ist einem schon überholenden Wagen vorgefahren.

Dieser Lastwagen hat in der Nähe einer Schwelle überholt.

Das Motorrad hat mich in der Kurve überholt.

Der Lastzug ist plötzlich auf meine Fahrbahn gefahren und hat mich gezwungen, rasch abzubremsen.

Der Wagen ist über den Grünstreifen gefahren.

Ich wurde durch die Scheinwerfer eines Fahrzeugs geblendet.

Der Fussgänger hat plötzlich die Strasse überquert.

Um rasch anhalten zu können, war ich gezwungen, auf den zweiten Gang zu schalten und habe ich dadurch das Getriebe beschädigt.

Dieser Radfahrer ist, während ich ihn überholte, plötzlich ins Schleudern gekommen.

Man konnte das Fahrrad in der Dunkelheit nicht sehen weil es keine Rückleuchte / kein Schlusslicht / keine Pedalrückstrahler hat.

Dieser Fussgänger hat die Strasse ausserhalb der Zebrastreifen überquert.

**I. Folgen** 1. Personenschaden 2. Sachschaden 3. Brand 4. Personenkraftwagen 5. Dreiradlieferwagen 6. Lieferwagen 7. Lastwagen 8. Fernlaster 9. Anhänger 10. Omnibus. **II. Hilfe** 1. Krankenwagen 2. Arzt 3. Tragbare 4. Verletzter 5. Mann 6. Frau 7. Kind 8. Fahrer 9. Insasse 10. Wunde 11. schwere Verletzung 12. innere Verletzung 13. Gehirnerschütterung 14. Bruch 15. Schädel 16. Arme 17. Beine 18. Hand 19. Gesicht 20. Brust 21. Mund-zu-Mund-Atmung. **III. Erhebungen und Verschulden** 1. Strassenpolizei 2. Führerschein 3. Zulassungsschein 4. Zuname 5. Vorname 6. **Anschrift** 7. Kennzeichen

**Español**

El conductor del otro coche no ha indicado a tiempo la maniobra.

Este coche tiene las señales de stop que no funcionan / las luces de posición apagadas / los neumáticos completamente gastados.

El coche ha patinado largamente antes de pararse.

Vd. iba, a pesar de la niebla / de la poca visibilidad con los faros apagados.

Este coche ha adelantado en tercera posición.

El camión ha adelantado en proximidad de un cambio de rasante.

La motocicleta ha adelantado en curva.

El camión ha ocupado de repente mi vía, obligándome a frenar bruscamente.

El coche ha superado la división de la carretera.

He sido deslumbrado por los faros de un vehículo.

El peatón ha cruzado de repente la carretera.

Para frenar más pronto he tenido que meter la segunda y he averiado el cambio.

El ciclista se ha desplazado de repente, mientras le estaba adelantando.

La bicicleta no era visibile en la obscuridad porque no lleva catafaros / luz roja posterior / señales fosforescentes en los pedales.

Este peatón no cruzaba la carretera por las rayas blancas.

**I Consecuencias** 1. daños a las personas 2. daños a las cosas 3. incendio 4. coche 5. furgoneta 6. furgón 7. autocar 8. camión con remolque 9. remolque 10. autobús. **II Socorros** 1. ambulancia 2. médico 3. camilla 4. herido 5. hombre 6. mujer 7. niño 8. conductor 9. pasajero 10. herida 11. herida grave 12. lesión interna 13. conmoción cerebral 14. rotura 15. cráneo 16. brazos 17. piernas 18. mano 19. cara 20. tórax 21. respiración boca a boca. **III Diligencias y responsabilidad** 1. policía de carretera 2. carnet de conducir 3. permiso de circulación 4. nombre 5. apellido 6. dirección

**Srpsko-hrvatski**

Vozač drugih kola nije na vrijeme uključio pokazivače smjera.

Ova kola imaju stop svjetla neispravna / poziciona svjetla ugašena / gume potpuno glatke.

Kola su klizila prije zaustavljanja.

Vi ste vozili u magli / mraku sa ugašenim svjetlima.

Ova su kola pretjecala u trećoj poziciji.

Kamion je pretjecao u blizini prijevoja.

Motocikl me je pretjecao u zavoju.

Vozni vlak je nenadano zauzeo moju stazu i primorao me da naglo kočim.

Kola su prešla centralnu linijn ceste.

Bio sam zasljepljen farovima jednog automobila.

Pjesak je nenadano prešao cestu.

Da bih što prije zakočio, bio sam primoran preći u drugu i time sam pokvario mjenjač.

Biciklista je nenadano skrenuo, dok sam ga pretjecao.

Bicikl nije bio vidljiv jer nije imao signalno-svjetlosna stakla / stražnje svjetlo / fosforescentne trake na pedalima.

Ovaj pješak nije prelazio ulicu na označenom mjestu.

**I Posljedice** 1. šteta na osobama 2. šteta na stvarima 3. požar 4. automobil 5. motofurgon 6. furgon 7. kamion 8. vozni vlak 9. prikolica 10. autobus. **II Pomoć** 1. kola hitne pomoći 2. liječnik 3. nosila 4. ranjenik 5. muškarac 6. žena 7. dijete 8. vozač 9. putnik 10. ranjena 11. teško ranjena 12. unutrašnja ozljeda 13. potres mozga 14. prijelom 15. lubanja 16. ruke 17. noge 18. šaka 19. lice 20. grudni koš 21. umjetno disanje usta na usta. **III Uvidjaj i odgovornost** 1. saobraćajna milicija 2. vozačka dozvola 3. saobraćajna knjižica 4. ime 5. prezime 6. adresa 7. registarski broj 8. udarac

**English**

9. head-on / sideways crash 10. braking marks 11. overtaking 12. overtaking on bend 13. ridge 14. hump 15. overtaking on the wrong side 16. overtaking lane 17. central reservation 18. side road 19. level crossing 20. dazzling 21. undipped headlamps 22. trafficators 23. side-lights 24. red tail-light 25. give-way sign 26. smooth / worn tyres 27. cyclist 28. bicycle 29. red reflectors 30. rear light 31. pedestrian 32. fog. 33. haze 45. darkness 35. rain 36. twilight 37. witness 38. to witness. **IV Insurance** 1. insurance company 2. name 3. address 4. policy 5. number of policy 6. third party insurance 7. maximum indemnity 8. declaration of accident 9. registered letter.

**Italiano**

rizzo 7. numero della targa 8. tamponamento 9. urto frontale / laterale 10. tracce di frenata 11. sorpasso 12. sorpasso in curva 13. dosso 14. cunetta 15. sorpasso sulla destra 16. corsia di sorpasso 17. aiuola spartitraffico 18. strada laterale 19. passaggio a livello 20. abbagliamento 21. fari abbaglianti 22. indicatori di direzione 23. luce di posizione 24. segnale di stop 25. segnale di precedenza 26. pneumatici lisci / consumati 27. ciclista 28. bicicletta 29. catarifrangente 30. luce posteriore 31. pedone 32. nebbia 33. foschia 34. buio 35. pioggia 36. crepuscolo 37. testimone 38. testimoniare. **IV Assicurazione** 1. compagnia d'assicurazione 2. nome 3. indirizzo 4. polizza 5. numero della polizza 6. assicurazione per la responsabilità civile 7. massimale di assicurazione 8. denuncia del sinistro 9. lettera raccomandata.

**Français**

mille 6. adresse 7. numéro d'immatriculation 8. tamponnement 9. collision de front / latérale 10. traces de coup de freins 11. dépassement 12. dépassement dans le virage 14. dos d'âne 14. cassis 15. dépassement à droite 16. couloir de dépassement 17. talus central 18. route latérale 19. passage à niveau 20. éblouissement par les phares 21. phares 22. indicateurs de direction 23. feux de position 24. signal de stop 25. signal de priorité 26. pneus lisses / usés 27. cycliste 28. bicyclette 29. cataphotes 30. feu arrière 31. piéton 32. brouillard 33. brume 34. obscurité 35. pluie 36. crépuscule 37. témoin 38. témoigner. **IV Assurances** 1. compagnie d'assurances 2. nom 3. adresse 4. police 5. numéro de la police 6. assurance pour la responsabilité civile 7. maximum d'assurance 8. déclaration de sinistre 9. lettre recommandée.

| DRIVING IN TOWNS | CIRCOLAZIONE URBANA | CIRCULATION EN VILLE |
|---|---|---|
| Does this road lead straight into the town? | Questa strada porta direttamente in città? | Cette route porte-t-elle directement en ville? |
| You can follow it for about a kilometre, then you'd better ask. | Può seguirla per un chilometro circa, poi le conviene chiedere. | Suivez-la pendant environ un kilomètre, puis demandez à nouveau. |
| If you follow this road, you'll come into the centre of the town. | Seguendo questa strada arriverà al centro della città. | En suivant cette route, vous arriverez au centre de la ville. |
| I have to go to this street. Can you show me the shortest way there on the map? | Devo andare in questa via. Può indicarmi il percorso più breve sulla cartina? | Je dois me rendre dans cette rue. Pourriez-vous s'il vous plaît m'indiquer le chemin le plus court sur le plan? |
| Can you show me where the station square is? | Può dirmi dov'è la piazza della stazione? | Pouvez-vous m'indiquer la place de la gare? |
| Go along this avenue for a couple of kilometres, then turn to the right / to the left at the first / second / third traffic lights. | Segua questo viale per un paio di chilometri, poi giri a destra / a sinistra al primo / secondo / terzo semaforo. | Suivez cette avenue pendant deux kilomètres environ, puis tournez à droite / à gauche au premier / deuxième / troisième feu rouge. |
| Take the second road to the left after the bridge / the level crossing. | Prenda la seconda strada a sinistra dopo il ponte / il passaggio a livello. | Prenez la deuxième rue à gauche après le pont / le passage à niveau. |
| I am looking for the Grand Hotel. What is the easiest way to get there? | Cerco il Grand Hotel. Qual è il modo più semplice per arrivarvi? | Je cherche le Grand Hôtel. Quelle est la façon la plus simple d'y arriver? |
| Go right round the square, take the road after the newspaper kiosk and follow the tramlines / bus route. | Faccia il giro della piazza, prenda la strada dopo l'edicola e segua la linea tranviaria / filoviaria. | Faites le tour de la place, prenez la rue après le kiosque et suivez la ligne du tramway / du trolleybus. |
| Which way must I go to get to the historical centre? | Dove devo passare per arrivare al centro storico? | Par où dois-je passer pour arriver au quartier historique? |
| Follow the wall all the way and you'll arrive in . . . Square. | Segua sempre le mura e si troverà a Piazza . . . | Suivez toujours les murs, et vous vous trouverez sur la place . . . |

8. Auffahren 9. frontaler / seitlicher Zusammenstoss 10. Bremsspuren 11. Überholen 12. Überholen in der Kurve 13. Schwelle 14. Querrinne 15. rechts Überholen 16. Überholspur 17. Grünstreifen 18. Seitenstrasse 19. Bahnübergang 20. Blendung 21. Fernlicht 22. Blinker 23. Standlicht 24. Bremslicht 25. Vorfahrtzeichen 26. glatte / abgenutze Reifen 27. Radfahrer 28. Fahrrad 29. Rückstrahler 30. Schlusslicht 31. Fussgänger 32. Nebel 33. Dunst 34. Dunkelheit 35. Regen 36. Dämmerung 37. Zeuge 38. zeugen. **IV. Versicherung** 1. Versicherungsgesellschaft 2. Name 3. Anschrift 4. Police 5. Policennummer 6. Haftpflichtversicherung 7. Versicherungs-Höchstbetrag 8. Unfallmeldung 9. eingeschriebener Brief.

7. número de matrícula 8. taponamiento 9. choque de frente / de lado 10. huellas de frenado 11. adelantamiento. 12. adelantamiento en proximidad de la curva 13. cambio de rasante 14. cuneta 15. adelantamiento por la derecha 16. via de adelantamiento 17. isla de división de la carretera 18. carretera lateral 19. paso a nivel 20. deslumbramiento 21. faros largos 22. indicadores de dirección 23. luces de posición 24. señal del freno 25. señal de prioridad 26. neumáticos lisos / gastados 27. ciclista 28. bicicleta 29. catafaros 30. luces posteriores 31. peatón 32. niebla 33. nieblina 34. obscuridad. 35. lluvia 36. atardecer 37. testigo 38. atestiguar. **IV Seguro** 1. casa de seguros 2. nombre 3. dirección 4. poliza 5. número de póliza 6. seguro contra la responsabilidad civil 7. capital asegurado 8. denuncia del accidente 9. carta certificada.

straga 9. frontalni udarac / bočni 10. tragovi kočenja 11. pretjecanje 12. pretjecanje u zavoju 13. prijevoj 14. arak 15. pretjecanje s desna 16. staza za pretjecanje 17. centralna diobena površina ceste 18. bočna cesta 19. prijelaz preko željezničke pruge 20. zasljepljenje 21. velika svjetla 22. pokazivači smjera 23. poziciona svjetla 24. znak stop 25. znak prednosti 26. gume glatke / istrošene 27. biciklista 28. bicikl 29. signalno-svjetlosna 30. stražnje svjetlo 31. pješak 32. magla 33. sumaglica 34. mrak 35. kiša 36. sumrak 37. svjedok 38. svjedočiti **IV Osiguranje** 1. osiguravajući zavod 2. naziv 3. adresa 4. polica 5. broj police 6. osiguranje za gradjansku odgovornost 7. maksimum osiguranja 8. prijava štete 9. preporučeno pismo.

| **STADTVERKEHR** | **CIRCULACION URBANA** | **GRADSKI SAOBRAĆAJ** |
|---|---|---|
| Führt diese Strasse direkt in die Stadt? | ¿Esta carretera lleva directamente a la ciudad? | Da li ova cesta vodi direktno u grad? |
| Fahren Sie ungefähr einen Kilometer weiter, dann wäre es ratsam, wieder zu fragen. | Puede continuar por casi un kilómetro, después le conviene preguntar. | Slijedite ovu cestu jedan kilometar, pa ponovno upitajte. |
| Diese Strasse führt zur Stadtmitte. | Siguiendo por esta carretera llegará justo al centro de la ciudad. | Slijedeći ovu cestu, stići ćete u centar grada. |
| Ich muss in diese Strasse. Würden Sie mir auf dem Plan den kürzesten Weg zeigen? | Tengo que ir a esta calle. ¿Me puede indicar en el mapa el recorrido más corto? | Moram ići u ovu ulicu. Možete li mi označiti najkraći put na planu grada? |
| Könnten Sie mir sagen, wo der Bahnhofsplatz ist? | ¿Puede decirme dónde está la plaza de la estación? | Možete li mi reći gdje se nalazi željeznička stanica? |
| Fahren Sie ungefähr zwei Kilometer dieser Allee entlang und biegen Sie dann nach der ersten / zweiten / dritten Verkehrsampel rechts / links ab. | Siga Vd. por esta calle y, después de un par de kilómetros, cruce a la derecha / a la izquierda / al primer / al segundo / al tercer semáforo. | Slijedite ovu ulicu nekoliko kilometara, zatim skrenite na desno / na lijevo kod prvog / drugog / trećeg semafora. |
| Biegen Sie in die zweite Strasse links nach der Brücke / dem Bahnübergang ein. | Tome Vd. por la segunda calle a la izquierda después del puente / del paso a nivel. | Podjite drugom cestom na lijevo poslije mosta / prelaza željezničke pruge. |
| Ich suche das Grand Hotel. Wie komme ich am besten hin? | Estoy buscando el Gran Hotel. ¿Cuál es la manera más sencilla para llegar? | Tražim Grand Hotel. Koji je najjednostavniji put? |
| Fahren Sie um den Platz, biegen Sie in die Strasse nach dem Zeitungskiosk ein und folgen Sie der Strassenbahnlinie / der O-Buslinie. | Dé la vuelta a la plaza, tome la calle a continuación del kiosko, y siga la línea del tranvía / del filobús. | Napravite krug oko trga, podjite cestom iza kioska i slijedite liniju tramvaja / trolejbusa. |
| Wie muss ich fahren, um in die Altstadt zu kommen? | ¿Qué calle debo tomar para llegar al centro histórico? | Gdje moram ići da bih stigao u historijski centar? |
| Fahren Sie den Mauern entlang, dann kommen Sie auf den ... Platz. | Siga la dirección de las murallas y llegará a la Plaza... | Slijedite stalno zidine i naći ćete se na Trgu ... |

| English | Italiano | Français |
|---|---|---|
| Are there any one-way streets along the way? | C'è qualche senso vietato lungo il percorso? | Y a-t-il des sens interdits sur le parcours? |
| Yes. You can't take the first turning to the left in this direction. | Sì. Non può percorrere la prima traversa a sinistra in questo senso. | Oui. Vous ne pouvez pas prendre la première à gauche dans ce sens. |
| You must turn back. | Deve tornare indietro. | Il vous faut revenir en arrière. |
| You've taken the wrong road. | Ha sbagliato strada. | Vous vous êtes trompé de route. |
| Which road must I follow to leave the town in the direction of . . . ? | Che strada devo fare per uscire dalla città in direzione di . . .? | Quel chemin dois-je prendre pour sortir de la ville en direction de . . . ? |
| How can I get to the motorway for . . . ? | Come posso raggiungere l'autostrada per . . .? | Comment rejoint-on l'autoroute pour |
| Where can I park the car? | Dove posso parcheggiare la macchina? | Où puis-je garer la voiture? |
| In a side road. | In una strada laterale. | Dans une rue latérale. |
| There is a supervised car-park near here. | C'è un parcheggio custodito qui vicino. | Il y a un parc surveillé tout près d'ici. |
| You have to pay to park in this street / square. | In questa via / piazza c'è il parcheggio a pagamento. | Dans cette rue / sur cette place, il y a un parking payant. |
| The supervision of this car-park ends at . . . o'clock / when the performance finishes at the nearby cinema. | La sorveglianza in questo parcheggio cessa alle ore . . . / al termine dello spettacolo del cinema vicino. | Le parking n'est plus surveillé à partir de . . . heures / après la fin du spectacle du cinéma voisin. |
| How much must I pay to stop in this car-park? | Quanto dovrò pagare per la sosta in questo parcheggio? | Quel est le tarif du stationnement dans ce parking? |
| You must pay . . . for the first hour, . . . for the second and . . . for each hour after that. | Dovrà pagare . . . per la prima ora, . . . per la seconda e . . . per ogni ora successiva. | Vous aurez à payer . . . pour la premièere heure, . . . pour la deuxième, et . . . pour chacune des heures suivantes. |
| Over there, as you see, is the "disc zone" sign. | Là, come vede, c'è il cartello della « zona disco ». | Comme vous le voyez, ce panneau indique que nous sommes dans la zone bleue. |
| Here parking time is restricted to one hour / half an hour / thirty minutes. | Qui la sosta è limitata a un'ora / mezz'ora / trenta minuti. | Ici, vous ne pouvez pas stationner plus d'une heure / d'une demi-heure / de trente minutes. |
| Where can I get a disc showing parking times? | Dove posso procurarmi un disco orario? | Où puis-je me procurer un disque de stationnement? |
| At any filling station. The disc must be placed so that it is clearly visible inside the windscreen. | Presso qualsiasi distributore di benzina. Il disco dovrà essere collocato in modo visibile all'interno del parabrezza. | Auprès de n'importe quel distributeur d'essence. Il vous faut placer le disque de manière bien visible derrière le parebrise. |
| It is forbidden to alter the time shown on the disc in order to extend the parking time. | E' vietato spostare l'indicazione oraria del disco per protrarre la sosta. | Il est absolument interdit de déplacer l'indication horaire du disque pour prolonger la durée du stationnement. |
| The parking time shown on the disc is up. | L'ora di sosta segnata dal disco è scaduta. | L'heure de stationnement indiquée par le disque est écoulée. |
| There are parking metres in this street. | In questa strada esistono parchimetri. | Dans cette rue, il y a un parking payant à compteur. |
| The parking time is up. | Il tempo di sosta è scaduto. | **Le temps de stationnement est écoulé.** |

| Deutsch | Español | Srpsko-hrvatski |
|---|---|---|
| Gibt es Einbahnstrassen längs der Strecke? | ¿Existe alguna dirección prohibida a lo largo del recorrido? | Postoji li koji zabranjeni smjer putem? |
| Ja. Sie dürfen die erste Seitenstrasse links nicht in dieser Richtung fahren. | Sí. No puede ir por la primera calle de la izquierda en esta dirección. | Da. Ne možete voziti prvom poprečnom na lijevo u ovome smjeru. |
| Sie müssen umkehren. | Tiene que volver atrás. | Morate se vratiti unazad. |
| Sie sind falsch gefahren. | Se ha equivocado de calle. | Pogriješili ste ulicu. |
| Welche Strasse führt aus der Stadt in Richtung . . .? | ¿Qué calle tengo que recorrer para salir de la ciudad en dirección de...? | Kojim putem moram voziti, da bih izašao iz grada u smjeru . . . ? |
| Wie komme ich zur Autobahn nach . . .? | ¿Cómo puedo llegar a la autopista por ...? | Na koji način mogu stići na autostradu za . . . ? |
| Wo kann ich den Wagen parken? | ¿Dónde puedo aparcar el coche? | Gdje mogu parkirati kola? |
| In einer Seitenstrasse. | En una calle lateral. | U jednoj pokrajnjoj ulici. |
| Hier in der Nähe ist ein bewachter Parkplatz. | Hay por aquí cerca un aparcamiento vigilado. | Postoji u blizini jedno čuvano parkiralište. |
| In dieser Strasse / auf diesem Platz ist das Parken gebührenpflichtig. | En esta calle / plaza hay un aparcamiento de pago. | U ovoj ulici / na trgu postoji parkiralište uz naplatu. |
| Dieser Parkplatz ist bis . . . Uhr / bis zum Ende der Vorführung im nebenanliegenden Kino bewacht. | La vigilancia en este aparcamiento termina a las... / al final de la funcion del cine más cercano. | Čuvanje ovog parkirališta prestaje u . . . sati / po završetku rada obližnjeg kina. |
| Wieviel muss ich für das Parken hier bezahlen? | ¿Cuánto tengo que pagar por estacionar el coche en este aparcamiento? | Koliko ću morati platiti za parkiranje na ovom parkiralištu? |
| Sie müssen . . . für die erste Stunde, . . . für die zweite und . . . für jede weitere Stunde bezahlen. | Tendrá que pagar... por la primera hora; ... por la segunda y ... por cada hora siguiente. | Platiti ćete . . . za prvi sat, . . . za drugi sat i . . . za svaki daljnji. |
| Wie Sie sehen, steht dort das Schild der « Kurzparkzone ». | Allá, como ve, hay un cartel que indica la « zona disco ». | Tamo, kao što vidite, postoji znak sa oznakom « disk » zone. |
| Hier ist das Parken auf eine Stunde / eine halbe Stunde / dreissig Minuten beschränkt. | Aquí la parada está limitada a una hora / media hora / treinta minutos. | Ovdje je zaustavljanje ograničeno na jedan sat / pola sata / trideset minuta. |
| Wo kann ich eine Parkscheibe bekommen? | ¿Dónde puedo encontrar un « disco horario »? | Gdje mogu nabaviti jedan satni disk? |
| An jeder Tankstelle. Die Parkscheibe muss an der Windschutzscheibe innen auf sichtbare Weise angebracht werden. | En una estación de servizio cualquiera. El disco deberá colocarlo en la parte interior del parabrisas, de manera que se vea. | Kod svake pumpne stanice. Disk mora biti smješten na vidnom mjestu iza prednjeg stakla. |
| Es ist verboten, die Stundenangabe auf der Scheibe zwecks Verlängerung der Parkzeit zu verstellen. | Está prohibido alterar la indicación horaria del disco para prolongar la parada. | Zabranjeno je pomicanje označenog vremena u cilju produženja parkiranja. |
| Die auf der Scheibe angezeigte Stunde ist abgelaufen. | La hora de parada indicada por el disco ha caducado. | Vrijeme parkiranja, označeno na disku, je isteklo. |
| Längs dieser Strasse gibt es Parkuhren. | En esta calle existen parquímetros. | U ovoj ulici postoji jedan parkirni sat. |
| Die Parkzeit ist abgelaufen. | El tiempo de parada ha caducado. | Vrijeme zaustavljanja je isteklo. |

| English | Italiano | Français |
|---|---|---|
| You will have to pay a second rate. | Dovrà pagare una nuova tariffa. | Vous devez payer une nouvelle période. |
| Put a coin of the correct value in the appropriate slot. | Inserisca una moneta del valore dovuto nell'apposita fessura. | Introduisez une pièce de monnaie de la valeur requise dans la fente aménagée à cet effet. |
| Can I stop here just for a minute? | Posso fermarmi qui per un solo minuto? | Puis-je m'arrêter un instant seulement? |
| I want to get out and buy some cigarettes / a newspaper. | Dovrei scendere per comprare delle sigarette / un giornale. | Je voudrais descendre acheter des cigarettes / un journal. |
| Very well, as long as it's really only for just a minute / just for a very short time. | Faccia pure, purché si tratti veramente di un solo minuto / di un tempo molto breve. | Vous le pouvez, mais à condition que vous ne restiez vraiment qu'une minute / un instant. |
| Your car is standing in a no-parking area. | La sua vettura è parcheggiata in divieto di sosta. | Votre voiture est garée dans un endroit interdit au stationnement. |
| Parking on the left-hand side / right-hand side is allowed only on even / odd days. | La sosta sul lato sinistro / destro è ammessa solo nei giorni pari / dispari. | Le stationnement du côté gauche / droit n'est autorisé que les jours pairs / impairs. |
| Please move your car because it is parked on a double line. | La prego di spostare la sua vettura perché è parcheggiata in doppia fila. | Votre voiture est garée en double file, veuillez la déplacer je vous prie. |
| You cannot leave the car here: there's a bus stop / a taxi rank here. | Non può lasciare qui la macchina: c'è la fermata dell'autobus / un posteggio di taxi. | Vous ne pouvez pas laisser votre voiture à l'arrêt d'autobus / à la station de taxis. |
| The lane defined by a yellow line is reserved for buses and taxis. | La corsia delimitata dalla striscia gialla è riservata ai mezzi pubblici e ai taxi. | La voie délimitée par la bande jaune est réservée aux transports publics et aux taxis. |
| You have stopped your car too close to the road junction / on the pedestrian crossing. | Ha fermato la sua vettura troppo vicino all'incrocio / sulle strisce pedonali. | Vous vous êtes arrêté trop près du croisement / sur le passage clouté. |
| Your car is holding up the traffic. | La sua vettura intralcia il traffico. | Votre voiture gêne la circulation. |
| You drove across the crossroads when the lights were red. | Ha attraversato l'incrocio con la luce rossa. | Vous avez traversé le croisement au feu rouge. |
| You have broken the traffic regulations. | Lei è in contravvenzione. | Vous êtes en contravention. |
| Your licence and registration book, please. | Favorisca la patente e il libretto di circolazione. | Veuillez me donner votre permis de conduire et votre carte grise. |
| You will have to pay a fine of . . . | Deve pagare una multa di . . . | Vous devez payer une amende de . . . |
| You cannot pay the fine immediately. | La contravvenzione non è conciliabile. | La contravention ne peut faire l'objet d'une conciliation. |
| Where is the headquarters of the town police / of the road police? | Dov'è il comando dei vigili urbani / della polizia stradale? | Où se trouve le poste des agents de ville / de police routière? |
| Where is the nearest police station? | Dov'è il più vicino commissariato di pubblica sicurezza? | Où se trouve le commissariat de police le plus proche? |

| Deutsch | Español | Srpsko-hrvatski |
|---|---|---|
| Sie müssen eine neue Gebühr zahlen. | Deberá pagar una nueva tarifa. | Morati ćete platiti novu tarifu. |
| Werfen Sie eine der Gebühr entsprechende Münze in den Schlitz. | Introduzca una moneda del valor correspondiente en esta ranura. | Ubacite kovani novac tražene vrijednosti u odgovarajući otvor. |
| Kann ich hier eine Minute halten? | ¿Puedo dejar aquí el coche por un solo minuto? | Mogu li se zaustaviti samo na jednu minutu? |
| Ich müsste aussteigen, um Zigaretten / eine Zeitung zu kaufen. | Tengo que comprar cigarrillos / un periódico. | Morao bih kupiti cigarete / novine. |
| Bitte, es darf sich aber nur um eine Minute / um eine sehr kurze Zeit handeln. | Vaya, pero que sea por un solo minuto / un tiempo muy breve. | Možete slobodno, ako se radi samo o jednoj minuti / o vrlo kratkom vremenu. |
| Wo ihr Wagen steht, ist Halteverbot. | Su coche está aparcado en zona prohíbida. | Vaša su kola parkirana na mjestu gdje je zabranjeno zaustavljanje. |
| Das Parken auf der linken / rechten Seite ist nur an gleichen / ungleichen Tagen erlaubt. | El aparcamiento en el lado izquierdo / derecho está autorizado sólo en los días pares / impares. | Zaustavljanje na lijevoj strani / desnoj je dozvoljeno u parne / neparne dane. |
| Bitte fahren Sie Ihren Wagen weg, er steht in zweiter Reihe. | Le ruego quite su coche, porque está estacionado en doble hilera. | Molim da pomaknete svoja kola, jer su parkirana u dvostrukom redu. |
| Sie dürfen Ihren Wagen hier nicht stehen lassen: hier ist eine Bus-Haltestelle / ein Taxistand. | No puede dejar aquí su coche: hay una parada del autobús / un aparcamiento de taxis. | Ovdje ne možete ostaviti kola; tu je autobusna stanica — parkiralište taksija. |
| Die durch den gelben Streifen begrenzte Fahrbahn ist den öffentlichen Verkehrsmitteln und den Taxis vorbehalten. | La banda limitada por un raya amarilla está reservada a los medios de transporte público y a los taxis. | Staza ograničena žutom linijom je rezervirana za javna prjevozna sredstva i taksi. |
| Sie haben Ihren Wagen zu nahe an der Kreuzung / auf dem Fussgängerüberweg geparkt. | Ha parado su coche demasiado cerca del cruce / sobre las rayas reservadas a los peatones. | Zaustavili ste svoja kola preblizu raskršću / pješačkom prelazu. |
| Ihr Wagen hindert den Verkehr. | Su auto obstruye el tráfico. | Vaša kola smetaju prometu. |
| Sie sind bei rotem Licht über die Kreuzung gefahren. | Ha pasado el cruce con la luz roja. | Prošli ste raskršće pod crvenim svjetlom. |
| Sie haben sich strafbar gemacht. | Vd. ha cometido una infracción. | Činite prekršaj. |
| Ihren Führerschein und den Zulassungsschein bitte. | Por favor su carnet de conducir y el permiso de circulación. | Pokažite mi vozačku dozvolu i saobraćajnu knjižicu. |
| Sie müssen eine Geldstrafe von . . . zahlen. | Vd. tiene que pagar una multa de... | Morate platiti globu od . . . |
| Es wird Ihnen das Strafmandat zugestellt werden. | La multa no es pagadera immediatamente. | Prekršaj se ne može platiti na licu mjesta. |
| Wo ist das Kommando der Verkehrspolizei / der Strassenpolizei? | ¿Dónde se encuentra la comandancia de los guardias municipales / de la policía de tráfico? | Gdje je Stanica milicije / Saobraćajne milicije? |
| Wo ist das nächste Kommissariat der Sicherheitspolizei? | ¿Dónde está la comisaría del cuerpo de Seguridad más cercana? | Gdje je najbliži Kriminalistički odsjek? |

**English**

Where can I find an interpreter?

You can speak to a traffic warden or a policeman who speaks your language. They wear a white arm-band showing the language they speak.

**I Routes** 1. town 2. street 3. avenue 4. square 5. bridge 6. walls 7. park 8. public gardens 9. centre of the town 10. historical centre 11. business centre 12. residential area 13. industrial area 14. railway station 15. airport 16. port 17. quay 18. docks 19. motorway 20. petrol station. **II Traffic regulations** 1. city policeman 2. infringement 3. fine 4. one-way street 5. no left turn / no right turn 6. roundabout 7. no-parking 8. left-hand side / right-hand side of the street 9. no parking on alternate days 10. even days 11. Tuesday 12. Thursday 13. Saturday 14. odd days 15. Monday 16. Wednesday 17. Friday 18. road junction 19. pedestrian crossing 20. traffic lights 21. red / green / amber light 22. car-park 23. supervised car-park 24. paying car-park 25. rate 26. holiday / night rate 27. parking metre 28. parking time 29. first / second / third hour 30. disc area 31. parking time disc. **III Public transport** 1. taxi 2. taxi rank 3. bus 4. trolley-bus 5. tram 6. line 7. stop.

**Italiano**

Dove posso trovare un interprete?

Può rivolgersi a un vigile urbano o a un agente di pubblica sicurezza che parlino la sua lingua. Essi portano una fascia bianca sul braccio con la indicazione della lingua.

**I Itinerari** 1. città 2. via 3. viale 4. piazza 5. ponte 6. mura 7. parco 8. giardini pubblici 9. centro della città 10. centro storico 11. centro degli affari 12. zona residenziale 13. zona industriale 14. stazione ferroviaria 15. aeroporto 16. porto 17. molo 18. banchina 19. autostrada 20. distributore di benzina. **II Norme del traffico** 1. vigile urbano 2. infrazione 3. multa 4. strada a senso unico 5. divieto di svolta a sinistra / a destra 6. circolazione rotatoria 7. divieto di sosta 8. lato sinistro / destro della strada 9. divieto di sosta a giorni alternati 10. giorni pari 11. martedì 12. giovedì 13. sabato 14. giorni dispari 15. lunedì 16. mercoledì 17. venerdì 18. incrocio 19. strisce pedonali 20. semaforo 21. luce rossa / verde / gialla 22. parcheggio 23. parcheggio custodito 24. parcheggio a pagamento 25. tariffa 26. tariffa festiva / notturna 27. parchimetro 28. tempo di sosta 29. prima / seconda / terza ora 30. zona disco 31. disco orario. **III Mezzi di trasporto pubblico** 1. taxi 2. posteggio di taxi 3. autobus 4. filobus 5. tram 6. linea 7. fermata.

**Français**

Où peut-on trouver un interprète?

Vous pouvez vous adresser à un sergent de ville ou à un agent de police parlant votre langue: ils portent un brassard blanc indiquant la langue qu'ils parlent.

**I Itinéraires** 1. ville 2. rue 3. avenue 4. place 5. pont 6. murs 7. parc 8. jardins publics 9. centre de la ville 10. centre historique 11. centre des affaires 12. quartiers résidentiels 13. zone industrielle 14. station de chemin de fer 15. aéroport 16. port 17. jetée 18. quai 19. autoroute 20. distributeur d'essence. **II Règlement de la circulation** 1. sergent de ville 2. contravention 3. amende 4. rue à sens unique 5. défense de tourner à gauche / à droite 6. sens giratoire 7. défense de stationner 8. côté gauche / droit de la rue 9. stationnement interdit un jour sur deux 10. jours pairs 11. mardi 12. jeudi 13. samedi 14. jours impairs 15. lundi 16. mercredi 17. vendredi 18. carrefour 19. passage clouté 20. feu rouge 21. lumière rouge / verte / jaune 22. parking 23. parking surveillé 24. parking payant 25. tarif 26. tarif des jours de fête / nocturne 27. parking payant à compteur 28. temps de stationnement 29. première / deuxième / troisième heure 30. zone bleue (disque) 31. disque de stationnement. **III. Transports publics** 1. taxi 2. station de taxis 3. autobus 4. trolleybus 5. tramway 6. ligne 7. arrêt.

## INFORMATION IN TOWNS

Can you tell me where to find the... embassy / the ... consulate / the stadium.

Is there a good restaurant / a cheap eating-place in these parts?

Is this the right way to get to the ... theatre / to the opera?

I am looking for the town picture-gallery / the gallery of modern art.

Is it open every day / at this time?

The museum is open from nine to one and from two to five.

It is closed on Tuesdays.

Who must I apply to for permission to visit the collection of ... ?

Where is the Catholic / Protestant church?

## INFORMAZIONI IN CITTA'

Sa dirmi dove si trova l'ambasciata / il consolato di ... / lo stadio?

C'è da queste parti un buon ristorante / una trattoria economica?

E' questa la strada giusta per arrivare al teatro ... / all'opera?

Cerco la pinacoteca civica / la galleria di arte moderna.

E' aperta tutti i giorni / a quèsta ora?

L'orario del museo è dalle nove all'una e dalle due alle cinque.

Il martedì è chiuso.

A chi devo rivolgermi per avere il permesso di visitare la collezione di ...?

Dov'è la chiesa cattolica / protestante?

## RENSEIGNEMENTS EN VILLE

Pourriez-vous me dire où se trouve l'ambassade de ... / le consulat de ... / le stade?

Y a-t-il dans ces parages un bon restaurant? un restaurant bon marché?

Suis-je sur le bon chemin pour le théâtre ... / l'opéra?

Je cherche le musée municipal / le musée d'art moderne.

Est-il ouvert tous les jours / à cette heure-ci?

Le musée est ouvert de neuf heures à treize heures, et de quatorze heures à dix-sept heures.

Le musée est fermé le mardi.

A qui dois-je m'adresser pour obtenir l'autorisation de visiter la collection de ... ?

Où se trouve l'église catholique / protestante?

**Deutsch**

Wo kann ich einen Dolmetscher finden?

Sie können sich an einen Verkehrspolizisten oder an einen Beamten der Sicherheitspolizei wenden, der Ihre Sprache spricht. Diese Beamten tragen eine weisse Armbinde mit der Angabe der Sprache.

**I. Stadtgebiet** 1. Stadt 2. Strasse 3. Allee 4. Platz 5. Brücke 6. Mauern 7. Park 8. Stadtgärten 9. Stadtzentrum 10. Altstadt 11. Geschäftsviertel 12. Wohnviertel 13. Industriezone 14. Bahnhof 15. Flughafen 16. Hafen 17. Mole 18. Hafendamm 19. Autobahn 20. Tankstelle. **II. Verkehrsregeln** 1. Verkehrspolizist 2. Übertretung 3. Geldstrafe 4. Einbahnstrasse 5. Verbot links / rechts abzubiegen 6. Kreisverkehr 7. Parkverbot 8. linker / rechter Strassenrand 9. Parkverbot an abwechselnden Tagen 10. gerade Tage 11. Dienstag 12. Donnerstag 13. Samstag 14. ungerade Tage 15. Montag 16. Mittwoch 17. Freitag 18. Kreuzung 19. Zebrastreifen 20. Verkehrsampel 21. rotes / grünes / gelbes Licht 22. Parkplatz 23. bewachter Parkplatz 24. gebührenpflichtiger Parkplatz 25. Tarif 26. Feiertagstarif / Nachttarif 27. Parkuhr 28. Parkzeit 29. erste / zweite / dritte Stunde 30. Kurzparkzone 31. Parkscheibe. **III. Öffentliche Verkehrsmittel** 1. Taxi 2. Taxistand 3. Bus 4. Obus 5. Strassenbahn 6. Linie 7. Haltestelle.

**Español**

¿Dónde podría encontrar un intérprete?

Puede dirigerse a un guardia municipal o a un agente de Seguridad, que hable su idioma. Llevan una faja blanca con la indicación del idioma que hablan.

**I Itinerarios** 1. ciudad 2. calle 3. calle ancha 4. plaza 5. puente 6. murallas 7. parque 8. jardines públicos 9. centro de la ciudad 10. centro histórico 11. centro de negocios 12. zona residencial 13. zona industrial 14. estación de ferrocarriles 15. aeropuerto 16. puerto 17. dique 18. muelle 19. autopista 20. surtidor de gasolina. **II Normas de tráfico** 1. guardia municipal 2. infracción 3. multa 4. calle de sentido único de marcha 5. prohíbido virar a la izquierda / a la derecha 6. circulación giratoria 7. prohibido parar 8. lado izquierdo / derecho de la calle 9. prohibido parar en días alternos 10. días pares 11. martes 12. jueves 13. sábado 14. días impares 15. lunes 16. miércoles 17. viernes 18. cruce 19. rayas reservadas a los peatones 20. semáforo 21. luz roja / verde / amarilla 22. aparcamiento 23. aparcamiento vigilado 24. aparcamiento de pago 25. tarifa 26. tarifa para los días de fiesta / nocturna 27. parquímetro 28. tiempo de parada 29. primera / segunda / tercera hora 30. zona disco 31. disco horario. **III Medios de transporte públicos** 1. taxi 2. aparcamiento de taxis 3. autobús 4. filobús 5. tranvía 6. línea 7. parada.

**Srpsko-hrvatski**

Gdje mogu naći jednog tumača?

Možete se obratiti na jednog milicionera, koji govori vaš jezik. Oni nose na rukavu jednu bijelu traku sa oznakom jezika koji govore.

**I Putopisi** 1. grad 2. ulica 3. bulevar 4. trg 5. most 6. zidine 7. park 8. javni parkovi 9. centar grada 10. historijski centar 11. poslovni centar 12. stambena zona 13. industrijska zona 14. željeznička stanica 15. zračna luka 16. luka 17. molo 18. gat 19. autostrada 20. pumpna stanica. **II Saobraćajne norme** 1. milicioner 2. prekršaj 3. globa 4. jednosmjerna ulica 5. zabranjeno skretanje u lijevo / u desno 6. obavezno kruženje 7. zabranjeno zaustavljanje 8. lijeva strana / desna strana ulice 9. zabranjeno zaustavljanje u naizmjenične dane 10. parni dani 11. utorak 12. četvrtak 13. subota 14. neparni dani 15. ponedjeljak 16. srijeda 17. petak 18. raskršće 19. pješački prijelaz 20. semafor 21. svjetlo crveno / zeleno / žuto 22. parkiralište 23. čuvano parkiralište 24. parkiralište uz naplatu 25. tarifa 26. tarifa praznična / noćna 27. parkirni sat 28. vrijeme parkiranja 29. prvi / drugi / treći sat 30. disk zona 31. satni disk. **III Javna sobraćajna sredstva** 1. taksi 2. parkiralište taksija 3. autobus 4. trolejbus 5. tramvaj 6. linija 7. stanica.

## AUSKÜNFTE IN DER STADT

Könnten Sie mir sagen, wo die ... Botschaft / das ... Konsulat / das Stadion ist?

Gibt es hier in der Nähe ein gutes Restaurant / ein nicht zu teures Gasthaus?

Fahre ich hier richtig zum ... Theater / zur Oper?

Ich suche die Städtische Pinakothek / die Galerie Moderner Kunst.

Ist sie täglich / zu dieser Zeit offen?

Das Museum ist von neun bis eins und von zwei bis fünf geöffnet.

Dienstag ist es geschlossen.

An wen muss ich mich wenden, um eine Eintrittserlaubis für die ... Sammlung zu bekommen?

Wo ist die katholische / die evangelische Kirche?

## INFORMACIONES EN LA CIUDAD

¿Sabe Vd. decirme dónde se halla la embajada de ... / el consulado de ... / el estadio? »

¿Hay por aquí cerca un buen restaurante / una casa de comidas económica?

¿Es ésta la calle precisa para ir al teatro... / a la ópera?

Busco la pinacoteca de la ciudad / la galería de arte moderno.

¿Está abierta todos los días / a esta hora?

El horario del museo es de nueve a una y de dos a cinco.

El martes está cerrado.

¿A quién debo dirigirme para obtener el permiso de visitar la colección de...?

¿Dónde se halla la iglesia católica / protestante?

## INFORMACIJE U GRADU

Da li znate objasniti gdje se nalazi ambasada ... / konzulat ... / stadion.

Postoji li u blizini jedna dobra restauracija / jeftinija gostionica?

Da li ova cesta vodi prema kazalištu / prema operi?

Tražim gradsku galeriju slika / galeriju moderne umjetnosti.

Da li je otvorena sve dane / u ovo vrijeme?

Radno vrijeme muzeja je od devet do trinaest i od četrnaest do sedamnaest.

Utorak je zatvoreno.

Na koga se moram obratiti za dozvolu razgledavanja kolekcije ... ?

Gdje je katolička crkva / pravoslavna?

| English | Italiano | Français |
|---|---|---|
| Where can I find a filling station / a garage / a tyre repair shop. | Dove posso trovare un distributore di benzina / un'officina / un vulcanizzatore? | Où puis-je trouver un distributeur d'essence / un atelier de réparations / un atelier de vulcanisation? |
| Carry-on in this direction and turn left / right in about twenty / thirty / a hundred metres. | Prosegua in questa direzione e volti a sinistra / a destra dopo circa venti / trenta / cento metri. | Continuez dans cette direction, puis tournez à gauche / à droite après vingt / trente / cent mètres environ. |
| Where can I find a post / telegraph office? | Dove posso trovare un ufficio postale / telegrafico? | Où puis-je trouver un bureau de poste / de télégraphe? |
| Where can I buy stamps? | Dove posso comprare dei francobolli? | Où peut-on acheter des timbres? |
| In a post office or at a tobacconist's. | In un ufficio postale o in una tabbaccheria. | A la poste ou dans un bureau de tabac. |
| What stamps must I put on a letter for abroad / by air mail? | Qual è l'affrancatura per una lettera per l'estero / via aerea? | Quel est l'affranchissement pour une lettre pour l'étranger / par avion? |
| I want to send this letter by registered express post. | Vorrei spedire questa lettera raccomandata espresso. | Je voudrais expédier cette lettre recommandée par exprès. |
| Give me the stamps for two postcards, with more than five words / with less than five words. | Mi dia i francobolli per due cartoline scritte / con saluti. | Je voudrais des timbres pour deux cartes postales toutes écrites / avec salutations seulement. |
| Where is the poste-restante counter? | Dov'è lo sportello del fermo-posta? | Où est le guichet de la poste restante? |
| I want to send a telegraphic money order / a telegram. | Dovrei spedire un vaglia telegrafico / un telegramma. | Je voudrais expédier un mandat télégraphique / un télégramme. |
| Is there a public telephone near here? | C'è un telefono pubblico qui vicino? | Y a-t-il un téléphone public dans les parages? |
| Please give me a counter for the telephone. | Mi dia, per favore, un gettone telefonico. | Voulez-vous me donner un jeton de téléphone, s'il vous plaît. |
| How much does it cost? | Quanto costa? | Combien est-ce? |
| Can you call this number at . . . for me? | Può chiamare questo numero a . . ? | Pourriez-vous appeler ce numéro à . . . ? |
| You can call it direct. This is the prefix. | Può parlare in teleselezione. Questo è il prefisso. | Vous pouvez parler sur l'automatique. Voici le préfixe. |
| How much do I owe you for this call? | Quanto devo per questa comunicazione? | Combien vous dois-je pour cette communication? |
| Could you direct me to a bank / an exchange office? | Potrebbe indicarmi una banca / un ufficio cambi? | Pourriez-vous nous indiquer une banque / un bureau de change? |
| What is the exchange rate today? | Qual è il cambio oggi? | A combien est le change aujourd'hui? |
| I should like to cash a traveller's cheque. | Vorrei incassare un traveller's cheque. | Je voudrais encaisser un traveller's chèque. |
| Has a remittance arrived for me? | E' arrivata una rimessa per me? | Est-il arrivé un virement pour moi? |
| Have you got a document on you? | Ha un documento? | Avez-vous une pièce d'identité? |
| What is your address in this town? | Qual è il suo indirizzo in questa città? | Quelle est votre adresse dans cette ville? |

| Deutsch | Español | Srpsko-hrvatski |
|---|---|---|
| Wo ist eine Tankstelle / eine Autowerkstatt / eine Reifenwerkstatt? | ¿Dónde puedo encontrar un surtidor de gasolina / un taller mecánico / un taller de recauchutado? | Gdje mogu naći jednu pumpnu stanicu / mehaničku radionicu / vulkanizera? |
| Fahren Sie in dieser Richtung weiter und biegen Sie nach ungefähr zwanzig / dreissig / hundert Metern links / rechts ab. | Siga por esta dirección y tuerza a la izquierda / a la derecha después de unos veinte / treinta / cien metros. | Nastavite ovim smjerom i zaokrenite na lijevo / na desno nakon dvadeset / trideset / sto metara. |
| Wo ist ein Postamt / ein Telegrafenamt? | ¿Dónde puedo encontrar una oficina de correos / de telegráfos? | Gdje mogu naći jedan poštanski ured / telegrafski ured? |
| Wo kann ich Marken kaufen? | ¿Dónde puedo adquirir sellos? | Gdje mogu kupiti poštanske marke? |
| In einem Postamt oder in einem Tabakladen. | En una oficina de correos o en una expendeduría de tabaco. | U poštanskom uredu ili u prodavaonici duhana. |
| Wie muss ich einen Brief ins Ausland / einen Luftpostbrief frankieren? | ¿Cuál es el franqueo de una carta para el extranjero / por avión? | Kolika je tarifa za jedno pismo za inozemstvo / avionski? |
| Ich möchte diesen Brief als eingeschriebenen Eilbrief aufgeben. | Quisiera enviar esta carta certificada urgente. | Želio bih poslati ovo pismo preporučeno, hitno. |
| Geben Sie mir bitte Marken für zwei vollgeschriebene Ansichtskarten / für zwei Ansichtskarten mit Grüssen. | Puede darme los sellos para dos tarjetas totalmente escritas / sólo con saludos. | Dajte mi marke za dvije razglednice popunjene / sa pozdravima. |
| Wo ist der Schalter für postlagernde Sendungen? | ¿Dónde está la ventanilla de la lista de correos? | Gdje se nalazi šalter za « posta restante ». |
| Ich müsste eine telegrafische Postanweisung / ein Telegramm aufgeben. | Deseo enviar un giro telegráfico / un telegrama. | Morao bih poslati jednu telegrafsku uputnicu / jedan telegram. |
| Gibt es hier in der Nähe eine Fernsprechstelle? | ¿Hay un teléfono público por aquí cerca? | Postoji li u blizini jedan javni telefon? |
| Geben Sie mir bitte eine Telefonmünze. | ¿Me da, por favor, una ficha telefónica? | Dajte mi molim jedan žeton za telefon. |
| Wierviel kostet sie? | ¿Cuánto cuesta? | Koliko košta? |
| Würden Sie mich mit dieser Nummer in . . . verbinden? | ¿Puede llamar a este número de...? | Možete li mi nazvati ovaj broj u . . . ? |
| Sie können durchwählen. Hier ist die Vorwahlnummer. | Puede comunicar por teleselección. Este es el prefijo. | Možete nazvati automatski. Ovo je prefiks. |
| Wieviel bin ich für dieses Gespräch schuldig? | ¿Cuánto tengo que pagar por esta cuomunicación? | Koliko sam dužan za ovaj razgovor? |
| Könnten Sie mir sagen, wo eine Bank / eine Wechselstube ist? | ¿Podría indicarme un banco / una oficina de cambio? | Možete li me uputiti u jednu banku / mjenjačnicu? |
| Wie ist der Kurs heute? | ¿Cuál es el cambio de hoy? | Koji je kurs danas? |
| Ich möchte einen traveller's cheque kassieren. | Quisiera cobrar un traveller's cheque. | Želio bih unovčiti jedan traveller's ček. |
| Ist eine Überweisung für mich angekommen? | ¿Ha llegado un depósito a mi nombre? | Da li je stigla jedna novčana pošiljka za mene? |
| Haben Sie einen Ausweis? | ¿Tiene Vd. un documento? | Imate li kakav dokument? |
| Wie ist Ihre Anschrift hier? | ¿Cuál es su dirección en esta ciudad? | Koja je vaša adresa u ovome gradu? |

| English | Italiano | Français |
|---|---|---|
| Please sign here. | Per cortesia, firmi qui. | Voulez-vous signer ici, je vous prie. |
| Where is the nearest hospital / first aid post. | Dov'è il piú vicino ospedale / pronto soccorso? | Où se trouve l'hôpital / le poste de secours le plus proche? |
| Could you take me there? I have a sick person / an injured person / a seriously injured person in the car. | Potrebbe accompagnarmi? Ho un ammalato / un ferito / un ferito grave a bordo. | Pourriez-vous m'accompagner? J'ai un malade / un blessé / un blessé grave à bord. |
| What is your blood group? | Qual è il suo gruppo sanguigno? | Quel est votre groupe sanguin? |
| Have you ever had an anti-tetanus injection? | Le è mai stata fatta un'iniezione antitetanica? | Vous a-t-on déjà fait une piqûre antitétanique? |
| Yes, two years ago. | Sí. due anni fa. | Oui, il y a deux ans. |
| Do you suffer from an allergy? | Soffre di allergia? | Etes-vous sujet aux allergies? |
| Where is there a chemist's? | Dov'è una farmacia? | Où y a-t-il une pharmacie? |
| Please give me something for a bad headache / toothache / stomach trouble. | Mi dia, per favore, qualche cosa contro un forte mal di testa / di denti / disturbi intestinali. | Donnez-moi, je vous prie, quelque chose pour un fort mal de tête / de dents / pour un dérangement intestinal. |
| What do you advice for a cold / a cough? | Cosa mi consiglia contro un raffreddore / contro la tosse? | Que me conseillez-vous contre le rhume / contre la toux? |
| I should like a tube of aspirins / a sedative / some sleeping pills. | Vorrei un tubetto di aspirina / un calmante / un sonnifero. | Je voudrais un tube d'aspirine / un calmant / un somnifère. |
| Have you got a prescription? | Ha la ricetta? | Avez-vous une ordonnance? |
| I cannot give you this medicine without a prescription. | Non posso darle questa medicina senza ricetta. | e ne peux pas vous vendre ce médicament sans ordonnance. |
| I should like some sticking plaster / an elastic bandage / a bandage / some sanitary towels. | Vorrei un cerotto / una fascia elastica / una benda / assorbenti. | Je voudrais du sparadrap / un bandage élastique / une bande / des serviettes hygiéniques. |
| Can you dress this cut? | Potrebbe medicare questo taglio? | Pourriez-vous panser cette coupure? |

**I Offices** 1. embassy 2. consulate 3. legation 4. police station 5. divisional police station 6. lost property office 7. bank 8. exchange office. **II Post, telegraph, telephone** 1. stamps 2. letter 3. postcard 4. registered letter 5. express 6. air mail 7. poste-restante counter 8. telegram counter 9. telegram form 10. letter telegram 11. urgent / reply-paid telegram 12. telegraphic money order 13. postal order 14. international money order 15. telephone box 16. counter for telephone 17. telephone directory 18. telephone number 19. trunk call. 20. S.T.D. 21. prefix. **III First aid and chemist's** 1. hospital 2. first aid post 3. doctor 4. nurse 5. blood group 6. high / low pressure 7. injection 8. anti-tetanus 9. anti-diphtheria 10. anti-typhoid 11. allergy 12. medication 13. stitches 14. night chemist's 15. prescription 16. pills 17. tablets 18. syrup 19. sedative 20. laxative 21. eyewash 22. ointment 23. gauze pads 24. cotton wool 25. sanitary towels 26. bandage 27. elastic bandage 28. alcohol 29. iodine 30. disinfectant 31. haemostatic 32. vaseline 33. cold 34. cough 35. headache 36. sore throat 37. toothache 38. stiff neck 39. lumbago 40.

**I Uffici** 1. ambasciata 2. consolato 3. legazione 4. questura 5. commissariato 6. ufficio oggetti smarriti 7. banca 8. ufficio cambi. **II Poste, telegrafo, telefono** 1. francobolli 2. lettera 3. cartolina 4. raccomandata 5. espresso 6. via aerea 7. sportello fermo-posta 8. sportello telegrammi 9. modulo telegrammi 10. telegramma lettera 11. telegramma urgente / con risposta pagata 12. vaglia telegrafico 13. vaglia postale 14. vaglia internazionale 15. cabina del telefono 16. gettone 17. elenco del telefono 18. numero di telefono 19. comunicazione interurbana 20. teleselezione 21. prefisso. **III Pronto soccorso e farmacia** 1. ospedale 2. posto di pronto soccorso 3. medico 4. infermiera 5. gruppo sanguigno 6. pressione alta / bassa 7. iniezione 8. antitetanica 9. antidifterica 10. antitifica 11. allergia 12. medicazione 13. punti 14. farmacia notturna 15. ricetta 16. pillole 17. pasticche 18. sciroppo 19. calmante 20. lassativo 21. collirio 22. pomata 23. tamponi di garza 24. cotone idrofilo 25. assorbenti 26. benda 27. fascia elastica 28. alcool 29. tintura di iodio 30. disinfettante 31. emostatico 32. vasellina

**I Bureaux** 1. ambassade 2. consulat 3. légation 4. poste de police 5. commissariat 6. bureau des objets trouvés 7. banque 8. bureau de change **II Postes, télégraphe, téléphone** 1. timbres 2. lettre 3. carte postale 4. lettre recommandée 5. exprès 6. par avion 7. guichet de la poste restante 8. guichet des télégrammes 9. formule de télégramme 10. télégramme lettre 11. télégramme urgent / avec réponse payée 12. mandat télégraphique 13. mandat postal 14. mandat international 15. cabine de téléphone 16. jeton 17. annuaire du téléphone 18. numéro de téléphone 19. communication interurbaine 20. appel automatique 21. préfixe. **III Secours d'urgence et pharmacie** 1. hôpital 2. poste de secours d'urgence 3. médecin 4. infirmière 5. groupe sanguin 6. tension élevée / basse 7. piqûre 8. antitétanique 9. antidiphtérique 10. contre la typhoïde 11. allergie 12. pansement 13. points de suture 14. pharmacie nocturne 15. ordonnance 16. pilules 17. comprimés 18. sirop 19. calmant 20. laxatif 21. collyre 22. pomade 23. tampons de gaze 24. coton hydrophile 25. serviettes hygiéniques 26. bande 27. bande élastique 28. alcool

| Deutsch | Español | Srpsko-hrvatski |
|---|---|---|
| Bitte unterzeichnen Sie hier. | Por favor, quiere Vd. firmar aquí. | Molim, potpišite ovdje. |
| Wo ist das nächstliegende Krankenhaus / die nächste Unfallstation? | ¿Dónde está el hospital más cercano / un puesto de socorro? | Gdje je najbliža bolnica / stanica za hitnu pomoć? |
| Würden Sie mich begleiten? Ich habe einen Kranken / einen Verletzten / einen Schwerverletzten an Bord. | ¿Podría Vd. acompañarme? En mi coche llevo un enfermo / un herido / un herido grave. | Možete li me otpratiti? Iman jednog bolesnika / ranjenika / teškog ranjenika u kolima. |
| Welcher Blutgruppe gehören Sie an? | /Cuál es su grupo sanguíneo? | Koja je vaša krvna grupa? |
| Wurde Ihnen schon einmal eine Tetanusspritze gemacht? | ¿Le han puesto alguna vez una inyección antitetánica? | Da li ste već primili injekciju protiv tetanusa? |
| Ja, vor zwei Jahren. | Sí, hace dos años. | Da, prije dvije godine. |
| Sind Sie allergisch? | ¿Padece de alergia? | Patite li od alergije? |
| Wo ist eine Apotheke? | ¿Dónde hay una farmacia? | Gdje se nalazi jedna apoteka? |
| Geben Sie mir bitte etwas gegen starke Kopfschmerzen / Zahnschmerzen / Darmbeschwerden. | Déme, por favor, algo contra un fuerte dolor de cabeza / de muelas / de vientre. | Dajte mi molim nešto protiv jake glavobolje / zubobolje / crjevnih smetnji. |
| Was würden Sie mir gegen eine Erkältung / gegen Husten raten? | ¿Qué me aconseja contra el resfriado / contra la tos? | Što mi preporučate protiv prehlade / protiv kašlja? |
| Ich möchte eine Tube Aspirin / ein Beruhigungsmittel / ein Schlafmittel. | Desearía un tubo de aspirinas / un calmante / un somnífero. | Želio bih jednu kutiju aspirina / sredstva za umirenje / sredstva za spavanje. |
| Haben Sie das Rezept? | ¿Tiene la receta? | Imate li recept? |
| Ich kann Ihnen dieses Medikament nur gegen Rezept geben. | No puedo darle esta medicina sin receta. | Ovaj lijek vam ne mogu dati bez recepta. |
| Ich möchte ein Pflaster / eine elastische Binde / eine Binde / Damenbinden. | Desearía un esparadrapo / una faja elástica / una venda / absorbentes. | Želim jedan flaster / elastični povez / zavoj / mjesečni uložak. |
| Würden Sie mir diese Schnittwunde verbinden? | ¿Podría curarme esta herida? | Možete li mi liječiti ovu posjekotinu? |

**I. Ämter** 1. Botschaft 2. Konsulat 3. Legation 4. Polizeidirektion 5. Kommissariat 6. Fundbüro 7. Bank 8. Wechselstube. **II. Post- und Telegrafenamt, Telefon** 1. Marken 2. Brief 3. Ansichtskarte 4. Einschreibebrief 5. Eilbrief 6. Luftpost 7. Schalter für postlagernde Sendungen 8. Telegrammschalter 9. Telegrammaufgabeschein 10. Brieftelegramm 11. Blitztelegramm / Telegramm Antwort bezahlt 12. telegrafische Postanweisung 13. Postanweisung 14. internationale Postanweisung 15. Fernsprechzelle 16. Münze 17. Telefonbuch 18. Telefonnummer 19. Ferngespräch 20. Selbstwählverkehr 21. Vorwahlnummer. **III. Erste Hilfe und Apotheke** 1. Krankenhaus 2. Unfallstation 3. Arzt 4. Pflegerin 5. Blutgruppe 6. hoher / niedriger Blutdruck 7. Injektion 8. Tetanusserum 9. Diphterieserum 10. Typhusimpfung 11. Allergie 12. ärztliche Behandlung 13. Naht 14. Nachtapotheke 15. Rezept 16. Pillen 17. Pastillen 18. Sirup 19. Beruhigungsmittel 20. Laxativ 21. Collyrium 22. Salbe 23. Gaze-Tampons 24. Watte 25. Dumenbinden 26. Binde 27. elastische Binde 28. Alkohol 29. Jodtinktur 30. Desinfektionsmittel 31. blutstillendes Mittel 32. Vaselin

**I Oficinas** 1. embajada 2. consulado 3. legación 4. dirección de Seguridad 5. comisaría 6. oficina de objetos perdidos 7. banco 8. oficina de cambio. **II Correos, telégrafo, teléfono** 1. sellos 2. carta 3. tarjeta 4. certificada 5. urgente 6. vía aérea 7. lista de correos 8. ventanilla para telegramas 9. módulo para telegramas 10. telegrama-carta 11. telegrama urgente / con respuesta pagada 12. giro telegráfico 13. giro postal 14. giro internacional 15. cabina de teléfono 16. ficha 17. guía de teléfonos 18. número de teléfono 19. comunicación interurbana 20. por teleselección 21. prefijo. **III Casa de socorro y farmacia** 1. hospital 2. puesto de socorro 3. médico 4. enfermera 5. grupo sanguíneo 6. tensión alta / baja 7. inyección 8. antitetánica 9. antidiftérica 10. antitífica 11. alergia 12. cura 13. puntos 14. farmacia nocturna 15. receta 16. píldoras 17. pastillas 18. jarabe 19. calmante 20. laxante 21. colirio 22. pomada 23. tapones de gasa 24. algodón hidrófilo 25 absorbentes 26. venda 27. faja elástica 28. alcohol 29. tintura de Yodo 30. desinfectante 31. hemostático 32. vaselina 33. resfriado 34. tos 35. jaqueca

**I Uredi** 1. ambasada 2. konzulat 3. poslanstvo 4. milicija 5. komesarijat 6. nalazni ured 7. banka 8. mjenjačnica **II Pošta, telegraf, telefon** 1. poštanske marke 2. pismo 3. razglednica 4. preporučeno 5. hitno 6. avionski 7. šalter za « posta restante » 8. šalter za telegrame 9. obrazac telegrama 10. pismo-telegram 11. hitni telegram / sa plaćenim odgovorom 12. telegrafska uputnica 13. poštanska uputnica 14. internacionalna uputnica 15. telefonska kabina 16. žeton 17. telefonski imenik 18. broj telefona 19. medjugradski razgovor 20. automatsko biranje medjugradske linije 21. prefiks. **III Hitna pomoć i apoteka** 1. bolnica 2. stanica za hitnu pomoć 3. liječnik 4. bolničarka 5. krvna grupa 6. pritisak visoki / niski 7. injekcija 8. protiv tetanusa 9. protiv difterije 10. protiv tifusa 11. alergija 12. liječenje 13. kopče 14. noćna apoteka 15. recept 16. pilule 17. tablete 18. sirup 19. sredstvo za umirenje 20. sredstvo za čišćenje 21. kapi za oči 22. krema 23. tamponi od gaze 24. hidronlni zavoj 25. mjesečni uložak 26. zavoj 27. elastični zavoj 28. alkohol 29. jodna tinktura 30. sredstvo za desinfekciju 31. hidrofilni pamuk

**English**

indigestion. **IV Art and monuments** 1. museum 2. picture gallery 3. gallery 4. collection 5. exhibition 6. church 7. cathedral 8. principal church. **V Entertainments** 1. theatre 2. opera 3. cinema 4. night club 5. stadium 6. football match 7. boxing match 8. race course.

**Italiano**

33. raffreddore 34. tosse 35. emicrania 36. mal di gola 37. mal di denti 38. torcicollo 39. lombaggine 40. indigestione. **IV Arte e monumenti** 1. museo 2. pinacoteca 3. galleria 4. collezione 5. mostra 6. chiesa 7. cattedrale 8. duomo. **V Spettacoli** 1. teatro 2. opera 3. cinema 4. locale notturno 5. stadio 6. partita di calcio 7. incontro di pugilato 8. ippodromo.

**Français**

29. teinture d'iode 30. désinfectant 31. hémostatique 32. vaseline 33. rhume 34. toux 35. migraine 36. mal de gorge 37. mal de dents 38. torticolis 39. lumbago 40. indigestion. **IV Art et monuments** 1. musée 2. pinacothèque 3. galerie 4. collection 5. exposition 6. église 7. cathédrale 8. dôme (cathédrale, en Italie). **V Spectacles** 1. théâtre 2. opéra 3. cinéma 4. night club 5. stade 6. partie de football 7. match de boxe 8. hippodrome.

## CAR HIRE

I should like to hire a car with / without driver.

How much does it cost a day?

Is there a supplement according to the mileage covered?

It costs . . . a day, everything included except petrol.

There is a supplement for every kilometre / every hundred kilometres.

Is the car insured?

You must leave a deposit of ...

Let me see your driving licence and give me your address in this town.

Sign this form, please.

**I Car** 1. small- / medium-sized car 2. make 3. model 4. four- / six-seater saloon 5. coupé 6. sports car 7. estate car 8. car fitted with radio / roof rack / ski-rack / snow chains 9. left-hand drive / right-hand drive car. **II Conditions** 1. car with / without driver 2. hire for one day / two days / a week 3. driving licence 4. rate per day / per kilometre 5. tachometer reading 6. mileage 7. deposit 8. supplement 9. fuel consumption 10. refund of expenditure for oil / greasing / repairs 11. presentation of invoice 12. third party insurance 13. insurance covering passengers.

## AUTONOLEGGIO

Vorrei noleggiare una macchina con / senza autista.

Quanto costa al giorno?

C'è un supplemento secondo i chilometri percorsi?

Costa . . . al giorno, tutto compreso eccetto la benzina.

C'è un supplemento per ogni chilometro / ogni cento chilometri.

La macchina è assicurata?

Deve versare un deposito di . . .

Mi faccia vedere la sua patente e mi dia il suo indirizzo in questa città.

Firmi questo modulo, per favore.

**I Vettura** 1. vettura di piccola / media cilindrata 2. marca 3. modello 4. berlina a quattro / sei posti 5. coupé 6. spider 7. giardiniera 8. vettura munita di autoradio / portabagagli supplementare / porta-sci / catene da neve 9. vettura con guida a sinistra / guida a destra. **II Condizioni** 1. vettura con / senza autista 2. noleggio per un giorno / due giorni / una settimana 3. patente 4. tariffa al giorno / per chilometro 5. lettura del contachilometri 6. chilometraggio 7. deposito 8. supplemento 9. consumo del carburante 10. rimborso spese per olio / ingrassaggio / riparazioni 11. esibizione fattura 12. assicurazione responsabilità civile 13. assicurazione per i trasportati.

## LOCATION DE VOITURES

Je voudrais louer une voiture avec / sans chauffeur.

Combien cela coûte-t-il par jour?

Y a-t-il un supplément selon les kilomètres parcourus?

Le prix est de . . . par jour, tout compris sauf l'essence.

Il y a un supplément pour chaque kilomètre / tous les cent kilomètres.

La voiture est-elle assurée?

Il vous faut verser une caution de .

Veuillez me montrer votre permis de conduire, et me donner votre adresse dans cette ville, s'il vous plaît.

Ayez l'obligeance de signer ce formulaire, je vous prie.

**I Voiture** 1. voiture de petite / moyenne cylindrée 2. marque 3. modèle 4. berline à quatre / six places 5. coupé 6. cabriolet 7. station-wagon 8. voiture avec radio / porte-bagages supplémentaire / porte-skis / chaînes pour la neige 9. voiture avec conduite à gauche / conduite à droite. **II Conditions** 1. voiture avec / sans chauffeur 2. location pour un jour / deux jours / une semaine 3. permis de conduire 4. tarif par jour / au kilomètre 5. lecture du compteur kilométrique 6. kilométrage 7. caution 8. supplément 9. consommation de carburant 10. remboursement des frais d'huile / de graissage / de réparations 11. présentation de la facture 12. assurance pour la responsabilité civile 13. assurance pour les passagers.

Erkältung 34. Husten 35. Migräne 36. Halsweh 37. Zahnweh 38. steifer Hals 39. Hexenschuss 40. Verdauungsstörungen. **IV. Kunst und Baudenkmäler** 1. Museum 2. Pinakothek 3. Galerie 4. Sammlung 5. Ausstellung 6. Kirche 7. Kathedrale 8. Dom. **V. Unterhaltung** 1. Theater 2. Oper 3. Kino 4. Nachtlokal 5. Stadion 6. Fussballpartie 7. Boxkampf 8. Rennplatz.

36. dolor de garganta 37. dolor de muelas 38. tortícolis 39. lumbago. 40. indigestión. **IV Arte y Monumentos** 1. museo 2. pinacoteca 3. galería 4. colección 5. exposición 6. iglesia 7. catedral 8. catedral. **V Espectáculos** 1. teatro 2. ópera 3. cine 4. local nocturno 5. estadio 6. partido de fútbol 7. encuentro de boxeo 8. hipódromo.

33. Erkältung 34. Husten 35. Migräne 36. 32. vazelin 33. prehlada 34. kašalj 35. glavobolja 36. upala grla 37. zubobolja 38. ukočenje vrata 39. lumbago 40. loša probava. **IV Umjetnost i spomenici** 1. muzej 2. galerija slika 3. galerija 4. kolekcija 5. izložba 6. crkva 7. katedrala 8. stolna crkva. **V Predstave** 1. kazalište 2. opera 3. kino 4. noćni lokal 5. stadion 6. nogometna utakmica 7. boksački susret 8. hipodrom.

## AUTOVERLEIH

## ALQUILER DE COCHES

## IZNAJMLJIVANJE AUTOMOBILA

| Deutsch | Español | Srpsko-hrvatski |
|---|---|---|
| Ich möchte einen Wagen mit / ohne Chauffeur mieten. | Quisiera alquilar un coche con / sin chofer. | Želio bih iznajmiti jedna kola sa / bez vozača. |
| Wieviel kostet es pro Tag? | ¿Cuánto cuesta por día? | Koliko košta na dan? |
| Zahlt man eine zusätzliche Gebühr je nach gefahrenen Kilometern? | ¿Hay un suplemento según el número de kilómetros? | Postoji li dodatak prema predjenim kilometrima? |
| Es kostet . . . pro Tag, alles inbegriffen ausser dem Kraftstoff. | Cuesta ... por día, incluído todo a excepción de la gasolina. | Košta . . . na dan, ukjučivši sve osim benzina. |
| Es ist eine Zusatzgebühr pro Kilometer / je hundert Kilometer zu zahlen. | Hay un suplemento por cada kilómetro / por cada cien kilómetros. | Postoji jedan dodatak za svaki kilometar / za svakih sto kilometara. |
| Ist der Wagen versichert? | ¿El coche está asegurado? | Da li su kola osigurana? |
| Sie müssen ein Depot von . . . erlegen. | Tiene que dejarnos un depósito de... liras. | Morate položiti kauciju od . . . |
| Darf ich Ihren Führerschein sehen? Wie ist Ihre Anschrift in dieser Stadt bitte? | Enséñeme su carnet de conducir y dígame su dirección en esta ciudad. | Pokažite mi svoju vozačku dozvolu i dajte mi svoju adresu u ovome gradu. |
| Bitte unterzeichnen Sie hier. | Firme este módulo, por favor | Molim, potpišite ovaj obrazac. |

**I. Wagen** 1. Kleinwagen / Mittelklassenwagen 2. Marke 3. Modell 4. viersitzige / sechssitzige Limousine 5. Coupé 6. Spider 7. Kombi 8. Wagen mit Radio / Gepäckrost / Skihalter / Schneeketten 9. linksgesteuerter / rechtsgesteuerter Wagen. **II. Bedingungen** 1. Wagen mit / ohne Chauffeur 2. Miete für einen Tag / zwei Tage / eine Woche 3. Führerschein 4. Gebuhrensatz pro Tag / pro Kilometer 5. Ablesen des Kilometerzählers 6. gefahrene Kilometer 7. Depot 8. Zusatzgebühr 9. Benzinverbrauch 10. Rückvergütung der Auslagen für Öl / Schmieren / Reparaturen 11. Rechnungsvorlage 12. Haftpflichtversicherung 13. Mitfahrer-Unfallversicherung

**I Coche** 1. coche de pequeña / media cilindrada 2. marca 3. modelo 4. berlina de cuatro / seis asientos 5. coupé 6. spider 7. rubia 8. coche con autoradio / con rejilla suplementaria / lleva-esquíes / cadenas para nieve. **II Condiciones** 1. alquiler con / sin chófer 2. alquiler por un dia / dos dias / por una semana 3. carnet de conducir 4. tarifa por día / por kilómetro 5. lectura del cuentakilómetros 6. kilometraje 7. depósito 8. suplemento 9. consumo de carburante 10. reembolso de los gastos por aceite / engrasado / reparaciones 11. presentación de la factura 12. seguro contra la responsabilidad civil 13. seguro para los pasajeros.

**I Vozilo** 1. vozilo male / srednje zapremnine 2. marka 3. model 4. luksuzna kola sa četiri / šest sjedišta 5. sportska kola 6. otvorena sportska kola 7. kola sa stražnjim vratima 8. kola opskrbljena autoradiom / dodatnim nosačem prtljage / nosačem za skije / lancima za snijeg 9. kola sa upravljačem na lijevoj / na desnoj strani. **II Uslovi** 1. kola sa / bez vozača 2. posudba na jedan dan / dva dana / jedan tjedan 3. vozačka dozvola 4. tarifa na dan / po kilometru 5. očitanje predjenih kilometara 6. kilometraža 7. kaucija 8. dodatak 9. potrošnja goriva 10. nadoknada troškova za ulje / podmazivanje / popravke 11. iskazivanje računa 12. osiguranje za gradjansku odgovornost 13. osiguranje za putnike u kolima.

**AT THE GARAGE**

**IN OFFICINA**

**A L'ATELIER DE REPARATIONS**

**IN DER WERKSTATT**

**EN EL TALLER MECANICO**

**U MAEHANIČKOJ RADIONICI**

| English | Italiano | Français |
|---|---|---|
| **AGREEMENT ON REPAIRS** | **ACCORDI PER LE RIPARAZIONI** | **ACCORDS CONCERNANT LES REPARATIONS** |
| Good morning, there is something wrong with my car. Can you put it right? | Buon giorno, ho un guasto alla macchina. Si può rimediare? | Bonjour, ma voiture a des ennuis, pouvez-vous m'arranger cela? |
| Yes, but it will take some time. | Sí, ma ci vorrà un po' di tempo. | Oui, mais il faudra un peu de temps. |
| No, we haven't got the necessary spare parts. You will have to go to a garage specializing in this make. | No, non abbiamo i pezzi di ricambio necessari. Deve andare in un'officina abilitata. | Non, nous n'avons pas les pièces de rechange nécessaires; il faut vous adresser à un atelier autorisé. |
| Can you do the essential repairs to allow me to get to the town? | Può fare le riparazioni essenziali per permettermi di arrivare in città? | Pouvez-vous me faire les réparations indispensables pour me permettre d'arriver en ville. |
| It is very dangerous to drive the car in this condition. | E' molto pericoloso viaggiare con la macchina in queste condizioni. | Il est très dangereux de marcher avec une voiture dans cet état. |
| It is rather risky. However, put in some oil and go on very slowly. | E' piuttosto rischioso. Aggiunga comunque dell'olio e proceda molto lentamente. | C'est plutôt risqué. Cependant ajoutez de l'huile, et marchez doucement. |
| Can you have the car towed to the specialized garage? | Può far rimorchiare la vettura fino all'officina abilitata? | Pouvez-vous faire remorquer la voiture jusqu'à l'atelier autorisé? |
| How much does it cost to have it towed? | Quanto costa farsi rimorchiare? | Combien en coûte-t-il pour se faire remorquer? |
| Begin the repairs at once, doing only the work that is absolutely necessary. | Cominci subito la riparazione, facendo solo i lavori strettamente necessari. | Commencez tout de suite la réparation en ne faisant que le strict nécessaire. |
| How long will the repair take? | Quanto tempo ci vorrà per la riparazione? | Combien de temps prendra la réparation? |
| Half an hour / an hour / half a day. | Mezz'ora / un'ora / mezza giornata. | Une demi-heure / une heure / une demi-journée. |
| What time will it be ready? | A che ora sarà pronta? | A quelle heure la voiture sera-t-elle prête? |
| After three o'clock, but don't come after seven because we close. | Dopo le tre, ma non venga dopo le sette perché chiudiamo. | A partir de trois heures, mais ne venez pas plus tard que sept heures, qui est l'heure de fermeture. |
| Telephone me at this hotel if there are any difficulties. | Mi telefoni in questo albergo se ci sono difficoltà. | Téléphonez-moi à cet hôtel s'il y a des difficultés. |
| Can you drive me to the hotel? | Può accompagnarmi in albergo? | Pourriez-vous m'accompagner jusqu'à l'hôtel? |

| Deutsch | Español | Srpsko-hrvatski |
|---|---|---|
| **AUFTRAGSANNAHME** | **ACUERDOS PARA LA REPARACION** | **DOGOVORI ZA POPRAVKE** |
| Guten Tag. Mein Wagen hat eine Panne. Könnten Sie mir behilflich sein? | Buenos días, tengo una avería en el coche. ¿Puede repararla? | Dobar dan, kola su u kvaru. Da li se mogu popraviti? |
| Ja, aber das erfordert etwas Zeit. | Sí, pero se necesitará un poco de tiempo. | Da, ali ćete morati malo sačekati. |
| Nein, leider haben wir nicht die erforderlichen Ersatzteile. Sie müssten sich an eine Vertragswerkstatt wenden. | No, no tenemos las piezas de repuesto necesarias. Tendrá que dirigirse a un taller autorizado. | Ne, nemamo potrebnih rezervnih dijelova. Morati ćete ići u jednu specijalnu radionicu. |
| Könnten Sie wenigstens die wichtigsten Arbeiten durchführen, damit ich bis in die Stadt komme? | ¿Puede Vd. hacer las reparaciones esenciales que me permitan llegar a la ciudad? | Možete li mi izvršiti potrebne popravke, da bih mogao stići u grad? |
| Es ist sehr gefährlich, den Wagen in diesem Zustand zu fahren. | Es muy peligroso viajar con el coche en estas condiciones. | Vrlo je opasno voziti se sa kolima u ovome stanju. |
| Es ist ziemlich riskant. Lassen Sie auf jeden Fall Öl auffüllen und fahren Sie sehr langsam. | Es un tanto arriesgado. Añada de todos modos aceite y vaya muy despacio. | Riskantno je. Dodajte ulje i nastavite vrlo polagano. |
| Könnten Sie den Wagen bis zur nächsten Vertragswerkstatt abschleppen? | ¿Puede remolcar el coche hasta un taller autorizado? | Možete li mi tegliti kola do specijalne radionice? |
| Wieviel kostet das Abschleppen? | ¿Cuánto cuesta remolcar el coche? | Koliko košta teglenje? |
| Beginnen Sie sofort mit der Reparatur und führen Sie nur die dringlichsten Arbeiten aus. | Empiece enseguida la reparación, haciendo solamente los arreglos estrictamente necesarios. | Počnite odmah sa popravkom, izvršivši samo najpotrebnije radove. |
| Wieviel Zeit wird die Reparatur erfordern? | ¿Cuánto tiempo necesita para la reparación? | Koliko će vremena iziskivati popravak? |
| Eine halbe Stunde / eine Stunde / einen halben Tag. | Media hora / una hora / medio día. | Pola sata / jedan sat / pola dana. |
| Um wieviel Uhr wird der Wagen fertig sein? | ¿A qué hora podré retirar el coche? | U koliko sati će biti gotova? |
| Nach drei Uhr. Kommen Sie aber bitte nicht nach sieben Uhr, denn um die Zeit schliessen wir. | Después de las tres y antes de las siete, porque a esa hora cerramos. | Poslije petnaest sati, ali nemojte doći poslije devetnaest, jer zatvaramo. |
| Sollten sich irgendwelche Schwierigkeiten ergeben, so rufen Sie mich bitte in diesem Hotel an. | Llámeme Vd. por teléfono a este hotel, si encuentra dificultades. | Ako dodje do komplikacija, telefonirajte mi u ovaj hotel |
| Könnten Sie mich zum Hotel bringen? | ¿Podría Vd. acompañarme al hotel? | Možete li me otpratiti u hotel? |

| English | Italiano | Français |
|---|---|---|
| How much is the repair? | Quanto costa la riparazione? | Combien coûtera la réparation? |
| Can you give me a detailed invoice? | Può darmi una fattura particolareggiata? | Pouvez-vous me faire une facture détaillée? |
| **I Duration of work** 1. half an hour 2. an hour 3. two hours 4. morning 5. afternoon 6. today 7. tomorrow 8. the day after tomorrow 9. one day 10. three days 11. urgent service. **II Estimate and invoice** 1. cost of spare parts 2. cost of labour 3. cost of towing service 4. rough estimate 5. part payment 6. discount 7. detailed invoice 8. stamp. | **I Durata del lavoro** 1. mezz'ora 2. un'ora 3. due ore 4. mattina 5. pomeriggio 6. oggi 7. domani 8. dopodomani 9. un giorno 10. tre giorni 11. servizio urgente. **II Preventivo e fattura** 1. costo dei pezzi di ricambio 2. costo della mano d'opera 3. costo del servizio di rimorchio 4. preventivo di massima 5. acconto 6. sconto 7. fattura particolareggiata 8. bollo. | **I Durée du travail** 1. une demi-heure 2. une heure 3. deux heures 4. matin 5. après-midi 6. aujourd'hui 7. demain 8. après-demain 9. un jour 10. trois jours 11. service urgent. **II Devis et facture** 1. prix des pièces de rechange 2. prix de la main d'oeuvre 3. prix du remorquage 4. devis de principe 5. accompte 6. rabais 7. facture détaillée 8. timbre. |

## ENGINE BLOCK / BLOCCO MOTORE / MOTEUR

| ENGINE BLOCK | BLOCCO MOTORE | MOTEUR |
|---|---|---|
| This engine is being run in. | Questo motore è in rodaggio. | Ce moteur est en rodage. |
| I'm having trouble with the engine. It knocks / doesn't pull / doesn't pick up / won't rev up. | Ho delle noie con il motore. Picchia in testa / non tira / non ha ripresa / non va su di giri. | J'ai des ennuis avec mon moteur. Il cogne / il ne tire pas / il manque de reprise / il plafonne. |
| I can feel a strange vibration in the engine | Sento una strana vibrazione nel motore. | J'entends une vibration bizarre dans le moteur. |
| I think that the cylinder head gasket has blown. | Credo che la guarnizione della testata sia bruciata. | Je crains que le joint de culasse ne soit brûlé. |
| Can you do this repair? | Può fare questa riparazione? | Pouvez-vous me faire cette réparation? |
| Yes. It's not advisable to go on like this. There's a danger of seizing. | Sí. Non è consigliabile proseguire in queste condizioni. C'è pericolo di grippare. | Oui. Je ne vous conseillerais pas de continuer dans ces conditions, vous pourriez gripper. |
| This engine is running on three / five cylinders. It's missing. | Questo motore va a tre / cinque cilindri. Perde colpi. | Ce moteur ne marche qu'à trois / cinq cylindres; il perd des coups. |
| The tappets need checking. | Bisogna controllare le punterie. | Il faudrait contrôler les culbuteurs des soupapes d'échappement. |
| The exhaust valves are blowing. | Sono bruciate le valvole di scarico. | Les soupapes d'échappement sont grillées. |
| The valves should be ground in. | Conviene smerigliare le valvole. | Il faudrait roder les soupapes. |
| The engine will have to be stripped down and the bearings renewed. | E' necessario smontare il motore e controllare le bronzine. | Il faut démonter le moteur et contrôler les coussinets. |
| The trouble is serious. The big end bearings and the main bearings will have to be replaced. | L'inconveniente è serio. Occorrerà sostituire le bronzine di biella e i cuscinetti di banco. | C'est un gros ennui. Il faudra remplacer les coussinets de bielle et les roulements de palier. |
| **I Cylinders and pistons** 1. cylinder block 2. gasket 3. head 4. wet / dry liner 5. piston 6. piston rings 7. scraper ring | **I Cilindri e pistoni** 1. blocco cilindri 2. guarnizione 3. testata 4. camicia umida / secca 5. pistone 6. fasce elasti- | **I Cylindres et pistons** 1. bloc cylindres 2. joint 3. tête 4. chemise humide / sèche 5. piston 6. colliers de caoutchouc |

| Deutsch | Español | Srpsko-hrvatski |
| --- | --- | --- |
| Wieviel kostet die Reparatur? | ¿Cuánto cuesta la reparación? | Koliko košta popravak? |
| Könnten Sie mir bitte eine detaillierte Kostenaufstellung geben? | ¿Puede proporcionarme una factura detallada? | Možete li mi dati račun sa navedenim radovima? |
| **I. Reparaturdauer** 1. eine halbe Stunde 2. eine Stunde 3. zwei Stunden 4. Morgen 5. Nachmittag 6. heute 7. morgen 8. übermorgen 9. ein Tag 10. drei Tage 11. Dringlichkeitskundendienst. **II. Kostenvoranschlag und Rechnung** 1. Preis der Ersatzteile 2. Arbeitskosten 3. Abschleppkosten 4. unverbindlicher Kostenvoranschlag 5. Anzahlung 6. Rabatt 7 detaillierte Kostenaufstellung 8. Stempelmarke. | **I Duración de la reparación** 1. media hora 2. una hora 3. dos horas 4. toda la mañana 5. toda la tarde 6. hoy 7. mañana 8. pasado mañana 9. un día 10. tres días 11. trabajo urgente. **II Presupuesto y factura** 1. coste de las piezas de repuesto 2. coste de la mano de obra 3. coste del servicio de remolque 4. presupuesto máximo 5. adelanto 6. descuento 7. factura detallada 8. sellos del impuesto. | **I Trajanje popravka** 1. pola sata 2. jedan sat 3. dva sata 4. prije podne 5. poslije podne 6. danas 7. sutra 8. prekosutra 9. jedan dan 10. tri dana 11. hitni popravak. **II Predračun i račun** 1. cijena rezervnih dijelova 2. cijena utrošenog radnog vremena 3. cijena teglenja 4. grubi predračun 5. akontacija 6. popust 7. detaljni račun sa nabrojenim radovima 8. porez. |
| **MOTORBLOCK** | **MOTOR** | **BLOK MOTORA** |
| Dieser Motor wird eingefahren. | Este motor está en rodaje. | Ovaj motor se još uhodava. |
| Irgend etwas ist mit dem Motor nicht in Ordnung. Er klingelt / zieht nicht / hat keine zügige Beschleunigung / kommt nicht auf Touren. | Tengo algunas dificultades con el motor. Pica de biela / no marcha / no arranca / no aumenta el número de revoluciones. | Imam poteškoće sa motorom. Udaraju ventili / ne vuče / nema ubrzanje / ne postiže broj okretaja. |
| Der Motor vibriert. | Oigo una vibración extraña en el motor. | U motoru osjećam jednu čudnu vibraciju. |
| Ich glaube, dass die Zylinderkopfdichtung durchgebrannt ist. | La junta de la culata se ha quemado | Vjerujem da je pregorjela brtva kućišta motora. |
| Können Sie diese Reparatur ausführen? | ¿Puede Vd. repararla? | Možete li izvršiti ovaj popravak? |
| Ja. Es wäre nicht ratsam, so die Fahrt fortzusetzen. Die Kolben könnten fressen. | Sí. No le aconsejo continuar en estas condiciones. El motor podría agarrotarse. | Da. Nije preporučljivo nastaviti pod ovim uslovima. Postoji opasnost zaribavanja. |
| Dieser Motor läuft mit drei / fünf Zylindern. Er setzt aus. | Este motor anda con tres / cinco cilindros. Crepita. | Motor radi sa tri / pet cilindara. Gubi udarce. |
| Das Ventilspiel muss geprüft werden. | Hay que controlar los empujadores. | Potrebno je kontrolirati podizaće ventila. |
| Die Auslassventile sind verbrannt. | Se han quemado las válvulas de escape. | Pregorjeli su ispušni ventili. |
| Die Ventile müssten eingeschliffen werden. | Se necesita esmerilar las válvulas. | Preporučljivo je prebrusiti ventile. |
| Der Motor muss ausgebaut werden, damit die Pleuellager nachgeprüft werden können. | Es preciso desmontar el motor y controlar los cojinetes antifricción. | Potrebno je rastaviti motor i kontrolirati ležajne košuljice. |
| Der Schaden ist erheblich. Die Pleuellager und die Hauptlager müssen ausgewechselt werden. | Es un inconveniente serio. Hay que cambiar los cojinetes antifricción de la biela y los cojinetes principales. | Kvar je ozbiljan. Potrebno je zamijeniti ležajne košuljice klipne motke i ležajeve bloka motora. |
| **I. Zylinder und Kolben** 1 Zylinderblock 2 Dichtung 3. Zylinderkopf 4 nasse trockene Zylinderlaufbuchse 5. Kolben | **I Cilindros y pistones** 1 bloque cilindros 2. junta 3. culata 4. camisa húmeda / seca 5. pistón 6. segmentos elás- | **I Cilindri i klipovi** 1. cilindarski blok 2. brtva 3. gornji blok 4. košuljica vlažna / suka 5. klip 6. elastični prstenovi |

| English | Italiano | Français |
|---|---|---|
| 8. engine revs 9. combustion chamber 10. stroke 11. bore 12. compression ratio. **II Crankshaft and bearing** 1. fly-wheel 2. pulley 3. bearings 4. big end bearings 5. main bearings 6. connecting rod 7. piston pin 8. bush. **III Timing system** 1. overhead / side / inclined valve 2. inlet valve 3. exhaust valve 4. valve seat 5. valve head 6. hydraulic tappets 7. tappet heads 8. tappet clearance 9. rod 10. rocker 11. camshaft 12. twin camshaft 13. timing chain. | che 7. raschia-olio 8. giri del motore 9. camera di scoppio 10. corsa 11. alesaggio 12. rapporto di compressione. **II Albero motore e biella** 1. volano 2. puleggia 3. supporti dell'albero motore 4. cuscinetti di biella 5. cuscinetti di banco 6. biella 7. spinotto 8. bronzina. **III Distribuzione** 1. valvola in testa / laterale / obliqua 2. valvola di aspirazione 3. valvola di scarico 4. sede della valvola 5. testa della valvola 6. punterie idrauliche 7. testa delle punterie 8. gioco delle punterie 9. asta 10. bilanciere 11. albero a camme 12. doppio albero a camme 13. catena di distribuzione. | 7. râcleur d'huile 8. révolutions du moteur 9. chambre d'explosion 10. course 11. alésage 12. rapport de compression. **II Arbre de transmission et bielle** 1. volant 2. poulie 3. supports de l'arbre moteur 4. coussinets de bielle 5. coussinets de palier 6. bielle 7. goujon 8. coussinet de pied de bielle. **III Distribution** 1. clapet de tête / latéral / oblique 2. clapet d'aspiration 3. clapet de décharge 4. siège de soupape 5. tête de soupape 6. culbuteurs hydrauliques 7. tête de culbuteurs 8. jeu des culbuteurs 9. tige 10. culbuteur de soupape 11. arbre à cames 12. arbre à cames double 13. chaîne de distribution. |

| FUEL SUPPLY AND CARBURATION | SISTEMA DI ALIMENTAZIONE | CARBURATION |
|---|---|---|
| The carburation is faulty. At least, that's my impression. | La carburazione non va. Questa è almeno la mia impressione. | La carburation ne va pas, du moins c'est mon impression. |
| What type of petrol do you use? Normal or premium? | Che tipo di carburante adopera? Normale o super? | Quel type de carburant utilisez-vous, normal ou super? |
| The petrol gauge doesn't work well. | L'indicatore del carburante non funziona bene. | L'indicateur de la jauge à essence ne marche pas bien. |
| The petrol warning light doesn't come on. | La spia della benzina non si accende. | Le voyant de réserve de l'essence ne s'allume pas. |
| The engine cuts out when idling. | Il motore non regge il minimo. | Le moteur ne tient pas le ralenti. |
| The idling speed must be adjusted. | Bisogna regolare il minimo. | Il faut régler le ralenti. |
| The engine gets too hot. | Il motore scalda. | Le moteur chauffe. |
| Clean the air filters. | Pulisca i filtri della presa d'aria. | Voulez-vous nettoyer les filtres à air, s'il vous plaît. |
| There is a strong smell of petrol. There must be a leak somewhere. | C'è un forte odore di benzina. Deve esserci una perdita nei raccordi. | On sent une forte odeur d'essence, il doit y avoir une fuite dans les raccords. |
| Black smoke comes out of the exhaust. | Dallo scarico esce fumo nero. | De la fumée noire sort de l'échappement. |
| There's a hole in the float. It must be replaced. | Il galleggiante è bucato. Va cambiato. | Le flotteur est percé, il faut le changer. |
| You will have to change the carburettor gasket, I see it's leaking. | Dovrà sostituire la guarnizione del carburatore, vedo che perde. | Il faudra remplacer le joint du carburateur, j'ai constaté qu'il fuit. |
| It would be a good idea to change the carburettor filters / the float chamber. | Sarà bene pulire i filtri del carburatore / la vaschetta del carburatore. | Il serait bon de nettoyer les filtres du carburateur / la cuve du carburateur. |
| The carburettor floods. | Il carburatore si ingolfa. | Le carburateur s'engorge. |
| The petrol pump doesn't work well. | La pompetta della benzina funziona male. | La pompe à essence fonctionne mal. |
| It may be necessary to check the lever controlling it. | Forse sarà necessario controllare la leva di comando. | Il sera peut-être nécessaire de contrôler la tringlerie de commande. |

6. Verdichtungsringe 7. Ölabstreifring 8. Motordrehzahl 9. Verbrennungsraum 10. Hub 11. Bohrung 12. Verdichtungsverhältnis. **II. Kurbelwelle und Pleuelstange** 1. Schwungrad 2. Schwungscheibe 3. Kurbelwellenlager 4. Pleuellager 5. Hauptlager 6. Pleuelstange 7. Kolbenbolzen 8. Bronzelager. **III. Steuerung** 1. hängendes / stehendes / schräghängendes Ventil 2. Einlassventil 3. Auslassventil 4. Ventilsitz 5. Ventilteller 6. hydraulische Ventilstössel 7. Stösselkopf 8. Stösselspiel 9. Stösselstange 10. Kipphebel 11. Nockenwelle 12. doppelt gelagerte Nockenwelle 13. Steuerkette

ticos 7. segmento rasca aceite 8. revoluciones del motor 9. cámara de explosión 10. recorrido 11. alisadura 12. relación de compresión. **II Eje motor y biela** 1. volante 2. polea 3. soportes del eje motor 4. cojinetes de biela 5. cojinetes principales 6. biela 7. aguja 8. cojinete antifricción. **III Distribución** 1. válvulas en culata / laterales / oblicuas 2. valvula de aspiración 3. válvula de escape 4. asiento de la válvula 5. cabeza de la válvula 6. pernos hidráulicos 7. cabeza de los pernos 8. juego de los pernos 9. vástago 10. balancín 11. árbol de balancín 12. doble árbol de balancín 13. cadena de distribución.

7. strugač ulja 8. okretaji motora 9. eksplozione komore 10. hod 11. promjer 12. kompresioni omjer. **II Radna osovina i klipna motka** 1. zamašnjak 2. remenica 3. nosači radne osovine 4. ležajevi klipne motke 5. ležajevi bloka motora 6. klipna motka 7. klipna osovina 8. ležajna košuljica. **III Razvod** 1. viseći ventili / bočni / « V » ventili 2. usisni ventil 3. ispušni ventil 4. sjedište ventila 5. glava ventila 6. hidraulički podizači ventila 7. glava podizača ventila 8. zračnost podizača ventila 9. motka 10. ravnotežna motka ventila 11. razvodna ventilska osovina 12. dvostruka razvodna ventilska osovina 13. razvodni lanac.

| **KRAFTSTOFFANLAGE** | **SISTEMA DE ALIMENTACION** | **SISTEM DOBAVE GORIVA** |
|---|---|---|
| Die Vergasung funktioniert nicht. Zumindest habe ich den Eindruck. | La carburación es irregular. Esta por lo menos es mi impresión. | Rasplinjavanje je nepravilno. To je naime moje mišljenje. |
| Welchen Krafstoff benutzen Sie? Normal- oder Superbenzin? | ¿Qué clase de carburante usa Vd.? ¿Normal o super? | Koju vrstu goriva upotrebljava? Normalni ili super? |
| Die Benzinuhr funktioniert nicht ordentlich. | El indicador del carburante no funciona bien. | Pokazivač rezerve goriva nije ispravan. |
| Die Benzinkontrolleuchte schaltet sich nicht ein. | El indicador de la gasolina no se enciende. | Signalna lampa rezerve goriva se ne upali. |
| Der Leerlauf ist unregelmässig und der Motor setzt aus. | El motor no gira al ralentí | Motor ne održava minimalni broj okretaja. |
| Der Leerlauf muss neu eingestellt werden. | Se necesita arreglar el ralentí. | Potrebno je regulirati minimum. |
| Der Motor wird zu warm. | El motor se calienta. | Motor se pregrijava. |
| Reinigen Sie bitte die Luftfilter. | Limpie los filtros de la toma de aire. | Očistite filtre otvora za zrak. |
| Es riecht stark nach Benzin. Ein Anschluss muss undicht sein. | Huele mucho a gasolina. Debe de perder una de las bridas. | Osjeća se jaki zadah benzina. Vjerojatno propuštaju spojevi. |
| Aus dem Auspuff kommt schwarzer Rauch. | Del escape sale humo negro. | Iz ispušne cijevi izlazi crni dim. |
| Der Schwimmer ist schadhaft und muss ausgewechselt werden. | El flotador está perforado. Hay que cambiarlo. | Plovak je probušen. Mora se izmijeniti. |
| Sie werden die Dichtung des Vergasers erneuern müssen. Sie ist offensichtlich schadhaft. | Tendrá que cambiar la junta del carburador, veo que pierde. | Morati ćete izmijeniti brtvu rasplinjača, jer vidim da propušta. |
| Es wäre ratsam, die Filter / das Schwimmergehäuse des Vergasers zu reinigen. | Será bien limpiar los filtros del carburador / de la pileta del carburador. | Bilo bi dobro očistiti filtre rasplinjača / kotlić rasplinjača. |
| Der Vergaser ist überflutet. | El carburador se ahoga. | Rasplinjač se zagušuje. |
| Die Kraftstoffpumpe funktioniert nicht ordentlich. | La bomba de la gasolina funciona mal. | Benzinska pumpa loše funkcionira. |
| Vielleicht sollte man den Pumpenhebel nachprüfen. | Quizás será necesario controlar la palanca de mando. | Možda će biti potrebno kontrolirati komandnu polugu. |

**English**

The pump washer is perished.

The diaphragm is broken.

The jets are faulty.

The inlet valve often remains open. It would be advisable to change the spring.

The valves should be checked.

Grease the accelerator controls.

Very well. But the wire must be changed.

**I Types of carburettors and injectors** 1. single carburettor / twin carburettor / four carburettor 2. downdraft / semi-downdraft / horizontal carburettor 3. direct / indirect injectors. **II Parts of carburettor** 1. float chamber 2. float 3. needle valve 4. pipes 5. carburation chamber 6. choke tube 7. butterfly valve 8. air intake 9. cleaner 10. spray nozzles 11. slow running / fast running jets 12. adjusting screw. **III Other parts of the system** 1. choke 2. fuel pump 3. electric / mechanical pump 4. diaphragm 5. carburettor filter 6. by-pass filter 7. air filter 8. cartridge 9. connexions 10. return spring 11. accelerator 12. accelerator controls 13. exhaust pipe 14. silencer.

## LUBRICATION SYSTEM

The engine overheats.

The oil pressure is low.

Check the oil pump / the filter / the valve of the filter.

The sparking plugs are always dirty.

The piston rings are broken / stuck.

The level of the engine oil in your car is above the maximum.

Half a litre must be drawn off.

The oil level is down to the minimum.

**Italiano**

La guarnizione della pompa è difettosa.

E' rotta la membrana.

I getti sono difettosi.

Questa valvola di ammissione rimane spesso aperta. E' consigliabile cambiare la molla.

Le valvole vanno messe a punto.

Lubrifichi i comandi dell'acceleratore.

Va bene. Però il filo deve essere cambiato.

**I Tipi di carburatori e iniettori** 1. carburatore monocorpo / doppio corpo / quadricorpo 2. carburatore invertito / semi-invertito / orizzontale 3. iniettori diretti / indiretti. **II Parti del carburatore** 1. vaschetta 2. galleggiante 3. valvola a spillo 4. condotti 5. camera di carburazione 6. tubo diffusore 7. valvola a farfalla 8. presa d'aria 9. depuratore 10. spruzzatori 11. getti del massimo / del minimo 12. vite di regolazione. **III Altre parti del sistema** 1. starter 2. pompa di alimentazione 3. pompa elettrica / meccanica 4. membrane 5. filtro del carburatore 6. filtro in derivazione 7. filtro dell'aria 8. cartuccia 9. raccordi 10. molla di richiamo 11. acceleratore 12. comandi dell'acceleratore 13. tubo di scappamento 14. marmitta.

## SISTEMA DI LUBRIFICAZIONE

Il motore scalda troppo.

La pressione dell'olio è bassa.

Controlli la pompa dell'olio / il filtro / la valvola del filtro.

Le candele sono sempre sporche.

I segmenti raschia-olio sono rotti / incollati.

Il motore della sua vettura ha l'olio oltre il livello massimo.

Occorre toglierne mezzo litro.

L'olio è al minimo.

**Français**

Le joint de la pompe est défectueux.

La membrane est percée.

Les gicleurs sont défectueux.

Cette soupape d'admission reste facilement ouverte. Il vaudrait mieux changer le ressort.

Il faut régler le jeu des soupapes.

Voudriez-vous graisser la pédale de l'accélérateur, s'il vous plaît.

D'accord, mais il faut changer le fil.

**I Types de carburateurs et d'injecteurs** 1. carburateur monocorps / double corps / quadruple corps 2. carburateur inversé / semi-inversé / horizontal 3. injecteurs directs / indirects. **III Eléments du carburateur** 1. cuve 2. flotteur 3. soupape à aiguille 4. conduits 5. chambre de carburation 6. diffuseur 7. papillon 8. prise d'air 9. épurateur 10. pulvérisateurs 11. gicleurs de démarrage / du ralenti 12. vis de réglage. **III Autres éléments du système** 1. démarreur 2. pompe d'alimentation 3. pompe électrique / mécanique 4. membrane 5. filtre du carburateur 6. filtre magnétique 7. filtre à air 8. cartouche 9. raccords 10. ressort de rappel 11. accélérateur 12. commandes de l'accélérateur 13. tuyau d'échappement 14. pot d'échappement.

## LUBRIFICATION

Le moteur chauffe trop.

La pression de l'huile est insuffisante.

Voudriez-vous vérifier la pompe à huile / le filtre / le clapet de décharge.

Les bougies sont constamment encrassées.

Les segments racleurs sont cassés / collés.

L'huile du moteur de votre voiture dépasse le niveau maximum.

Il faudrait en ôter un demi-litre.

L'huile est au minimum.

| Deutsch | Español | Srpsko-hrvatski |
|---|---|---|
| Die Dichtung der Kraftstoffpumpe ist defekt. | La junta de la bomba es defectuosa. | Brtva pumpe je neispravna. |
| Die Membrane ist gebrochen. | La membrana está rota. | Membrana je neispravna. |
| Die Düsen sind schadhaft. | Los surtidores son defectuosos. | Sapnice su neispravne. |
| Das Einlassventil schliesst nicht immer. Es wäre ratsam, die Ventilfeder auszuwechseln. | Esta válvula de aspiración queda a menudo abierta. Creo que se necesita cambiar el muelle. | Ovaj usisni ventil ostaje često otvoren. Preporučljivo je izmijeniti oprugu. |
| Die Ventile müssen nachgestellt werden. | Hay que ajustar las válvulas. | Ventili se moraju regulirati. |
| Schmieren Sie bitte das Vergasergestänge. | Lubrifique los mandos del acelerador. | Podmažite elemente akceleratora |
| Ohne weiteres. Aber der Gaspedaldraht muss erneuert werden. | Está bien. Pero tiene que cambiar el cable de mando. | U redu; ali vučna žica mora biti izmijenjena. |
| **I. Verschiedene Arten von Vergasern und Einspritzdüsen** 1. Einzelvergaser / Doppelvergaser / Vierfachvergaser 2. Fallstromvergaser / Halbfallstromvergaser / Flachstromvergaser 3. direkte / indirekte Einspritzdüse **II. Bauteile des Vergasers** 1. Schwimmergehäuse 2. Schwimmer 3. Nadelventil 4. Rohrleitungen 5. Mischkammer 6. Lufttrichter 7. Drosselklappe 8. Lufteintritt 9. Luftfilter 10. Einspritzdüsen 11. Hauptdüse / Leerlaufdüse 12. Leerlaufeinstellschraube **III. Sonstige Bauteile** 1. Starter 2. Kraftstoffpumpe 3. Elektropumpe / mechanisch betätigte Pumpe 4. Membrane 5. Filter des Vergasers 6. Abzweigfilter 7. Luftfilter 8. Einsatz 9. Leitungen 10. Rückholfeder 11. Beschleunigungsvorrichtung 12. Gaspedal 13. Auspuffrohr 14. Auspufftopf | **I Tipos de carburadores e inyectores** 1. carburador simple / de doble cuerpo / cuadricuerpo 2. carburador descendiente / semidescendiente / horizontal 3. inyectores directos / indirectos. **II Piezas del carburador** 1. pileta 2. flotador 3. válvula de aguja 4. juntas 5. cámara de carburación 6. difusor 7. válvula de mariposa 8. toma de aire 9. depurador 10. pulverizadores 11. surtidor de máxima / del ralentí 12. tornillo de regulación. **III Otras partes del sistema** 1. stárter 2. bomba de alimentación 3. bomba eléctrica / mecánia 4. membranas 5. filtro del carburador 6. filtro derivado 7. filtro del aire 8. cartucho 9. bridas 10. muelle de retracción 11. acelerador 12. mandos del acelerador 13. escape (tubo de) 14. escape. | **I Tipovi rasplinjača i injektora** 1. rasplinjač jednostruki / dvostruki / četverostruki 2. silazni rasplinjač / polusilazni / horizontalni 3. direktni injektori / indirektni. **II Dijelovi rasplinjača** 1. kotlić 2. plovak 3. ventil sa iglom 4. kanali 5. komora rasplinjavanja 6. difuzor 7. ventil sa zaklopcem 8. otvor za zrak 9. pročistač 10. štrcaljke 11. sapnica maksimuma / minimuma 12. vijak za regulaciju. **III Ostali dijelovi sistema** 1. starter 2. pumpa za dobavu 3. pumpa električna / mehanička 4. membrane 5. filtar rasplinjača 6. derivacioni filtar 7. filtar za zrak 8. ulozak 9. spojevi 10. povratna opruga 11. akcelerator 12. komandni elementi akceleratora 13. ispušna cijev 14. ispušni lonac. |

| SCHMIERUNG | SISTEMA DE LUBRIFICACION | SISTEM ZA PODMAZIVANJE |
|---|---|---|
| Der Motor wird zu warm. | El motor se calienta demasiado. | Motor se pregrijava. |
| Der Öldruck ist zu niedrig. | La presión del aceite es baja. | Pritisak ulja je nizak. |
| Prüfen Sie bitte die Ölpumpe / den Filter / das Filterventil. | Revise la bomba del aceite / el filtro / la válvula del filtro. | Kontrolirajte pumpu za ulje / filtar / ventil filtra. |
| Die Kerzen sind ständig verschmutzt. | Les bujías están siempre sucias. | Svjećice su uvijek zamazane. |
| Die Ölabstreifringe sind gebrochen / verklebt. | Los segmentos rasca aceite están rotos / pegados. | Elementi strugača ulja su polomljeni / sljepljeni. |
| Der Ölstand Ihres Motors ist zu hoch. | El aceite de su motor está sobre el nivel máximo. | Motor vaših kola ima ulje iznad maksimalne razine. |
| Es muss ein halbes Liter abgelassen werden. | Hay que sacar medio litro. | Potrebno je ukloniti pola litre |
| Der Ölstand ist bis zur unteren Marke abgesunken. | El aceite está por debajo del nivel. | Ulje je na minimumu. |

| English | Italiano | Français |
|---|---|---|
| Put in a litre / two litres. | Aggiunga un litro / due litri. | Il faut en rajouter un litre / deux litres. |
| The oil temperature is too high. | La temperatura dell'olio è troppo elevata. | Le température de l'huile est trop élevée. |
| You must change over from winter-grade to summer-grade. | Bisogna passare dalla gradazione invernale a quella estiva. | Il faudrait remplacer l'huile d'hiver par de l'huile d'été. |
| The internal pipes are blocked. | I condotti interni sono ostruiti. | Les canalisations internes sont obstruées. |
| The oil sump is cracked. | Si è rotta la coppa dell'ólio. | Le carter inférieur est cassé. |
| The oil warning light stays on all the time. | La spia dell'olio resta sempre accesa. | La lampe témoin de l'huile est constamment allumée. |
| The oil gets very hot and I can hear a strange noise that gets worse as the revs are increased. | L'olio si scalda molto e sento uno strano rumore che aumenta con il numero dei giri. | L'huile surchauffe, et j'entends un cliquetis dans le moteur, qui augmente avec le nombre de tours. |
| Probably a bearing has seized. | Probabilmente si è fusa una bronzina. | Un coussinet a dû couler. |
| **I Parts of the system** 1. oil sump 2. oil pump 3. gear / eccentric / rotor pump 4. pipes 5. pressure adjusting valve 6. adjusting screw 7. oil cap 8. drain plug 9. register nut 10. inlet pipe 11. centrifugal / mesh / by-pass filter 12. cartridge 13. oil-water heat exchanger 14. pressure gauge. **II Lubricants** 1. thin / thick / medium / heavy oil 2. winter / summer oil 3. multigrade oil 4. clean / dirty oil 5. detergent oil. | **I Parti del sistema** 1. coppa dell'olio 2. pompa dell'olio 3. pompa a ingranaggi / a eccentrici / a rotori 4. condotti 5. valvola regolatrice della pressione 6. vite di regolazione 7. tappo di carico 8. tappo di scarico 9. dado di registro 10. tubo di aspirazione 11. filtro centrifugo / a rete / in derivazione 12. cartuccia 13. scambiatore di calore olio-acqua 14. manometro. **II Lubrificanti** 1. olio fluido / denso / semidenso 2. olio invernale / estivo 3. olio multigrade 4. olio pulito / sporco 5. olio di lavaggio. | **I Eléments du système** 1. carter inférieur 2. pompe à huile 3. pompe à engrenages / à cames / à rotors 4. conduits 5. soupape régulatrice de pression 6. vis de réglage 7. bouchon de remplissage 8. bouchon de vidange 9. écrou de réglage 10. tuyau d'arrivée 11. filtre centrifuge / à crépine / magnétique 12. cartouche 13. échangeur de température huile-eau 14. manomètre. **II Lubrifiants** 1. huile fluide / épaisse / semi-visqueuse 2. huile d'hiver / d'été 3. huile multigrade 4. huile propre / sale 5. huile de rinçage. |

| **COOLING SYSTEM** | **SISTEMA DI RAFFREDDAMENTO** | **REFROIDISSEMENT** |
|---|---|---|
| The radiator is leaking. There's a hole in it. | Il radiatore perde. E' bucato. | Le radiateur perd. Il est percé. |
| I think the water pump is out of order. | Credo che sia guasta la pompa dell'acqua. | Je crois que la pompe à eau ne fonctionne plus. |
| The water pump is noisy. | La pompa dell'acqua è rumorosa. | La pompe à eau est bruyante. |
| It only needs greasing. | Basterà lubrificarla. | Il suffit de la graisser. |
| The bearing of the water pump has had it. | Il cuscinetto della pompa dell'acqua è sballato. | Le coussinet de la pompe à eau est détérioré. |
| The washer of the pump has gone. | La guarnizione della pompa è rotta. | Le joint de la pompe est coupé. |
| The water cooling pipes are blocked. | Le tubazioni di raffreddamento dell'acqua sono ostruite. | Les tuyaux du circuit de refroidissement sont obstrués. |
| The radiator is clogged. | Il radiatore è intasato. | Le radiateur est entartré. |
| The engine overheats. | Il motore scalda troppo. | Le moteur chauffe trop. |

| Deutsch | Español | Srpsko-hrvatski |
|---|---|---|
| Setzen Sie ein Liter / zwei Liter zu. | Eche un litro / dos litros de aceite. | Dodajte jednu litru / dvije litre. |
| Die Temperatur des Öls ist zu hoch. | La temperatura del aceite está demasiado alta. | Temperatura ulja je previsoka. |
| Statt des Winteröls müsste nun Sommeröl benutzt werden. | Hay que pasar de la gradación de invierno a la de verano. | Potrebno je prijeći sa zimskog na ljetno ulje. |
| Die Ölleitungen sind verstopft. | Los conductos están obstruídos. | Unutrašnji cjevovodi su začepljeni. |
| Die Ölwanne ist undicht. | Se ha roto la cubeta del aceite. | Pumpa za ulje je neispravna. |
| Die Öldruckkontrolleuchte schaltet sich nicht aus. | La lámpara indicadora del aceite permanece encendida. | Signalna lampa za ulje ostaje stalno zapaljena. |
| Das Öl erhitzt sich zu stark. Ausserdem höre ich ein Geräusch, das sich mit zunehmender Drehzahl verstärkt. | El aceite del motor se calienta demasiado y oigo un repiqueteo que crece al aumentar el número de revoluciones. | Ulje se pregrijava i osjećam čudnu buku sa povećanjem broja okretaja. |
| Wahrscheinlich ist ein Lager ausgelaufen. | Es posible que se haya fundido un cojinete antifricción. | Vjerojatno se rastopila jedna ležajna košuljica. |
| **I. Bauteile** 1. Olwanne 2. Ölpumpe 3. Zahnradpumpe / Nockenpumpe / Laufradpumpe 4. Ölleitungen 5. Überdruck-Ölventil 6. Einstellschraube 7. Öleinfüllstutzen 8. Ölablasschraube 9. Einstellmutter 10. Ansaugrohr 11. Zentrifugalölfilter / Siebfilter / Abzweigfilter 12. Patrone 13. Wärmeaustauscher 14. Öldruckmesser. **II. Schmiermittel** 1. dünnflüssiges / dickflüssiges / mittleres Öl 2. Winteröl / Sommeröl 3. Mehrbereichsöl 4. sauberes / verschmutztes Öl 5. Spülöl. | **I Partes del sistema** 1. cubeta 2. bomba del aceite 3. bomba de engranajes / de excéntrica / de ruptores 4. conductos 5. válvula reguladora de la presión 6. tornillo de regulación 7. tapón de llenado 8. tapón de vaciado 9. tuerca de ajuste 10. tubo de aspiración 11. filtro centrífugo / de malla / derivado 12. cartucho 13. dispositivo intercambio calor aceite / agua 14. manómetro. **II Lubrificantes** 1. aceite flúido / denso / semidenso 2. aceite de invierno / de verano 3. aceite multigrado 4. aceite limpio / sucio 5. aceite de lavado. | **I Dijelovi sistema** 1. sabirnik ulja 2. pumpa za ulje 3. zupčasta pumpa / ekscentrična / sa rotorom 4. cjevovodi 5. ventil za regulaciju pritiska 6. vijak za regulaciju 7. čep za punjenje 8. čep za ispust 9. vijak za registraciju 10. usisna cijev 11. centrifugalni filtar / mrežni / derivacioni 12. uložak 13. izmjenjivač topline ulje-voda 14. manometar. **III Maziva** 1. ulje tekuće / gusto / polugusto 2. ulje zimsko / ljetno 3. univerzalno ulje 4. ulje čisto / onečišćeno 5. ulje za ispiranje. |
| **KÜHLUNG** | **SISTEMA DE ENFRIAMIENTO** | **RASHLADNI SISTEM** |
| Der Kühler ist undicht. Er muss beschädigt sein. | El radiador pierde. Está agujereado. | Hladnjak propušta. Probušen je. |
| Ich glaube, dass die Wasserpumpe defekt ist. | Creo que esté estropeada la bomba del agua. | Vjerujem da je pumpa za vodu neispravna. |
| Die Wasserpumpe ist laut. | La bomba del agua hace ruido. | Pumpa za vodu stvara buku. |
| Sie braucht nur abgeschmiert zu werden. | Bastará lubrificarla. | Dovoljno je podmazati je. |
| Das Lager der Wasserpumpe ist defekt. | El cojinete de la bomba del agua se ha estropeado. | Ležaj pumpe za vodu je neuravnotežen. |
| Die Abdichtung der Pumpe ist defekt. | La junta de la bomba del agua está rota. | Brtva pumpe je oštećena. |
| Die Kühlerschlauchverbindungen sind verstopft. | Los tubos de enfriamiento del agua están obstruídos. | Cjevovodi rashladne tekućine su začepljeni. |
| Der Kühler ist verschlammt. | El radiador está atascado. | Hladnjak je začepljen. |
| **Der Motor läuft heiss.** | **El motor se calienta demasiado.** | **Motor se pregrijava.** |

**English**

The cooling system is all right. The trouble may stem from several other causes (faulty carburation, poor mixture, insufficient lubrication, retarded ignition, badly adjusted tappets, incorrect timing).

It would be a good idea to wash through the radiator and scale it.

The fan belt is broken.

The belt is too slack.

Have a look at the electromagnetic control of the fan.

Change the fan belt.

It would be a good idea to check the pulley groove, too. It may be worn.

Check the pipes of the sealed circuit.

The cylinder head gasket has blown. There is water in the sump.

The radiator cap needs replacing. The spring is broken.

**I Parts of the system** 1. radiator 2. honeycomb-type 3. with vertical tubes 4. radiator cap 5. grill 6. cell 7. connexion 8. coupling 9. water pump 10. centrifugal pump 11. bearing 12. gasket 13. pipes 14. drainage tap 15. water circuit 16. electromagnetic control 17. thermostat 18. thermometer 19. warning light 20. fan 21. fan belt 22. sealed circuit 23. two-way valve 24. extra tank. **II Liquids** 1. cold / hot water 2. boiling point 3. freezing point 4. anti-freeze 5. anti-rust.

**Italiano**

Il circuito di raffreddamento è a posto. L'inconveniente può dipendere da parecchie altre cause (carburazione difettosa, miscela povera, scarsa lubrificazione, accensione ritardata, punterie non registrate, distribuzione fuori fase).

Sarà bene lavare il radiatore e disincrostarlo.

Si è rotta la cinghia del ventilatore.

La cinghia è troppo lenta.

Dia un'occhiata al comando elettromagnetico del ventilatore.

Cambi la cinghia del ventilatore.

Sarà bene verificare anche la gola della puleggia. Può essere consumata.

Controlli la tubazione del circuito sigillato.

La guarnizione della testata si è rotta. Vedo acqua in fondo alla coppa dell'olio.

Il tappo del radiatore va cambiato. Si è rotta la molla.

**I Parti del sistema** 1. radiatore 2. a nido d'ape 3. a tubetti verticali 4. tappo del radiatore 5. griglia 6. elemento 7. raccordo 8. manicotto 9. pompa dell'acqua 10. pompa centrifuga 11. cuscinetto 12. guarnizione 13. tubazione 14. rubinetto di scarico 15. circuito dell'acqua 16. comando elettromagnetico 17. termostato 18. termometro 19. spia 20. ventilatore 21. cinghia del ventilatore 22. circuito sigillato 23. valvola a doppio effetto 24. serbatoio supplementare. **II Liquidi** 1. acqua fredda / calda 2. temperatura di ebollizione 3. temperatura di congelamento 4. anticongelante 5. antiruggine.

**Français**

Le circuit de refroidissement est en bon état. L'inconvénient constaté peut avoir une autre origine (carburation défectueuse, mélange pauvre, lubrification insuffisante, retard à l'allumage, culbuteurs non réglés, distribution non calée).

Il faudrait laver le radiateur et le désincruster.

La courroie du ventilateur est cassée.

La courroie n'est pas assez tendue.

Pourriez-vous donner un coup d'oeil à la commande électromagnétique du ventilateur?

Changez, s'il vous plaît, la courroie du ventilateur.

Il faudrait aussi vérifier la gorge de la poulie, elle est peut-être usée.

Voulez-vous contrôler la tuyauterie du circuit scellé?

Le joint de culasse est brûlé, dans le carter huile il y a de l'eau.

Il faudrait changer le bouchon du radiateur, le ressort est cassé.

**I Eléments du système** 1. radiateur 2. à faisceaux 3. à tuyaux verticaux 4. bouchon du radiateur 5. grille 6. élément 7. raccord 8. manchon 9. pompe à eau 10. pompe centrifuge 11. coussinet 12. joint 13. tuyauterie 14. robinet de vidange 15. circuit d'eau 16. commande électromagnétique 17. thermostat 18. thermomètre 19. lampe témoin 20. ventilateur 21. courroie du ventilateur 22. circuit scellé 23. soupape à double effet 24. réservoir supplémentaire. **II Liquides** 1. eau froide / chaude 2. température d'ébullition 3. température de congélation 4. antigel 5. antirouille.

## ELECTRICAL SYSTEM

Look and see if all the cells of the battery are all right.

Add some distilled water.

The battery doesn't charge properly / is flat / has a faulty cell.

The battery is charged, but there is no output / it won't turn the engine over.

## IMPIANTO ELETTRICO

Guardi se sono a posto tutti gli elementi della batteria.

Aggiunga acqua distillata.

La batteria non si carica completamente / è scarica / ha un elemento guasto.

La batteria è carica, ma non dà corrente / non riesce a far girare il motorino.

## INSTALLATION ELECTRIQUE

Voudriez-vous vérifier tous les éléments de la batterie?

S'il vous plaît, ajoutez de l'eau distillée.

La batterie ne se charge pas complètement / est déchargée / a un élément défectueux.

La batterie est chargée, mais le courant ne passe pas / mais elle ne fait pas tourner le démarreur.

**Deutsch**

Der Wasserumlauf ist einwandfrei. Die Störung kann verschiedene andere Ursachen haben (mangelhafte Vergasung, armes Gemisch, unzulängliche Schmierung, Spätzündung, falsche Ventileinstellung, falsche Einstellung).

Der Kühler muss gereinigt und entkalkt werden.

Der Keilriemen ist gerissen.

Der Keilriemen ist zu locker.

Prüfen Sie bitte den elektromagnetischen Antrieb des Ventilators.

Wechseln Sie bitte den Keilriemen aus.

Es wäre ratsam, auch die Rille der Riemenscheibe nachzuprüfen. Sie könnte abgenutzt sein.

Prüfen Sie bitte die Leitung des geschlossenen Kühlwasserkreislaufs nach.

Die Zylinderkopfdichtung ist defekt. Auf dem Boden der Ölwanne ist Wasser.

Der Kühlerverschluss muss erneuert werden, denn die Feder ist gebrochen.

**I. Bauteile** 1. Kühler 2. Lamellenkühler 3. Röhrenkühler 4. Kühlerverschluss 5. Kühlergrill 6. Kühlerteilblock 7. Kühlerschlauch 8. Muffe 9. Wasserpumpe 10. Schleuderpumpe 11. Lagerpackung 12. Abdichtung 13. Leitung 14. Wasserablasshahn 15. Wasserumlauf 16. elektromagnetischer Antrieb 17. Thermostat 18. Thermometer 19. Kontrollleuchte 20. Ventilator 21. Keilriemen 22. geschlossener Kühlwasserkreislauf 23. doppelt wirkendes Ventil 24. Hilfsbehälter **II. Flüssigkeiten** 1. kaltes warmes Wasser 2. Siedepunkt 3. Gefriertemperatur 4. Frostschutzmittel 5. Rostschutzmittel.

## ELEKTRISCHE ANLAGE

Sehen Sie bitte nach, ob alle Batteriezellen in Ordnung sind.

Füllen Sie bitte destilliertes Wasser nach.

Die Batterie lädt sich nicht voll auf / ist entladen / eine Zelle ist defekt.

Die Batterie ist geladen, gibt aber keinen Strom ab / der Anlasser dreht nicht.

**Español**

El circuito está bien. El inconveniente puede depender de otras causas (carburación defectuosa, mezcla pobre, escasa lubrificación, encendido retrasado, pernos no ajustados, distribución a destiempo).

Convendría lavar el radiador y quitar las incrustaciones.

Se ha roto la correa del ventilador.

La correa está demasiado floja.

Podría echar una ojeada al mando electromagnético del ventilador.

Cambie la correa del ventilador.

Sería conveniente revisar también la garganta de la polea. Puede estar gastada.

Revise los tubos del circuito registrado.

La junta de la culata se ha roto. Veo agua en el fondo de la cubeta del aceite.

Se necesita cambiar el tapón del radiador. Está roto el muelle.

**I Partes del sistema** 1. radiador 2. de nido de abejas 3. de tubos verticales 4. tapón del radiador 5. parrilla 6. elemento 7. uniones 8. manguito 9. bomba del agua 10. bomba centrífuga 11. cojinete 12. junta 13. tubo 14. grifo de desagüe 15. circuito del agua 16. mando engrane electromangético 17. termóstato 18. termómetro 19. luz indicadora 20. ventilador 21. correa del ventilador 22. circuito registrado 23. válvulas de doble empleo 24. depósito suplemental. **II Liquidos** 1. agua fría / caliente 2. temperatura de abullición 3. temperatura de congelación 4 anticongelante 5. antioxido

## INSTALACION ELECTRICA

Controle si están bien todos los elementos de la batería.

Añada agua destilada.

La batería no carga del todo / está descargada / tiene un elemento averiado.

La batería está cargada, pero no produce corriente / no logra hacer girar el motor de arranque.

**Srpsko-hrvatski**

Rashladni ciklus je u redu. Neispravnost može ovisiti o raznim uzrocima (rasplinjavanje neispravno, siromašna smjesa, nedovoljno podmazivanje, kasno paljenje, neregulirani podizači ventila, razvod izvan faze).

Bilo bi dobro oprati hladnjak i ukloniti kamenac.

Remen ventilatora se prekinuo.

Remen je prelabav.

Ispitajte elektromagnetsku komandu ventilatora.

Promijenite remen ventilatora.

Bilo bi dobro pregledati glavčinu remenice. Može biti istrošena.

Pregledajte cjevovode zatvorenog rashladnog sistema.

Brtva bloka motora je oštećena. U sabirniku ulja se nalazi voda.

Potrebno je izmijeniti poklopac hladnjaka. Oštećena je opruga.

**I Dijelovi sistema** 1. hladnjak 2. u obliku pčelinjeg saća 3. sa vertikalnim cijevima 4. poklopac hladnjaka 5. rešetka 6. elemenat 7. spoj 8. naglavak cijevi 9. pumpa za vodu 10. centrifugalna pumpa 11. ležaj 12. brtva 13. cjevovod 14. slavina za ispust 15. cirkulacija vode 16. elektromagnetska komanda 17. termostat 18. termometar 19. signalna lampa 20. ventilator 21. remen ventilatora 22. zatvoreni sistem 23. ventil sa dvostrukim djelovanjem 24. rezervni spremnik **II Tekučine** 1. voda hladna topla 2 temperatura vrenja 3. temperatura zaledjivanja 4. sredstvo protiv zamrzavanja 5. sredstvo protiv korozije

## ELEKTRIČNI UREDJAJ

Pregledajte, da li su ispravni elementi akumulatora.

Dodajte destilirane vode.

Akumulator se ne puni potpuno / ispražnjen je / ima jedan neispravan elemenat.

Akumulator je napunjen, ali ne daje struju / ne uspijeva pokrenuti motor.

| English | Italiano | Français |
|---|---|---|
| The terminals are corroded. They need to be cleaned. | I morsetti sono ossidati. Bisogna pulirli. | Les cosses sont oxydées, il faudrait les nettoyer. |
| The dynamo warning light doesn't go out. | La spia della dinamo non si spegne. | Le voyant de la dynamo reste allumé. |
| There's probably a short circuit. | E' probabile che ci sia un corto circuito | Il doit y avoir un court-circuit. |
| The dynamo brushes may be worn. | Forse le spazzole della dinamo sono consumate. | Les balais de la dynamo sont peut-être usés |
| Check the voltage regulator. | Controlli il regolatore di tensione. | Veuillez contrôler le régulateur de tension. |
| It's as well to look at the starting motor brushes, too. | E' bene guardare anche le spazzole del motorino di avviamento. | Il faudrait contrôler également les balais du démarreur. |
| It's necessary to check the armature / the pinion of the starting motor. | Occorre controllare l'indotto / il pignoncino del motorino di avviamento. | Il faut vérifier l'induit / le pignon du démarreur. |
| The starter commutator must be cleaned. | Il collettore del motorino deve essere pulito. | Je vous prie de nettoyer le collecteur du démarreur. |
| Check the contacts of the rotor arm / the coil ignition / the platinum points. | Verifichi i contatti della spazzola di distribuzione / lo spinterogeno / le puntine platinate. | S'il vous plaît, vérifiez les contacts du balai de distribution / l'allumeur / les vis platinées. |
| The spindle of the distributor needs greasing. | Occore lubrificare l'alberino dello spinterogeno. | Il faudrait graisser l'axe de l'allumeur. |
| I think the ignition coil has blown. | Credo che sia bruciata la bobina. | Je crains que la bobine ne soit brûlée. |
| The trouble may be in the windings of the coil. | L'inconveniente può dipendere dai cavetti della bobina. | Cet ennui peut dépendre des fils de la bobine. |
| The sparking plugs are dirty / worn. | Le candele sono sporche / consumate. | Les bougies sont encrassées / usées. |
| The porcelain is cracked. | La porcellana è incrinata. | La porcelaine est fêlée. |
| The tappets are worn. | Le punterie sono consumate. | Les marteaux sont usés. |
| The spark gap is incorrect. The electrodes are too close / far apart. | La distanza tra gli elettrodi non è regolare. Sono troppo vicini / distanti. | La distance entre les électrodes n'est pas réglementaire; ils sont trop rapprochés / éloignés. |
| When I turn off the engine, it runs on irregularly. Can this cause damage? | Quando tolgo il contatto il motore continua a girare irregolarmente. Può verificarsi qualche danno? | Quand j'enlève le contact, le moteur continue à tourner irrégulièrement. Est ce dangereux? |
| The sparking plugs get overheated. They must be replaced by a harder grade of plug. | Le candele scaldano troppo. Bisogna sostituirle con altre piú fredde. | Les bougies surchauffent, il faut les remplacer par d'autres plus froides. |
| The engine has a very high compression; it needs very hard plugs. | Il motore è molto compresso, ha bisogno di candele molto fredde. | Le moteur est très comprimé, il lui faut des bougies très froides. |
| The engine has very low compression, and needs soft (hot running) plugs. | Il motore ha scarsa compressione, perciò conviene usare candele calde. | Le moteur est peu comprimé, il vaut mieux utiliser des bougies chaudes. |
| The headlamps are not well aligned. They need adjusting | I fari non sono bene orientati. Bisogna regolarli. | Les phares sont mal orientés, il faudrait les régler. |

| Deutsch | Español | Srpsko-hrvatski |
| --- | --- | --- |
| Die Klemmen sind oxydiert und müssen gereinigt werden. | Los bornes están oxidados. Hay que limpiarlos. | Priključni polovi su oksidirani. Potrebno ih je oćistiti. |
| Die Ladestromkontrolleuchte brennt beim Fahren weiter. | La lámpara de la dínamo no se apaga. | Signalna lampa dinama se ne gasi. |
| Wahrscheinlich handelt es sich um einen Kurzschluss. | Es probable que haya un corto circuito. | Postoji mogućnost kratkog spoja. |
| Vielleicht sind die Bürsten der Lichtmaschine abgenutzt. | Quizás las escobillas de la dínamo estén gastadas. | Možda su istrošene četke dinama. |
| Prüfen Sie bitte den Spannungsregler. | Revise el regulador de tensión. | Pregledajte regulator napona. |
| Es wäre ratsam, auch die Bürsten des Anlassers zu prüfen. | Sería conveniente revisar también las escobillas del motor de arranque. | Dobro je pregledati takodjer četke elektropokretača. |
| Der Anker / das Ritzel des Anlassers muss geprüft werden. | Hay que revisar el inducido / el piñón del motor de arranque. | Potrebno je pregledati kotvu / zupčanik elektropokretača. |
| Der Kollektor des Anlassers muss gereinigt werden. | Hay que limpiar el colector del motor de arranque. | Kolektor motora se mora oćistiti. |
| Prüfen Sie bitte die Kontakte der Verteilerbürsten / den Zündverteiler / die Unterbrecherkontakte. | Revise los contactos de la escobilla de distribución / el distribuído del encendido / los platinos. | Pregledajte kontakte četke razvodnika / razvodnik paljenja / platinske kontakte. |
| Die Zündverteilerwelle muss geschmiert werden. | Hay que engrasar el eje del distribuidor del encendido. | Potrebno je podmazati osovinu razvodnika paljenja. |
| Ich glaube, dass die Zündspule durchgebrannt ist. | Creo que se ha quemado la bobina. | Vjerujem da je pregorio pretvarač napona. |
| Die Störung kann von den Kabeln herrühren. | El inconveniente puede depender de los cables de la bobina. | Kvar može ovisiti o električnim sprovodnicima pretvarača napona. |
| Die Zündkerzen sind verschmutzt / korrodiert. | La bujías están sucias / gastadas. | Svjećice su zamazane / istrošene. |
| Der Isolator ist rissig. | La porcelana está agrietada. | Porculanski izolator je napuknut. |
| Die Stössel sind abgenutzt | Los platinos están gastados. | Istrošeni su električni kontakti. |
| Der Elektrodenabstand ist nicht richtig. Er ist zu klein / zu gross. | La luz entre los electrodos es irregular. Están demasiado cerca / alejados. | Razmak elektroda nije ispravan. Suviše su primaknute / razmaknute. |
| Wenn ich die Zündung ausschalte, dreht der Motor unregelmässig weiter. Können dadurch irgendwelche Schäden entstehen? | Al quitar el contacto, el motor sigue girando irregularmente. ¿Puede causar alguna avería? | Kada prekinem kontakt, motor se nastavi nepravilno okretati. Možete li ustanoviti razlog. |
| Die Zündkerzen erwärmen sich zu stark. Sie müssen durch andere, mit höherem Wärmewert ersetzt werden. | Las bujías se calientan demasiado. Hay que cambiarlas por otras más frías. | Svjećice se previše zagrijavaju. Potrebno ih je zamijeniti sa hladnijima. |
| Der Motor ist hoch verdichtet und verlangt Kerzen mit hohem Wärmewert. | El motor está muy comprimido, necesita bujías muy frías. | Motor ima visoku kompresiju, i potrebne su vrlo hladne svjećice. |
| Der Verdichtungsdruck des Motors ist niedrig, so dass man am besten Kerzen mit niederem Wärmewert verwendet. | El motor tiene escasa compresión, por eso sería conveniente montar bujías calientes. | Motor ima slabu kompresiju, pa se preporuča upotreba toplih svjećica. |
| Die Scheinwerfer sind nicht ordentlich eingestellt. Sie müssen nachgestellt werden. | Los faros no están bien orientados. Hay que arreglarlos. | Farovi su nepravilno orjentirani. Potrebno ih je regulirati. |

| English | Italiano | Français |
|---|---|---|
| The bulb of the right headlamp is fused. | La lampadina del faro destro è fulminata. | L'ampoule du phare de droite est grillée. |
| The glass of the fog lamp is broken. Have you got one the same? | Si è rotto il vetro del faro antinebbia. Ne ha uno uguale? | Le verre du phare antibrouillard est cassé, en avez-vous un pareil? |
| The main beam warning light doesn't come on. | La spia degli abbaglianti non si accende. | Le voyant des feux de route ne s'allume pas. |
| The dipswitch controlling the lights isn't working. | Non funziona la leva per il cambio delle luci. | Le levier pour changer les feux ne fontionne pas. |
| When I change gear, the reversing light comes on. | Quando cambio si accende la luce della retromarcia. | Quand je change, le feu de marche arrière s'allume. |
| The red tail-lights do not light up. | Le luci di stop non si accendono. | Les stops ne fonctionnent pas. |
| The horn often fails to work. It seems to me that it depends on the position of the steering-wheel. | Spesso non funziona il clacson. Mi pare che ciò dipenda dalla posizione del volante. | Souvent l'avertisseur ne fonctionne pas: il me semble que cela vient de la position du volant. |
| The horns don't work. They may be full of mud. | Le trombe non suonano. Forse si sono riempite di fango. | Les trompes de l'avertisseur ne marchent pas. Elles sont peut-être pleines de boue. |
| There must be a short circuit. | Ci deve essere un contatto. | Il doit y avoir un court-circuit. |
| The windscreen wipers don't work / work too slowly / often stick. | Il tergicristallo non si muove / va troppo piano / spesso si blocca. | L'essuie-glace ne bouge pas / va trop doucement / se bloque souvement. |
| The trouble is in the motor. | Il difetto sta nel motorino. | Il a un moteur défectueux. |
| The spray-jet is clogged. | Lo spruzzatore è ostruito. | Le pulvérisateur est bouché. |
| The liquid container is empty. | Il contenitore del liquido è vuoto. | Le réservoir du liquide pour l'essuie-glace est vide. |
| The blades don't wipe clean. | Le spazzole non puliscono bene. | Les balais ne nettoient pas bien. |
| The rubbers need to be changed. | Bisogna sostituire le guarnizioni di gomma. | Il faudra changer leurs caoutchoucs. |
| The dashboard light doesn't come on. | La luce del cruscotto non si accende. | La lumière du tableau de bord ne s'allume pas. |
| Only the valve needs changing. | Basta cambiare la valvolina. | Il suffit de changer le coupe-circuit. |
| The courtesy light comes on on bends. | La luce interna si accende in curva. | La lumière intérieure s'allume dans les virages. |
| The switch is broken. | E' rotto l'interruttore. | L'interrupteur est cassé. |
| The petrol gauge has got very inaccurate. | L'indicatore della benzina è diventato molto impreciso. | L'indicateur du niveau d'essence est devenu très peu précis. |
| The reserve warning light doesn't come on. | La spia della riserva non si accende. | Le voyant de la réserve ne s'allume pas. |
| The anti-theft device has jammed. | Si è bloccato l'antifurto. | L'antivol est bloqué. |
| The heating isn't working properly. | L'impianto di riscaldamento non va. | Le chauffage ne marche pas. |

| Deutsch | Español | Srpsko-hrvatski |
|---|---|---|
| Die Birne des rechten Scheinwerfers ist durchgebrannt. | La bombilla del faro dereeho se ha fundido. | Žarulja desnog fara je pregorjela. |
| Die Scheibe der Nebelleuchte ist zerbrochen. Haben Sie einen passenden Ersatz? | Se ha roto el cristal del faro antiniebla. ¿Tiene Vd uno igual? | Polomilo se staklo fara protiv magle. Imate li jedno rezervno? |
| Die Fernlichtkontrollampe leuchtet nicht auf. | El indicador de los faros deslumbrantes no se enciende. | Signalna lampa velikog svjetla se ne upali. |
| Der Abblendschalter funktioniert nicht. | La palanca del cambio de las luces no funciona. | Neispravna je poluga za izmjenu svjetla. |
| Beim Umschalten schalten sich die Rückfahrscheinwerfer ein. | Cuando engrano una marcha se enciende la luz de la marcha atrás. | Kada mjenjam, upali se svjetiljka za vožnju unazad. |
| Die Bremslichter schalten sich nicht ein. | Las luces del « stop » no se encienden. | Stop svjetla se ne upale. |
| Häufig funktioniert die Hupe nicht. Ich habe den Eindruck, dass das an der Stellung des Steuers liegt. | A menudo no funciona el claxon. Me parece que depende de la posición del volante. | Često ne funkcionira sirena. Čini mi se da to zavisi o položaju upravljača. |
| Die Hörner funktionieren nicht. Vielleicht sind sie verschlammt. | Las bocinas no funcionan. Tal vez estén llenas de barro. | Trube ne sviraju. Možda su se ispunile blatom. |
| Da ist gewiss ein Wackelkontakt. | Habrá un contacto. | Mora da je po srijedi jedan kontakt. |
| Der Scheibenwischer kommt nicht in Bewegung / bewegt sich zu langsam / verklemmt sich häufig. | El limpia parabrisas no funciona / va demasiado lento / a menudo se para. | Brisač stakla je neprokretan / radi prepolako / često se zaustavi. |
| Das liegt am Scheibenwischermotor. | La avería está en su motor. | Kvar je u motoru. |
| Die Spritzdüse ist verstopft. | El pulverizador está obstruído. | Začepljena je štrcaljka za staklo. |
| Der Vorratsbehälter ist leer. | El contenedor del líquido está vacío. | Spremnik za tekućinu je prazan. |
| Die Scheibenwischer reinigen nicht ordentlich. | Las rasquetas no limpian bien. | Četke ne čiste dobro. |
| Die Wischblätter müssen erneuert werden. | Hay que substituir las juntas de goma. | Potrebno je izmijeniti gumene brtve. |
| Die Instrumentenbeleuchtung schaltet sich nicht ein. | La luz del tablero no se enciende. | Neispravno je osvjetljenje table s instrumentima. |
| Da braucht nur die Sicherung ausgewechselt zu werden. | Basta cambiar el fusible. | Dovoljno je izmijeniti osigurač. |
| Die Deckenleuchte schaltet sich in der Kurve ein. | La luz interior del auto se enciende en curva. | Unutrašnje osvjetljenje se upali u zavoju. |
| Der Schalter ist defekt. | Se ha estropeado el interruptor. | Oštećen je prekidač. |
| Die Kraftstoffanzeige ist sehr ungenau geworden. | El indicador del nivel de combustible es muy impreciso. | Indikator benzina je postao vrlo neprecizan. |
| Die Reservetankkontrolleuchte schaltet sich nicht ein. | La luz que indica la reserva del carburante no se enciende. | Signalna lampa rezerve se ne upali. |
| Das Lenkschloss hat sich verklemmt. | Se ha atascado el antifurto. | Blokirala se je sigurnosna brava. |
| Die Heizungsanlage funktioniert nicht. | El sistema de calefacción está estropeado. | Uredjaj za zagrijavanje je neispravan. |

**English**

The warm air doesn't reach the rear seats.

The warm air can't be turned off.

The windscreen steams up.

The ventilator has stuck.

**I Generator and starting motor** 1. dynamo 2. brushes 3. manifold 4. armature 5. automatic cut-out 6. magnetic field 7. belt 8. alternator 9. rotor arm 10. windings 11. diodes 12. voltage regulator 13. electromagnetic engagement 14. pinion 15. bearing. **II Battery** 1. cells 2. plates 3. lead 4. sulphuric acid 5. distilled water 6. terminals 7. leads 8. positive / negative pole 9. cap 10. ammeter 11. amperes-hour 12. battery capacity 13. measure of voltage 14. corrosion. **III Ignition coil and distributor** 1. condenser 2. rotor arm 3. contact breaker 4. socket 5. brush 6. lead 7. distributor 8. distributor cap 9. platinum points 10. distributor shaft 11. charcoal 12. spark advance control 13. spring 14. cam 15. coil 16. winding 17. leads 18. contact. **IV Sparking plugs** 1. electrodes 2. distance of electrodes 3. porcelain 4. hot / cold sparking plugs 5. dirty / cracked / corroded plugs. **V Lights** 1. headlamp 2. main / dipped beams 3. fog lamps 4. bulb 5. filament 6. reflector 7. rim 8. glass 9. front / rear sidelights 10. trafficators 11. red tail-light 12. number plate light 13. reversing light 14. control for lights 15. blinking light 16. engine inspection light 17. boot light 18. door light 19. dashboard light 20. switch 21. warning light for sidelights 22. dynamo warning light 23. oil pressure warning light 24. petrol reserve warning light 25. heating warning light. **VI Other parts** 1. windscreen wiper 2. windscreen wiper switch 3. motor 4. blades 5. rubber elements 6. jet 7. anti-theft gadget 8. petrol / oil pressure gauge 9. oil / water temperature gauge 10. oil pressure gauge 11. clock 12. tachometer 13. total mileage indicator 14. trip-counter 15. rev. counter 16. radio 17. antenna 18. cigarette lighter 19. resistance 20. heating system 21. heating control 22. electric fan 23. cooling fan 24. anti-fogging resistance 25. de-icers 26. horn 27. horn 28. diaphragm 29. air conductor 30. switch.

**Italiano**

L'aria calda non raggiunge i sedili posteriori.

Non si riesce a chiudere l'aria calda.

I parabrezza si appanna.

Il ventilatore è bloccato.

**I Generatore e motorino d'avviamento** 1. dinamo 2. spazzole 3. collettore 4. indotto 5. interruttore di minima 6. campo magnetico 7. cinghia 8. alternatore 9. rotore 10. avvolgimenti 11. diodi 12. regolatore di tensione 13. innesto elettromagnetico 14. pignoncino 15. cuscinetto. **II Batteria** 1. elementi 2. piastre 3. piombo 4. acido solforico 5. acqua distillata 6. morsetti 7. cavi 8. polo positivo / negativo 9. tappo 10. amperometro 11. ampère-ora 12. capacità della batteria 13. misura della tensione 14. ossidazione. **III Spinterogeno e distributore** 1. condensatore 2. martelletto 3. ruttore 4. presa di corrente 5. spazzola 6. cavo 7. distributore 8. calotta 9. puntine platinate 10. alberino di comando 11. carboncino 12. comando dell'anticipo 13. molla 14. camma 15. bobina 16. avvolgimento 17. cavetti 18. contatto. **IV Candele** 1. elettrodi 2. distanza degli elettrodi 3. porcellana 4. candele calde / fredde 5. candele sporche / incrinate / corrose. **V Luci** 1. faro 2. fari abbaglianti / anabbaglianti 3. fari antinebbia 4. lampadina 5. filamento 6. riflettore 7. ghiera 8. vetro 9. luci di posizione anteriori / posteriori 10. indicatori di direzione 11. fanalino stop 12. luce della targa 13. luce retromarcia 14. comando delle luci 15 lampeggiatore 16. luce vano motore 17. luce portabagagli 18. luce portiere 19. luce cruscotto 20. interruttore 21. spia luci città 22. spia della dinamo 23. spia dell'olio 24. spia della riserva 25. spia del riscaldamento. **VI Altre parti** 1. tergicristallo 2. comando tergicristallo 3. motorino 4. spazzole 5. guarnizioni di gomma 6. spruzzatore 7. antifurto 8. indicatore della benzina / dell'olio 9. indicatore temperatura olio / acqua 10. indicatore pressione olio 11. orologio 12. tachimetro 13. contachilometri totale 14. contachilometri parziale 15. contagiri 16. radio 17. antenna 18. accendisigaro 19. resistenza 20. impianto di riscaldamento 21. comando riscaldamento 22. elettroventilatore 23. ventola di raffreddamento 24. resistenza antiappannamenti 25. sbrinatori 26. clacson 27. tromba 28. membrana 29. condotta d'aria 30. interruttore.

**Français**

L'air chaud n'arrive pas jusqu'à la banquette arrière.

Il est impossible de fermer l'arrivée d'air chaud.

Le parebrise se couvre de buée.

Le ventilateur est bloqué.

**I Générateur et démarreur** 1. dynamo 2. balais 3. collecteur 4. induit 5. interrupteur du disjoncteur 6. champ magnétique 7. courroie 8. alternateur 9. rotor 10. enroulements 11. diodes 12. régulateur de tension 13. électro-aimant 14. pignon 15. coussinet. **II Batterie** 1. éléments 2. plaques 3. plomb 4. acide sulfurique 5. eau distillée 6. cosses 7. câbles 8. pôle positif / négatif 9. bouchon 10. ampèremètre 11. ampère-heure 12. charge de la batterie 13. mesure de la tension 14. oxydation **III Allumeur et distributeur** 1. condensateur 2. marteau 3. rupteur 4. prise de courant 5. balai 6. câble 7. distributeur 8. tête d'allumeur 9. vis platinées 10. arbre de commande 11. charbon 12. commande de l'avance 13. ressort 14. came 15. bobine 16. enroulement 17. fils 18 contact. **IV Bougies** 1. électrodes 2. pas polaire 3. porcelaine 4. bougies chaudes / froides 5. bougies sales / fêlées / corrodées. **V Feux** 1. phare 2. phares de route / de croisement 3. phares antibrouillard 4. ampoule 5. filament 6. réflecteur 7. douille 8. verre 9. feux de position antérieurs / postérieurs 10. indicateurs de direction 11. stops 12. feu de plaque 13. feux de recul 14. commande des feux 15. clignotant 16. éclairage du logement du moteur 17. éclairage du coffre à bagages 18. feux des portières 19. lumière du tableau de bord 20. interrupteur 21. voyant de l'éclairage lanternes 22. voyant de la dynamo 23. voyant de l'huile 24. voyant de la réserve de carburant 25. voyant du chauffage. **VI Autres éléments** 1. essuie-glace 2. commande de l'essuie-glace 3. moteur de l'essuie-glace 4. balais 5. caoutchoucs 6. pulvérisateur 7. antivol 8. indicateur jauge d'essence / d'huile 9. indicateur de température de l'huile / l'eau 10. indicateur de pression de l'huile 11. montre 12. tachymètre 13. compteur kilométrique total 14. compteur kilométrique partiel 15. compte-tours 16. radio 17. antenne 18. allume-cigares 19. résistance 20. système de chauffage 21. commande du chauffage 22. ventilateur électrique 23. écran de refroidissement 24. résistance anti-buée 25. dégivreurs 26. avertisseur 27. trompe 28. membrane 29. conduit d'air 30. interrupteur.

## TRANSMISSION AND STEERING

Can you adjust the clutch pedal?

The clutch is jerky / slips.

The play in the clutch pedal needs taking up.

## TRASMISSIONE E STERZO

Può regolare il pedale della frizione?

La frizione strappa / slitta.

Bisogna controllare il gioco della frizione.

## TRANSMISSION ET DIRECTION

Pourriez-vous vérifier la pédale de l'embrayage?

L'embrayage accroche / patine.

Il faudrait contrôler le jeu de l'embrayage.

| Deutsch | Español | Srpsko-hrvatski |
|---|---|---|
| Die Warmluft erreicht nicht den Fond. | El aire caliente no alcanza los asientos posteriores. | Topli zrak ne stiže do stražnjih sjedala. |
| Die Warmluftzufuhr lässt sich nicht abstellen. | No consigo cerrar el flujo de aire caliente. | Ne može se zatvoriti topli zrak. |
| Die Windschutzscheibe beschlägt. | El parabrisas se empaña. | Prednje staklo se zamagljuje. |
| Der Lüfter ist verklemmt. | El ventilador se ha atascado. | Ventilator je blokiran. |

**I. Generator und Anlasser** 1. Lichtmaschine 2. Bürsten 3. Kollektor 4. Anker 5. Regler-Schalter 6. Magnetfeld 7. Riemen 8. Wechselstromgenerator 9. Läufer 10. Wicklung 11. Dioden 12. Spannungsregler 13. Magnetkupplung 14. Ritzel 15. Kugellager. **II. Batterie** 1. Zellen 2. Platten 3. Blei 4. Schwefelsäure 5. destilliertes Wasser 6. Klemmen 7. Kabel 8. Pluspol / Minuspol 9. Verschlussstopfen 10. Amperemesser 11. Amperestunde 12. Kapazität der Batterie 13. Spannungsmessung 14. Oxydation. **III. Zündverteiler und Verteiler** 1. Kondensator 2. Unterbrecherhebel 3. Unterbrecher 4. Anschluss 5. Verteilerfinger 6. Kabel 7. Verteiler 8. Verteilerscheibe 9. Unterbrecherkontakte 10. Antriebswelle 11. Kohle 12. Zündhebel 13. Feder 14. Nocke 15. Zündspule 16. Wicklung 17. Zündkabel 18. Kontakt. **IV Zündkerzen** 1. Elektroden 2. Elektrodenabstand 3. Isolator 4. heisse / kalte Zündkerzen 5. verschmutzte / gesprungene / korrodierte Zündkerzen. **V. Beleuchtungsanlage** 1. Scheinwerfer 2. Fernlicht / Abblendlicht 3. Nebelscheinwerfer 4. Birne 5. Glühfaden 6. Reflektor 7. Tragring 8. Scheibe 9. vordere / hintere Parkleuchten 10. Richtungsanzeiger 11. Bremslicht 12. Kennzeichenbeleuchtung 13. Rückfahrscheinwerfer 14. Lichtschalter 15. Blinklicht 16. Motorraumlampe 17. Kofferraumlampe 18. Türleuchte 19. Instrumentenbeleuchtung 20. Einstell-Knopf 21. Standlichtkontrolleuchte 22. Ladestromkontrolleuchte 23. Öldruckkontrolleuchte 24. Reservetankkontrolleuchte 25. Heizungskontrolleuchte. **VI. Sonstige Teile** 1. Scheibenwischer 2. Scheibenwischer-Schalter 3. Scheibenwischermotor 4. Wischerarme 5. Wischblätter 6. Scheibenwascher-Spritzdüse 7. Lenkschloss 8. Kraftstoff-Vorratsanzeiger / Ölstandanzeiger 9. Öl- / Kühlmittel-Fernthermometer 10. Öldruckanzeiger 11. Uhr 12. Tachometer 13. Gesamtkilometerzähler 14. Tageskilometerzähler 15. Drehzahlmesser 16. Radio 17. Antenne 18. Zigarren-Anzünder 19. Widerstand 20. Heizungsanlage 21. Schalter für Heizung 22. Elektrolüfter 23. Lüfterrad 24. Klarsichtwiderstand 25. Entfroster 26. Hupe 27. Horn 28. Membrane 29. Luftschlauch 30. Unterbrecher.

**I Dinamo y motor de arranque** 1. dinamo 2. escobillas 3. colector 4. inducido 5. interruptor de mínima 6. campo magnético 7. correa 8. alternador 9. ruptor 10. arrollamiento 11. diodos 12. regulador de tensión 13. acoplamiento electromagnético 14. piñoncito 15. cojinete. **II Batería** 1. elementos 2. placas 3. plomo 4. ácido sulfúrico 5. agua destilada 6. bornes 7. cables 8. polo positivo / negativo 9. fichas de enchufe 10. amperímetro 11. amperios/hora 12. capacidad de la batería 13. medida de la tensión 14. oxidación. **III Distribuidor del encendido** 1. condensador 2. contacto móvil 3. ruptor 4. toma de corriente 5. escobilla 6. cable 7. distribuidor 8. cúpula 9. platinos 10. eje de mando 11. carboncillo 12. mando del avance 13. resorte 14. excéntrica 15. bobina 16. arrollamiento 17. cables 18. contacto. **IV Bujías** 1. electrodos 2. paso de rosca de los electrodos 3. porcelana 4. bujías calientes / frías 5. bujías sucias / agrietadas / desgastadas. **V Luces** 1. faro 2. faros deslumbrantes / de luz atenuada 3. faros antiniebla 4. bombilla 5. filamento 6. reflector 7. virola 8. espejo 9. luces de posición delantera / traseras 10. indicadores de dirección 11. luz de stop 12. luz de la placa 13. luz de la marcha atrás 14. mando de las luces 15. intermitente 16. luz del departamento motor 17. luz del departamento equipaje 18. luz de la portezuela 19. luz del tablero 20. interruptor 21. indicador luces de posición 22. indicador de la dínamo 23. indicador del aceite 24. indicador de la reserva del carburante 25. indicador de la calefacción. **VI Otras partes** 1. limpia parabrisas 2. mando del limpia parabrisas 3. motor 4. rasquetas 5. juntas de goma 6. pulverizador 7. antifurto 8. indicador de la gasolina / del aceite 9. indicador de la temperatura aceite / agua 10. indicador presión aceite 11. reloj 12. taquímetro 13. cuentakilómetros total 14. cuentakilómetros parcial 15. cuentarrevoluciones 16. radio 17. antena 18. encendedor 19. resistencia 20. sistema de calefacción 21. mando de la calefacción 22. electroventilador 23. rotor ventilador refrigeración 24. resistencia antifuscamiento 25. descongelador 26. claxon 27. bocinas 28. membrana 29. conducto del aire 30. interruptor.

**I Dinamo i električni pokretač** 1. dinamo 2. četke 3. kolektor 4. kotva 5. prekidač minimuma 6. magnetsko polje 7. remen 8. ispravljač 9. rotor 10. namotaj 11. dioda 12. regulator napona 13. elektromagnetsko ukapčanje 14. zupčanik elektropokretača 15. ležaj. **II Akumulator** 1. elementi 2. ploče 3. olovo 4. sumporna kiselina 5. destilirana voda 6. priključni polovi 7. električni provodnici 8. pozitivni pol / negativni 9. čep 10. ampermetar 11. amper-sat 12 kapacitet akumulatora 13. mjera napona 14. oksidacija. **III Električni razvodnik** 1. kondenzator 2. čekić 3. ekscentar razvodnika 4. priključna kutija 5. četka 6. električni provodnik 7. razvodnik 8. poklopac razvodnika 9. platinski kontakti 10. osovina razvodnika 11. ugljeni kontakt 12. podešivač paljenja 13. opruga 14. grba 15. strujni pretvarač 16. namotaj 17. električni sprovodnici 18. kontakt. **14. Svjećice** 1. elektrode 2. razmak elektroda 3. porculanski izolator 4. svjećice tople / hladne 5. svjećice zamazane / napuknute / korodirane. **V Svjetla** 1. far 2. farovi veliki / srednji 3. farovi protiv magle 4. žarulja 5. žarna nit 6. reflektor 7. bradavica žarulje 8. staklo 9. poziciona svjetla prednja / stražnja 10. pokazivači smjera 11. stop svjetla 12. svjetlo registarske table 13. svjetlo brzine unazad 14. prekidač za svjetlo 15. prekidač velikog i srednjeg svjetla 16. svjetlo motornog prostora 17. svjetlo prtljažnog prostora 19. svjetlo table s instrumentima 20. prekidač 21. signalna lampa gradskog svjetla 22. signalna lampa dinama 23. signalna lampa pritiska ulja 24. signalna lampa rezerve goriva 25. signalna lampa uredjaja za zagrijavanje. **VI Ostali dijelovi** 1. brisač stakla 2. prekidač brisača 3. motor 4. četke 5. gumena brtva 6. štrcaljka 7. sigurnosna brava 8. indikator benzina / ulja 9. indikator temperature ulja / vode 10. indikator pritiska ulja 11. sat 12. brzinomjer 13. brojčanik totalno predjenih kilometara 14. parcijalni brojčanik kilometara 15. brojač okretaja 16. radio 17. antena 18. upaljač za cigarete 19. otpornik 20. uredjaj za zagrijavanje 21. komande uredjaja za zagrijavanje 22. električni ventilator 23. ventilator za hladjenje 24. grijač stakla 25. odledjivači 26. sirena 27. truba 28. membrana 29. cjevovod za zrak 30. prekidač.

| KRAFTÜBERTRAGUNG UND LENKUNG | TRANSMISION Y VOLANTE | PREIJENOS I UPRAVLJAČKI UREDJAJ |
|---|---|---|
| Könnten Sie bitte das Kupplungspedal neu einstellen? | ¿Puede revisar el recorrido del pedal del embrague? | Možete li mi regulirati pedalu spojke. |
| Die Kupplung rupft / schleift. | El embrague renguea / patina. | Spojka trga / kliže. |
| Das Kupplungsspiel muss geprüft werden. | Hay que controlar el juego del embrague. | Potrebno je prekontrolitari zračnost spojke. |

| English | Italiano | Français |
|---|---|---|
| The clutch isn't adiustable. | La frizione non è regolabile. | L'embrayage n'est pas réglable. |
| The clutch doesn't engage gradually | L'innesto della frizione non è progressivo. | L'embrayage n'est pas progressif. |
| The clutch doesn't disengage properly. | La frizione non stacca bene. | L'embrayage ne décroche pas bien. |
| The friction lining of the plate is worn. I suggest you replace it as soon as possible. | La guarnizione del disco è logora. Consiglierei di sostituirla appena possibile. | La garniture du disque est usée, je vous conseille de la remplacer au plus vite. |
| The oil-seal too is worn. | Anche la guarnizione para-olio è consumata. | La garniture anti-huile est usée, elle aussi. |
| There's no fluid in the master cylinder. That's why the clutch isn't working properly. | Manca olio nella pompa di comando della frizione. Per questo non funziona bene. | La pompe de commande de l'embrayage manque d'huile, c'est pourquoi elle fonctionne mal. |
| The pressure springs are slack. | Le molle spingidisco sono scariche | Les ressorts du mécanisme d'embrayage sont détériorés. |
| When the car is running, the gearbox makes a lot of noise. | Quando la vettura corre il cambio fa molto rumore. | La boîte de vitesse est très bruyante lorsque la voiture marche vite. |
| The gearbox oil is too far below / above the correct level. | Nella scatola del cambio l'olio è troppo al di sotto / al di sopra del livello. | La boîte de vitesse n'a pas assez / a trop d'huile. |
| It's impossible to engage reverse gear. | Non si riesce a innestare la retromarcia. | Je n'arrive pas à engrener la marche arrière. |
| Third often slips out. | La terza molte volte sfugge. | La troisième saute souvent. |
| The gears are worn. | Gli ingranaggi sono consumati. | Les pignons sont usés. |
| Some teeth on the gears are broken. The spare parts will have to be found. | Alcuni denti degli ingranaggi sono rotti. Bisogna trovare i pezzi di ricambio. | Les pignons ont des dents cassées, il faudrait trouver des pièces de rechange. |
| The gearchange is very stiff. The gearshift fork needs changing. | Il cambio è molto duro. Occorre sostituire la forcella. | Le changement de vitesse est très dur, il faut changer la fourchette. |
| The return springs are broken. | Sono rotte le molle di rimando. | Les ressorts de rappel sont cassés. |
| The rubber buffer is broken. | E' rotto il tampone di gomma di appoggio. | Le tampon de support en caoutchouc est détérioré. |
| The gearbox nuts are slack. They only need to be tightened. Everything else is all right. | I dadi della scatola del cambio si sono allentati. Non c'è che da stringerli. Tutto il resto è a posto. | Les écrous de la boîte de vitesse ne sont pas assez serrés. Il suffit de les resserrer, tout le reste peut aller. |
| The propeller shaft is noisy / vibrates. | L'albero di trasmissione è rumoroso / vibra. | L'arbre de transmission est bruyant / vibre. |
| The central bearing of the shaft has gone. | Il cuscinetto centrale dell'albero è sballato. | Le palier central de l'arbre est défectueux. |
| The flexible couplings are worn. | I giunti elastici sono consumati. | Les joints élastiques sont usés. |
| The universal joints are dry / worn. | I giunti cardanici sono senza grasso / logori. | Les joints de cardan ne sont pas graissés / sont usés. |
| The nipples of the universal joints are dry. | Gli ingrassatori dei giunti cardanici sono asciutti. | Les graisseurs des joints de cardan sont secs. |

| Deutsch | Español | Srpsko-hrvatski |
|---|---|---|
| Die Kupplung ist nicht nachstellbar. | El embrague no es regulable. | Spojka se ne može regulirati. |
| Das Einrücken der Kupplung ist nicht progressiv. | El engrane del embrague no es progresivo. | Uključivanje spojke nije progresivno. |
| Die Kupplung trennt nicht gut. | El embrague no desengancha bien. | Spojka ne isključuje dobro. |
| Die Kupplungsbeläge sind verschlissen. Ich würde Ihnen raten, sie möglichst bald erneuern zu lassen. | La junta del disco está gastada. Le aconsejo substituirla cuanto antes. | Brtva diska spojke je izlizana. Preporučam vam da je što prije izmijenite. |
| Auch die Ölabdichtung ist abgenutzt. | También la junta de la chapa de retención del aceite está deteriorada. | Takodjer uljna brtva je istrošena |
| Im Pumpenrad der Kupplung fehlt Öl; daher funktioniert sie nicht ordentlich. | Falta aceite en la bomba de mando del embrague. Por esto no funciona bien. | U pumpi komande spojke nedostaje ulje. Zbog toga ne funkcionira ispravno. |
| Die Druckfedern sind entspannt. | Los resortes del plato de apriete están deteriorados. | Opruge spojke su omlohavljele. |
| Beim Fahren ist das Getriebe sehr laut. | Cuando aumento de velocidad el cambio mete ruido. | Kada kola voze velikom brzinom, mjenjač pravi buku. |
| Der Ölstand im Getriebe ist zu niedrig / zu hoch. | En la caja del cambio, el aceite está muy por debajo / muy por arriba del nivel. | U mjenjačkoj kutiji ulje je ispod / iznad odredjene razine. |
| Der Rückwärtsgang lässt sich nicht einlegen. | No consigo engranar la marcha atrás. | Ne uspijeva se uključiti brzina unazad |
| Der dritte Gang springt häufig aus. | La tercera muchas veces no agarra. | Treća se često isključi. |
| Die Zahnräder sind abgenutzt. | Los engranajes están gastados. | Zupčanici su istrošeni. |
| Einige Zähne sind abgebrochen. Wir müssen die entsprechenden Ersatzteile besorgen. | Algunos dientes de los engranajes están rotos. Hay que comprar las piezas de repuesto. | Nekoji zupci zupčanika su polomljeni. Potrebno je naći rezervne dijelove. |
| Das Wechselgetriebe ist sehr schwergängig. Die Schaltgabel muss ausgewechselt werden. | El cambio está demasiado duro. Hay que substituir la horquilla. | Mjenjač je jako tvrd. Potrebno je izmijeniti vilicu. |
| Die Rückzugfedern sind gebrochen. | Los resortes de reenvío están rotos. | Oštećene su povratne opruge. |
| Das Gummilager ist defekt. | El cabezal de goma de apoyo está roto. | Oštećen je gumeni odbojnik. |
| Die Muttern des Getriebegehäuses haben sich gelockert; sie brauchen nur angezogen zu werden. Ansonsten ist alles in Ordnung. | Las tuercas de la caja del cambio están flojas. Non hay más que cerrarla a fondo. Todo lo demás está bien. | Matice mjenjačke kutije su labave. Potrebno je samo zategnuti ih. Ostalo je u redu. |
| Die Gelenkwelle ist laut / vibriert. | El eje de transmisión hace ruido / vibra. | Prjenosna osovina stvara buku / vibrira. |
| Das mittlere Wellenlager ist defekt. | El cojinete central del eje está deteriorado. | Centralni ležaj osovine je labav. |
| Die Wellengelenke sind abgenutzt. | Las juntas elásticas están gastadas. | Elastične spojke su istrošene. |
| Die Kardangelenke sind trocken / abgenutzt. | Las juntas cardán está sin grasa / gastadas. | Kardanski zglobovi su bez podmaza / oštećeni. |
| Die Schmiernippel der Kardangelenke sind trocken. | Los engrasadores de las juntas cardán están secos. | Mazalice kardanskih zglobova su suhe. |

| English | Italiano | Français |
|---|---|---|
| The propellor shaft is cracked. | L'albero di trasmissione è incrinato. | L'arbre de transmission est fêlé. |
| The level of the oil in the rear axle must be checked. | Bisogna controllare il livello dell'olio al differenziale. | Il faudrait contrôler le niveau d'huile du différentiel. |
| It's better to change the oil. It's advisable to drain off the old oil while it's still hot. | Meglio cambiare l'olio. Conviene scaricare quello vecchio finché è ancora caldo. | Il vaut mieux changer l'huile, et vidanger l'huile usée pendant qu'elle est encore chaude. |
| The rear axle is noisy. The level gear needs checking. | Il ponte posteriore è rumoroso. Dipende dal gruppo conico, che va registrato. | Le pont arrière est bruyant. Cela vient du couple conique, il faudrait le vérifier. |
| The final drive has been running for a long time without oil. | Il differenziale ha funzionato a lungo senza olio. | Le différentiel a travaillé longtemps sans huile. |
| One of the halfshafts / bearings is faulty. | E' rotto uno dei semiassi / un cuscinetto. | Un des demi-arbres est cassé / un roulement est cassé. |
| The whole axle will have to be stripped down and the gears checked. | Tutto il ponte va smontato e gli ingranaggi vanno controllati. | Il faut démonter tout le pont et contrôler les pignons. |
| It will probably be necessary to replace the crown wheel and pinion. | Probabilmente sarà necessario sostituire la corona e il pignone. | Il faudra probablement changer la couronne et le pignon. |
| The steering is stiff / noisy. | Lo sterzo è duro / rumoroso. | La direction de cette voiture est dure / bruyante. |
| The car tends to pull to the right / to the left. | La vettura tende ad andare a destra / a sinistra. | La voiture tire à droite / à gauche. |
| The steering vibrates. | Lo sterzo vibra. | La direction vibre. |
| The toe-in needs checking. | E' necessario controllare la convergenza delle ruote. | Il faudrait contrôler la convergence des roues. |
| The wheels should be balanced. | Sarà bene equilibrare le ruote. | Il vaudra mieux équilibrer les roues. |
| There's no oil in the steering box. Some very heavy oil will have to be put in. | La scatola dello sterzo è asciutta. Bisogna metterci dell'olio molto denso. | Le boîtier de direction est sec, il y faudrait de l'huile très épaisse. |
| The pins and joints of the steering arms are worn. | I perni e gli snodi della tiranteria sono consumati. | Les pivots et les rotules de la timonerie sont usés. |
| These are the nipples of the pins and joints. They need greasing. | Ecco gli ingrassatori dei perni e degli snodi. Occorre aggiungere grasso. | Voici les graisseurs des pivots et des rotules. il faut y rajouter de la graisse. |
| The flexible coupling of the steering is broken. | Il giunto elastico dello sterzo è rotto. | Le joint élastique de la direction est cassé. |
| The steering column is out of true. It's certainly the result of a bump. | Il piantone dello sterzo è deformato. E' sicuramente la conseguenza di un urto. | Le tube de la direction est déformé, c'est certainement la conséquence d'un choc. |

**I Clutch** 1. clutch pedal 2. play of pedal 3. single dry plate 4. engagement 5. disengagement 6. plate 7. oil seal 8. pressure springs 9 friction lining 10. lever 11. link 12. thrust bearing 13. automatic gearbox 14. hydraulic drive. **II Gearbox** 1. gear lever 2. mechanical / automatic gearbox 3. manual / automatic selection 4. main / auxiliary / driven shaft 5. first / second / third / fourth / fifth gear 6. reverse gear 7. synchronized

**I Frizione** 1. pedale della frizione 2. gioco del pedale 3. monodisco a secco 4. innesto 5. disinnesto 6. disco 7. guarnizione 8. molla spingidisco 9. ferodo 10. leva 11. tirante 12. cuscinetto reggispinta 13. frizione automatica 14. comando idraulico. **II Cambio** 1. leva del cambio 2. cambio meccanico / automatico 3. selezione manuale / automatica 4. albero primario / ausiliario / secondario 5. prima / seconda / terza /

**I Embrayage** 1. pédale de l'embrayage 2. jeu de la pédale 3. monodisque à sec 4. embrayage 5. débrayage 6. disque 7. garniture. 8. ressort pousse-disque 9. férodo 10. levier 11. tirant 12. butée tournante 13. embrayage automatique 14. jeu de l'embrayage hydraulique. **II Boîte de vitesses** 1. levier de vitesses 2. changement de vitesse mécanique / automatique 3. sélection à main / automatique 4. arbre primaire / auxiliaire /

| Deutsch | Español | Srpsko-hrvatski |
|---|---|---|
| Die Gelenkwelle hat Risse. | El eje de transmisión está hendido. | Prjenosna osovina je napukla. |
| Der Ölstand im Ausgleichsgetriebe muss geprüft werden. | Hay que controlar el nivel del aceite del diferencial. | Potrebno je kontrolirati razinu ulja u diferencijalu. |
| Das Öl müsste gewechselt werden. Am besten lassen wir das alte Öl ab, solange es noch heiss ist. | Es mejor cambiar el aceite. Conviene sacar el viejo, mientras aún está caliente. | Bolje je promijeniti ulje. Preporučljivo je istočiti staro, dok je toplo. |
| Die Hinterachse ist laut. Das liegt an dem Kegelradgetriebe, das nachgestellt werden muss. | El puente trasero hace ruido. Depende del grupo cónico, que es preciso reglar. | Stražnji most pravi buku. Ovisi o koničnom paru, koji treba registrirati. |
| Das Ausgleichsgetriebe hat lange Zeit ohne Öl gearbeitet. | El diferencial ha trabajado mucho tiempo sin aceite. | Diferencijal je dugo vremena funkcionirao bez ulja. |
| Eine der Achswellen / ein Lager ist gebrochen. | Se ha roto uno de los semiejes / un cojinete. | Ostećena je jedna od poluosovina / jedan ležaj. |
| Die ganze Achse muss ausgebaut werden, damit die Zahnräder nachgeprüft werden können. | Hay que desmontar todo el puente y revisar los engranajes. | Potrebno je rastaviti most i kontrolirati zupčanike. |
| Wahrscheinlich müssen Tellerrad und Ritzel erneuert werden. | Con toda probabilidad habrá que cambiar la corona y el piñón. | Vjerojatno će biti potrebno izmijeniti zupčastu krunu i zupčanik. |
| Die Lenkung ist schwergängig / laut. | El volante está duro / mete ruido. | Upravljač je tvrd / pravi buku. |
| Der Wagen zieht nach rechts / nach links. | El coche tiende a ir hacia la derecha / la izquierda. | Kola vuku na desno / na lijevo. |
| Das Lenkrad vibriert. | El volante vibra. | Upravljač vibrira |
| Der Radsturz muss geprüft werden. | Es necesario controlar la convergencia de las ruedas. | Potrebno je kontrolirati konvergenciju kotača. |
| Die Räder müssen ausgewuchtet werden. | Será bien equilibrar las ruedas. | Biti će dobro, da se uravnoteže kotači. |
| Das Lenkgehäuse ist trocken. Es müsste sehr dickflüssiges Öl eingefüllt werden. | El cárter de la dirección está seco. Hay que añadir aceite muy denso. | Upravljačka kutija je suha. Potrebno je staviti jako gusto ulje. |
| Die Zapfen und Gelenke des Lenkgestänges sind abgenutzt. | Los pernos y los torniquetes de los tirantes están consumidos. | Osovine i zglobovi vućnih elemenata su istrošeni. |
| Hier sind die Schmiernippel der Zapfen und Gelenke. Es muss Fett hinzugefügt werden. | Mire cómo están los engrasadores de los pernos y de los torniquetes. Hay que añadir grasa. | Eto mazalica osovina i zglobova. Potrebno je nadodati podmaz. |
| Die Federkupplung der Lenkung ist gebrochen. | El acoplamiento elastico del volante está roto. | Elastični zglob upravljača je polomljen. |
| Die Lenksäule ist verbogen. Das ist gewiss die Folge eines Stosses. | La barra de la dirección está deformada. Con toda seguridad es la consecuencia de un choque. | Motka upravljača je deformirana. To je sigurno posljedica jednog udara. |

**I. Kupplung** 1. Kupplungspedal 2. Kupplungsspiel 3. Einscheibentrockenkupplung 4. Einrückvorrichtung 5. Ausrückvorrichtung 6. Kupplungsscheibe 7. Dichtring 8. Kupplungsdruckfeder 9. Belag 10. Druckhebel 11. Druckstange 12. Drucklager 13. automatische Kupplung 14. hydraulische Kupplungsbetätigung. **II. Getriebe** 1. Getriebeschalthebel 2. mechanisches / automatisches Getriebe 3. Handschaltung / automatische Schaltung

**I Embrague** 1. pedal del embrague 2. juego del pedal 3. monodisco seco. 4. enganche 5. desenganche 6. disco 7. junta 8. resorte de apriete 9. ferodo 10. palanca 11. tirante 12. cojinete parachoques 13. embrague automático 14. mando hidráulico. **II Cambio** 1. palanca del cambio 2. cambio mecánico / automático 3. selección marchas manual / automática 4. árbol primario / auxiliar / secundario 5. marcha primera / se-

**I Spojka** 1. pedala spojke 2. zračnost pedale 3. jednodjelni disk 4. uključivanje 5. isključivanje 6. disk 7. brtva 8. povratna opruga 9. feroda 10. poluga 11. vučni element 12. ležaj 13. automatska spojka 14. hidraulička komanda. **II Mjenjač** 1. poluga mjenjača 2. mjenjač mehanički / automatski 3. mijenjanje ručno / automatsko 4. osovina primarna / pomoćna / sekundarna 5. prva / druga / treća / četvrta / peta brzina

**English**

gearbox 8. synchronizer 9. unsynchronized gear 10. neutral 11. gearbox 12. gear box ratio 13. gears 14. teeth 15. gearshift fork 16. return spring 17. rubber buffer 18. nuts 19. coupling 20. oil 21. oil level 22. drainage plug. **III Transmission shaft and final drive** 1. flexible coupling 2. universal joint 3. slip joint 4. bearing 5. connexion 6. slip coupling 7. bevel drive 8. pinion 9. crown wheel 10. final drive 11. sun wheel 12. planet wheel 13. half shaft 14. differential casing. **IV Steering** 1. spoke 2. column 3. damper 4. rack-andpinion 5. worm screw 6. recirculating ball 7. rod 8. stub axle 9. pins 10. track rod 11. helical sector 12. steering-box 13. adjusting screw 14. flexible coupling 15. oil 16. oil tank 17. servo-steering 18. hydraulic pump 19. pump cylinder. **V Wheels** 1. hub 2. rim 3. bolt 4 alignment 5. toe-in 6. balancing.

**Italiano**

quarta / quinta marcia 6. retromarcia 7. cambio sincronizzato 8. sincronizzatore 9. marcia non sincronizzata 10. cambio in folle 11. scatola del cambio 12. rapporto del cambio 13. ingranaggi 14. denti 15. forcella 16. molla di rimando 17. tampone di gomma 18. dadi 19. manicotto 20. olio 21. livello dell'olio 22. tappo di scarico. **III Albero di trasmissione e differenziale** 1. giunto elastico 2. giunto cardanico 3. giunto scorrevole 4. cuscinetto 5. raccordo 6. manicotto scorrevole 7. coppia conica 8. pignone 9. corona dentata 10. differenziale 11. planetari 12. satelliti 13. semiasse 14. scatola del differenziale. **IV Sterzo** 1. razza 2. piantone 3. ammortizzatore 4. cremagliera 5. vite senza fine 6. circolazione di sfere 7. tirante 8. fuso a snodo 9. perni 10. barra di accoppiamento 11. settore elicoidale 12. scatola dello sterzo 13. vite di registrazione 14. giunto elastico 15. olio 16. serbatoio dell'olio 17. servosterzo 18. pompa idraulica 19. cilindro della pompa. **V Ruote** 1. mozzo 2. cerchione 3. bullone 4. allineamento 5. convergenza 6. equilibratura.

**Français**

secondaire 5. première / seconde / troisième / quatrième / cinquième vitesse 6. marche arrière 7. changement de vitesse synchronisé 8. synchronisateur 9. vitesse non synchronisée 10. point mort 11. boîte de vitesses 12. rapport de vitesse 13. pignons 14. dents 15. fourchette 16. ressort de rappel 17. tampon de caoutchouc 18. écrous 19. manchon 20. huile 21. niveau d'huile 22. bouchon de vidange. **III Arbre de transmission et différentiel** 1. joint élastique 2. joint de cardan 3. joint coulissant 4. coussinet 5. raccord 6. manchon coulissant 7. couple conique 8. pignon 9. couronne dentée 10. différentiel 11. planétaires 12. satellites 13. demi-arbre 14. boîtier de différentiel. **IV Direction** 1. bras 2. tube de direction 3. amortisseur 4. crémaillère 5. vis sans fin 6. roulement à billes 7. tirant 8. fusée d'essieu 9. pivots 10. barre d'accouplement 11. galet hélicoïdal 12. boîtier de direction 13. vis de réglage 14. joint élastique 15. huile 16. réservoir d'huile 17. direction assistée 18. pompe hydraulique 19. cylindre de la pompe. **V Roues** 1. moyeu 2. jante 3. boulon 4. alignement 5. convergence 6. équilibrage.

| SUSPENSION AND BRAKES | SOSPENSIONI E FRENI | SUSPENSIONS ET FREINS |
|---|---|---|
| The springs are noisy. | Le balestre sono rumorose. | Les ressorts sont bruyants. |
| They need greasing / some graphite on them. | Vanno lubrificate / grafitate. | Il faut les lubrifier / les graphiter. |
| The brackets need tightening. | Occorre stringere le staffette. | Il faudrait resserrer les étriers. |
| The leafsprings are slack. They will have to be stripped down and reset. | Le balestre sono scariche. Occorre smontarle e ricaricarle. | Les ressorts sont mous. Il faut les démonter et les bander. |
| The silent block of the leafsprings has gone. | Gli spessori dei perni delle balestre sono rotti. | Les cales des pivots des ressorts sont cassées. |
| The dampers are noisy. There's not much oil. | Gli ammortizzatori sono rumorosi. C'è poco olio. | Les amortisseurs sont bruyants, ils manquent d'huile. |
| The noise is coming from the couplings. | Il rumore dipende dagli attacchi. | Le bruit vient des attaches. |
| The holding nuts are slack. | I dadi di ritegno sono allentati. | Les écrous de fixation sont desserrés. |
| The dampers are slack. But they cannot be repaired. They must be replaced. | Gli ammortizzatori sono scarichi. Ma non possono essere riparati. Vanno sostituiti. | Les amortisseurs sont déchargés, mais ils ne peuvent pas être réparés, il faut les remplacer. |
| It is dangerous to open them: the pneumatic system is by compressed nitrogen. | E' pericoloso aprirli: il sistema pneumatico è composto di azoto compresso. | Il est dangereux de les ouvrir, le système pneumatique est composé d'azote comprimé. |
| The swinging arms are very noisy. Should they be greased? | I bracci oscillanti sono molto rumorosi. Bisogna lubrificarli? | Les bras oscillants font beaucoup de bruit. Faut-il les lubrifier? |
| The longest spring has moved out of place. | Il mollone è uscito dalla sua sede. | Le ressort est sorti de son logement. |

| Deutsch | Español | Srpsko-hrvatski |
|---|---|---|
| 4. Antriebswelle / Vorlegewelle / Abtriebswelle 5. erster / zweiter / dritter / vierter / fünfter Gang 6. Rückwärtsgang 7. Synchrongetriebe 9. nicht synchronisierter Gang 10. Leergang 11. Getriebegehäuse 12. Übersetzungsverhältnis 13. Zahnräder 14. Zähne 15. Schaltgabel 16. Rückholfeder 17. Gummipuffer 18. Muttern 19. Schaltmuffe 20. Öl 21. Ölstand 22. Ölablasschraube. **III. Gelenkwelle und Ausgleichsgetriebe** 1. Keilnabengelenk 2. Kardangelenk 3. Schiebegelenk 4. Lager 5. Anschlusstück 6. Schiebemuffe 7. Kegelradtrieb 8. Antriebsritzel 9. Tellerrad 10. Ausgleichsgetriebe 11. Planetenrad 12. Ausgleichssatellit 13. Achswelle 14. Differentialgehäuse. **IV. Lenkung** 1. Lenkradspeiche 2. Lenksäule 3. Lenkungsdämpfer 4. Zahnstange 5. Lenkschnecke 6. Kugelumlauf 7. Schubstange 8. Achsschenkel 9. Lenkbolzen 10. Spurstange 11. Schnekkensegment 12. Lenkgehäuse 13. Einstellschraube 14. Federkupplung 15. Öl 16. Ölbehälter 17. Servolenkung 18. Hydraulikpumpe 19. Zylinder der Hydraulikpumpe. **V. Räder** 1. Nabe 2. Felge 3. Bolzen 4. Spur 5. Sturz 6. Auswuchten. | gunda / tercera / cuarta / quinta 6. marcha atrás 7. cambio sincronizado 8. sincronizador 9. marcha no sincronizada 10. cambio en posición neutra. 11. cárter del cambio 12. relación del cambio 13. engranajes 14. dientes 15. horquilla 16. resorte de reenvío 17. cabezal de goma 18. tuercas 19. manguito 20. aceite 21. nivel del aceite 22. tapón del vaciado. **III Arbol de transmisión y diferencial** 1. junta elástica 2. junta cardán 3. junta corrediza 4. cojinete 5. collar 6. manguito corredizo 7. par cónico 8. piñón 9. corona dentada 10. diferencial 11. planetarios 12. satélites 13. semiejes 14. cárter del diferencial. **IV Volante de dirección** 1. radio 2. barra de dirección 3. amortiguadores 4. cremallera 5. tornillo sin fin 6. circulación de bolas 7. tirante 8. fuso de torniquete 9. pernos 10. barra de acoplamiento 11. sector helicoidal 12. cárter de la dirección 13. tornillo de registro 14. acoplamiento elástico 15. aceite 16. depósito aceite 17. servoguía 18. bomba hidráulica 19. cilindro de la bomba. **V Ruedas** 1. cubo 2. llanta 3. perno 4. alineación 5. convergencia 6. calibraje. | 6. brzina unazad 7. sinhronizirani mjenjač 8. sinhronizator 9. nesinhronizirana brzina 10. mjenjač izvan brzine 11. mjenjačka kutija 12. prjenosni omjer mjenača 13. zupčanici 14. zupci 15. naglavak 20. ulje 21. razina ulja 22. čep za ispust. **III Prjenosna osovina i diferencijal** 1. elastični zglob 2. kardanski zglob 3. klizni zglob 4. ležaj 5. spoj 6. klizni naglavak 7. konični par 8. zupčanik 9. zupčasti vijenac 10. diferencial 11. planetarni zupčanici 12. sateliti 13. poluosovine 14. kućište diferencijala. **IV Upravljač** 1. žbica 2. motka upravljača 3. amortizer 4. zubna letva 5. pužni vijak 6. sferno kruženje 7. vučni elemenat 8. vreteno sa zglobom 9. klinovi 10. spojna opruga 11. spiralni sektor 12. upravljačka kutija 13. vijak za registraciju 14. elastični zglob 15. ulje 16. spremnik za ulje 17. pomoćni uredjaj za upravljanje 18. hidraulična pumpa 19. cilindar pumpe. **V Kotači** 1. glavčina 2. čelični obruč kotača 3. vijak 4. mjerenje 5. konvergencija 6. uravnoteženje. |

| AUFHÄNGUNG UND BREMSEN | SUSPENSIONES Y FRENOS | VJEŠANJE I KOČNICE |
|---|---|---|
| Die Blattfedern sind laut. | Las ballestas son ruidosas. | Lučne opruge stvaraju buku. |
| Sie müssen mit Fett / mit Graphit bestrichen werden. | Hay que lubrificarlas / grafitarlas. | Moraju se podmazati / premazati grafitom. |
| Die Federklammern müssen angezogen werden. | Es menester apretar las bridas. | Protebno je stegnuti obruče. |
| Die Blattfedern sind zu schlaff. Sie müssen ausgebaut und neu gespannt werden. | Las ballestas están descargadas. Es necesario desmontarlas y recargarlas. | Lučni nosači su omlohavljeli. Potrebno je rastaviti ih i napeti. |
| Die Scheiben der Federbolzen sind gebrochen. | Los elevadores de los pernos de las ballestas están rotos. | Umetači klinova lučnog nosača su uništeni. |
| Die Stossdämpfer sind laut. Sie sind nur ungenügend geölt. | Los amortiguadores meten ruido. Hay poco aceite. | Amortizeri stvaraju buku. Imaju malo ulja. |
| Das Geräusch kommt von den Befestigungsösen. | El ruido se debe a los anclajes. | Buka ovisi o učvršćenju. |
| Die Muttern haben sich gelockert. | Las tuercas de retención están flojas. | Pritezne matice su labave. |
| Die Stossdämpfer sind defekt. Leider können sie nicht mehr instandgesetzt und müssen daher erneuert werden. | Los amortiguadores están descargados. Pero no tienen arreglo. Hay que cambiarlos. | Amortizeri su prazni. Ne mogu se popraviti. Moraju se izmijeniti. |
| Es ist gefährlich, sie zu öffnen, denn das Luftfederungssystem enthält hochgradig verdichteten Stickstoff. | Es peligroso abrirlos: el sistema neumático está compuesto de nitrógeno comprimido. | Opasno je otvoriti ih: sistem je pneumatski, napunjen dušikom. |
| Die Schwingarme sind sehr laut. Müssen sie abgeschmiert werden? | Los brazos oscilantes meten mucho ruido. ¿Hay que lubrificarlos? | Oscilirajući krakovi stvaraju buku. Potrebno ih je podmazati? |
| Die Feder ist aus ihrem Sitz gesprungen. | El muelle se ha salido del asiento. | Opruga je iskočila iz svoga sjedišta. |

| English | Italiano | Français |
| --- | --- | --- |
| The car has lost a bump stop. A new one is necessary. | La vettura ha perso un tampone paracolpi. Ce ne vuole uno nuovo. | La voiture a perdu un tampon antichocs. Il faut en mettre un neuf. |
| The reservoir of the hydraulic suspension is leaking. | Il serbatoio della sospensione elastica perde. | Le réservoir de la suspension élastique fuit. |
| One of the plastic reservoirs of the pneumatic suspension needs to be replaced. | E' necessario sostituire uno dei serbatoi di plastica delle sospensioni pneumatiche. | Il faut changer un des réservoirs de plastique des suspensions pneumatiques. |
| There's a leak in the pipes. | C'è una perdita nella tubazione. | Il y a une fuite dans la tuyauterie. |
| Please check the play of the pedal. | Controlli, per favore, la corsa del pedale. | Pourriez-vous, je vous prie, régler la course de la pédale? |
| The brakes aren't working well. | I freni non funzionano bene. | Les freins ne fonctionnent pas bien. |
| They need adjusting / bleeding. | Bisogna registrarli / spurgarli. | Il faut les régler / les purger. |
| There isn't much brake fluid in the reservoir. | C'è poco liquido nel serbatoio dei freni. | Il n'y a pas beaucoup de liquide dans le réservoir des freins. |
| The linings are worn. | I ferodi sono consumati. | Les garnitures de freins sont usées. |
| The drums get hot. The shoes need adjusting. | I tamburi si scaldano. Bisogna registrare i perni. | Les tambours chauffent. Il faut régler les moyeux. |
| The drums have distorted. They need skimming. | I tamburi sono ovalizzati. Bisogna rettificarli. | Les tambours sont ovalisés. Il faut les rectifier |
| After the drums have been skimmed, the thickness of the linings must be increased. | Dopo la rettifica dei tamburi si dovranno maggiorare le guarnizioni. | Après la rectification des tambours, il faudra renforcer les garnitures. |
| A pipe in the circuit is leaking. | Una tubazione del circuito perde liquido. | Un tuyau du circuit de freinage fuit. |
| The three- / four-way pipe is faulty. | Il raccordo a tre / quattro vie è difettoso. | Le raccord à trois / quatre voies est défectueux. |
| It must be changed. The thread is worn. | Occorre cambiarlo. La filettatura è consumata. | Il faut le changer, le filetage est usé. |
| The red tail-lights aren't working. There must be a short circuit because the bulbs aren't fused. | Non funziona lo stop. Dev'esserci un difetto nel contatto perché le lampadine non sono fulminate. | Le stop ne marche pas. Il doit s'agir d'un défaut du contacteur, car les ampoules sont en bon état. |
| The handbrake isn't working. | Non funziona il freno a mano. | Le frein à main ne marche pas. |
| The wing-nuts / brake rods need tightening. | E' necessario stringere i galletti / i tiranti. | Il faut serrer les écrous / les tirants. |
| The pads are only a couple of millimetres thick. They must be changed. | Le pasticche hanno soltanto uno spessore di un paio di millimetri. Occorre cambiarle. | Les plaquettes n'ont que deux millimètres d'épaisseur, il faut les changer. |

**I Chassis and suspension** 1. long member 2. cross member 3. central backbone 4. leafspring 5. leaf 6. main leaf 7. bracket 8. pin 9. shackle 10. anti-roll bar 11. rubber buffers 12. damper 13. coupling 14. plunger 15. external / internal cylinder 16. inlet / compression

**I Telaio e sospensioni** 1. longherone 2. traverse 3. trave centrale 4. balestra 5. foglia 6. foglia maestra 7. staffetta 8. perno 9. biscottino 10. barra stabilizzatrice 11. tamponi di gomma 12. ammortizzatore 13. attacco 14. stantuffo 15. cilindro esterno / interno

**I Châssis et suspensions** 1. longeron 2. palonnier 3. barre centrale 4. ressort 5. lame 6. lame maîtresse 7. étrier 8. pivot 9. jumelle de ressort 10. barre stabilisatrice 11. tampons de caoutchouc 12. amortisseur 13. attache 14. piston 15. cylindre extérieur / interieur

| Deutsch | Español | Srpsko-hrvatski |
|---|---|---|
| Der Wagen hat einen Gummianschlag verloren. Es muss ein neuer eingebaut werden. | El coche ha perdido un tope parachoques. Necesita uno nuevo. | Kola su izgubila jedan čep-odbojnik. Potrebno je staviti jedan novi. |
| Ein Behälter der Federaufhängung ist durchlässig. | El depósito de la suspensión elástica pierde. | Spremnik elastičnog vješanja propušta. |
| Einer der Plastikbehälter der Luftfederung muss ausgewechselt werden. | Es necesario substituir uno de los depósitos de plástica de las suspensiones neumáticas. | Potrebno je zamijeniti jedan od plastičnih spremnika pneumatskog vješanja. |
| Die Rohrleitung muss irgendwo undicht sein. | Hay una fuga en el tubo. | Cjevovod propušta. |
| Prüfen Sie bitte den Bremspedalweg. | Controle, por favor, el recorrido del pedal. | Kontrolirajte molim hod pedala. |
| Die Bremsen funktionieren nicht ordentlich. | Los frenos no funcionan bien. | Kočnice ne funkcioniraju dobro. |
| Sie müssen nachgestellt / entlüftet werden. | Hay que reajustarlos / purgarlos. | Potrebno ih je registrirati / očistiti. |
| Im Bremsflüssigkeitsbehälter ist nur wenig Flüssigkeit. | Hay poco líquido en el depósito de los frenos. | U spremniku ima premalo tekućine za kočenje. |
| Die Beläge sind abgenutzt. | Los ferodos están gastados. | Ferode su istrošene. |
| Die Bremstrommeln erhitzen sich zu stark. Die Bolzen müssen angezogen werden. | Los tambores se calientan. Habrá que reajustar los frenos. | Bubnjevi se pregrijavaju. Potrebno je registrirati osovine. |
| Die Trommeln sind unrund geworden und müssen geschliffen werden. | Los tambores están ovalados. Hay que rectificarlos. | Bubnjevi su ovalni. Potrebno ih je nanovo obraditi. |
| Nach dem Schleifen der Trommeln müssen die Beläge erneuert werden. | Después de la rectificación de los tambores, habrá que agrandar las guarniciones. | Poslije obrade bubnjeva potrebno je povećati brtve. |
| Eine Bremsleitung lässt Flüssigkeit durch. | Uno de los tubos del circuito de los frenos pierde líquido. | Jedan cjevovod sistema propušta tekućinu. |
| Die Dreiweg- / Vierwegverschraubung ist schadhaft. | El enchufe de tres / cuatro caños está deteriorado | Trostruka / četverostruka spojnica je neispravna. |
| Sie muss ausgewechselt werden. Das Gewinde ist verschlissen | Hay que cambiarlo. El fileteado está gastado. | Potrebno ju je zamijeniti. Navoj je istrošen. |
| Das Bremslicht funktioniert nicht. Mit dem Kontakt muss etwas nicht in Ordnung sein, denn die Birnen sind nicht durchgebrannt. | No funciona el « stop ». Debe de haber un defecto en el contacto, porque las bombillas no están fundidas. | Stop svjetlo je neispravno. Kvar mora biti u kontaktima, jer žarulje nisu pregorjele. |
| Die Handbremse funktioniert nicht. | El freno de mano no funciona. | Ručna kočnica je neispravna. |
| Die Nachstellmuttern / die Bremsstangen müssen angezogen werden. | Es necesario apretar las charnelas / los tirantes. | Potrebno je stegnuti matice / vučne elemente. |
| Die Beläge sind nur noch zwei / drei Millimeter stark. Sie müssen erneuert werden. | Las pastillas tienen solamente un par de milímetros de espesor. Hay que cambiarlas. | Pastile imaju debljinu od samo nekoliko milimetara. Potrebno ih je izmijeniti. |

**I. Fahrwerk und Aufhängung** 1. Längsträger 2. Querträger 3. Mittelrohr 4. Blattfeder 5. Federblatt 6. Hauptblatt 7. Federbügel 8. Bolzen 9. Federlasche 10. Stabilisator 11. Gummipuffer 12. Stossdämpfer 13. Befestigungsöse 14. Kolben 15. äussere Hülse / inneres Rohr

**I Chasis y suspensiones** 1. larguero 2. travesaño 3. viga central 4. ballesta 5. hoja 6. hoja maestra 7. brida 8. perno 9. gemela 10. barra estabilizadora 11. tope de goma 12. amortiguador 13. anclaje 14. émbolo 15. cilindro exterior / interior 16. válvula de aspiración

**I Okvir i vješanje** 1. uzdužni nosač 2. nosači 3. centralni nosač 4. lučna opruga 5. list opruge 6. noseći list opruge 7. obruč 8. klin 9. nosač lučne opruge 10. stabilizirajuća traka 11. gumeni odbojnici 12. amortizer 13. spojnica 14. klip 15. cilindar vanjski / unutrašnji 16. usis-

**English**

valve 17. gasket 18. liquid 19. independent suspension 20. upper / lower swinging arms 21. coil spring 22. lubrication 23. pressure greaser. **II Brakes** 1. brake pedal 2. play of pedal 3. drum brakes 4. disc brakes 5. pads 6. linings 7. release spring 8. linings 9. shoes 10. two leading shoes 11. upper / lower toggle 12. pin 13. brake adjusters 14. adjustable brake rod 15. cooling fin 16. hydraulic brakes 17. tank 18. pump 19. pipes 20. bracket 21. circuit 22. three / four-way pipe 23. cylinders 24. plunger 25. adjusting screw 26. bleeder screw 27. release spring 28. servo-brake 29. pneumatic pump 30. hydraulic pump 31. hand brake 32. wing nuts 33. pull rods.

**Italiano**

16. valvola di aspirazione / compressione 17. guarnizione 18. liquido 19. sospensioni a ruote indipendenti 20. braccio oscillante inferiore / superiore 21. molla elicoidale 22. lubrificazione 23. ingrassatore a pressione. **II Freni** 1. pedale del freno 2. corsa del pedale 3. freni a tamburo 4. freni a disco 5. pasticche 6. guarnizioni 7. molla di richiamo 8. ferodo 9. ganasce 10. ganasce autofrenanti 11. eccentrico superiore / inferiore 12. perno 13. perni di registrazione 14. tirante di registro 15. alette di raffreddamento 16. freni idraulici 17. serbatoio 18. pompa comando 19. tubazione 20. staffetta 21. circuito 22. raccordo a tre / quattro vie 23. cilindretti 24. stantuffo 25. vite di registro 26. vite spurgo aria 27. molla di richiamo 28. servo-freno 29. pompa pneumatica 30. pompa idraulica 31. freno a mano 32. galletti 33. tiranti.

**Français**

16. soupape d'aspiration / de compression 17. garniture 18. liquide 19. suspensions à roues indépendantes 20. bras oscillant inférieur / supérieur 21. ressort hélicoïdal 22. lubrification 23. graisseur à pression. **II Freins** 1. pédale du frein 2. course de la pédale 3. freins à tambour 4. freins à disque 5. plaquettes 6. garnitures 7. ressort de rappel 8. férodo 9. mâchoires 10. mâchoires de freinage automatique 11. excentrique supérieur / inférieur 12. pivot 13. pivots de réglage 14. tirant de réglage 15. volets de refroidissement 16. freins hydrauliques 17. réservoir 18. pompe de commande 19. tuyauterie 20. étrier 21. circuit 22. raccord à trois / quatre voies 23. petits cylindres 24. piston 25. vis de réglage 26. vis de purge d'air 27. ressort de rappel 28. servo-frein 29. pompe pneumatique 30. pompe hydraulique 31. frein à main 32. écrous 33. tirants.

| COACHWORK | CARROZZERIA | CARROSSERIE |
|---|---|---|
| Can you give me an estimate for re-spraying this door? I should like to know if it's possible to get exactly the same colour blue / charcoal / light grey / dark grey. | Può farmi un preventivo per riverniciare questo sportello? Vorrei sapere se è possibile riprendere esattamente il coloro blu / antracite / grigio chiaro / grigio scuro. | Pourriez-vous m'établir un devis pour la réfection de la peinture de cette portière? Peut-on retrouver la couleur exacte, bleu / gris anthracite / gris clair / gris foncé? |
| I should like to have the whole front / rear / right / left wing repaired. | Vorrei rimettere a posto tutto il parafango anteriore / posteriore / destro / sinistro. | Je voudrais faire remettre en état tout le garde-boue antérieur / postérieur / droit / gauche. |
| Is it enough to re-spray just one part? | Basta verniciare solo una parte? | Peut-on ne repeindre qu'une partie? |
| It isn't possible. It's a metallized paint which is difficult to match. | Non è possibile, si tratta di una ver nice metallizzata, difficile da accompagnare. | Ce n'est pas possible, cette peinture métallisée est très difficile à réassortir. |
| How long will it take? | Quanto tempo ci vorrà? | Combien de temps faudra-t-il? |
| Two or three days. It's necessary to hammer out the plate, wait until the stopper dries and then spray it. | Due o tre giorni. Bisogna ribattere la lamiera, attendere che si asciughi lo stucco e poi fare la verniciatura a spruzzo. | Deux ou trois jours. Il faut marteler la tôle, laisser sécher le mastic, puis peindre au pistolet. |
| Can I use the car in the meantime? | Potrei usare la vettura nel frattempo? | Est-ce que je peux utiliser la voiture entre temps? |
| Yes, but you'll have to call in every day to have the fresh coats of stopper applied. | Sí, però dovrà passare ogni giorno per far applicare le nuove mani di stucco. | Oui, mais il faudra passer ici tous les jours pour vous faire mettre une nouvelle couche de mastic. |
| Is it a job that takes a very long time? | E' un lavoro che richiede molto tempo? | Est-ce une opération longue? |
| No, not more than ten minutes | No, bastano dieci minuti. | Non, environ dix minutes. |
| Won't the paint you use change colour with time? | La vernice che lei usa, con il tempo, non cambierà colore? | La peinture que vous employez ne risque pas de virer à la longue? |

16. Saugventil / Verdichtungsventil 17. Dichtung 18. Flüssigkeit 19. Einzelradaufhängung 20. unterer / oberer Schwingarm 21. Schraubenfeder 22. Schmierung 23. Druckschmierkopf. **II. Bremsen** 1. Bremspedal 2. Bremsweg 3. Trommelbremsen 4. Scheibenbremsen 5. Bremsbeläge der Scheibenbremse 6. Bremsbeläge 7. Rückzugfeder 8. Bremsbeläge 9. Bremsbacken 10. selbsttätige Backen 11. obere / untere Nocke 12. Bolzen 13. Nachstellbolzen 14. Nachstellzugstange 15. Kühlrippen 16. hydraulische Bremsen 17. Behälter 18. Hauptbremszylinder 19. Leitung 20. Bügel 21. Bremskreis 22. Dreiweg- / Vierwegverschraubung 23. Bremszylinder 24. Bremskolben 25. Nachstellschraube 26. Luftablasschraube 27. Rückzugfeder 28. Servobremse 29. pneumatisch betätigte Pumpe 30. Hydraulikpumpe 31. Handbremse 32. Nachstellmuttern 33. Seilzüge.

/ compresión 17. junta 18. líquido 19. suspensión de ruedas independientes 20. brazo oscilante inferior / superior 21. resorte helicoidal 22. lubrificación 23. engrasador de presión. **II Frenos** 1. pedal del freno 2. recorrido del pedal 3. frenos de tambor 4. frenos de disco 5. pastillas 6. juntas 7. resorte de retracción 8. ferodo 9. mordaza 10. mordazas autofrenantes 11. excéntrica superior / inferior 12. perno 13. pivote de ajuste 14. tirante de ajuste 15. aletas de refrigeración 16. frenos hidráulicos 17. depósito 18. bomba 19. tubo 20. brida 21. circuito 22. enchufe de tres / cuatro caños 24. émbolo 25. tornillo de regulación 26. tornillo de purga de aire 27. muelle de retracción 28. servofreno 29. bomba neumática 30. bomba hidráulica 31. freno de mano 32. charnelas 33. tirantes.

ni ventil / kompresioni 17. brtva 18. tekučina 19. vješanje sa neovisnim kotačima 20. oscilirajuči krak donji /gornji 21. spiralna opruga 22. podmazivanje 23. mazalica na pritisak. **II Kočnice** 1. pedala kočnice 2. hod pedala 3. bubanj kočnice 4. disk kočnice 5. pastile 6. brtve 7. povratna opruga 8. feroda 9. čeljusti 10. samokočeće čeljusti 11. ekscentar gorni / donji 12. klin 13. klin za registraciju 14. vučni elemenat registracije 15. rashladna rebra 16. hidrauličke kočnice 17. spremnik 18. kočnička pumpa 19. cjevovodi 20. obruč 21. circulacija 22. trostruka / četverostruka spojnica 23. cilindri 24. klip 25. vijak za registraciju 26. vijak za ispust zraka 27. povratna opruga 28. pomočni uredjaj za kočenje 29. pneumatska pumpa 30. hidraulična pumpa 31. ručna kočnica 32. krilaste matice 33. vučni elementi.

## KAROSSERIE / CARROCERIA / KAROSERIJA

Könnten Sie mir einen Kostenvoranschlag für die Lackierung dieser Tür machen? Liesse sich der gleiche anthrazitfarbene / hellgraue / dunkelgraue Farbton erreichen?

¿Puede hacerme el presupuesto para pintar esta portezuela? Quisiera saber si es posible darle exactamente el mismo color azul / antracita / gris claro / gris obscuro.

Možete li mi napraviti predračun za lakiranje ovih vrata? Želio bih znati, da li je moguće točno pogoditi ton plave boje / antracit / svijetlo sive / tamno sive.

Ich möchte den ganzen vorderen / hinteren / rechten / linken Kotflügel neu spritzen lassen.

Quisiera que me arreglara todo el guardabarros delantero / trasero / derecho / izquierdo.

Želio bih popraviti blatobran prednji / stražnji / desni / lijevi.

Genügt es, wenn nur ein Teil lackiert wird?

¿Es suficiente pintar sólo una parte?

Dovoljno je lakirati samo jednu stranu.

Das ist leider nicht möglich; es handelt sich um einen Metalleffekt-Lack, der sich nur schwer beilackieren lässt.

No es posible, porque se trata de pintura metalizada difícil de dar.

Nemoguće je, jer se radi o metaliziranom laku, ćiji je ton teško pogoditi.

Wieviel Zeit benötigen Sie für die Arbeit?

¿Cuánto tiempo se necesita?

Koliko vremena će iziskivati?

Zwei oder drei Tage. Das Blech muss zuerst ausgehämmert und gespachtelt werden. Dann muss der Spachtelkitt trocknen und erst dann kann gespritzt werden.

Dos o tres días. Hay que desabollar bien la chapa, esperar a que se seque el estuco y luego pintarla a pistola.

Dva ili tri dana. Potrebno je ispraviti lim, sačekati dok se osuši štuko, i zatim lakirati sa štrcaljkom.

Könnte ich den Wagen zwischendurch benutzen?

¿Puedo, entretanto, utilizar el coche?

Da li bih mogao u medjuvremenu upotrebljavati kola?

Ja, aber Sie müssten jeden Tag vorbeikommen, damit wir jedesmal eine neue Schicht Spachtelkitt auftragen können.

Sí, pero deberá pasar por aquí todos los días para dar las otras manos de estuco.

Da, ali ćete morati navratiti svaki dan, da bi se nanio novi sloj štuka.

Erfordert das viel Zeit?

¿Esta operación exige mucho tiempo?

Da li je to posao, koji iziskuje mnogo vremena?.

Nein, zehn Minuten reichen.

No, bastarán diez minutos.

Ne, dovoljno je deset minuta.

Wird der Lack, den Sie benutzen, mit der Zeit nicht die Farbe wechseln?

¿La pintura que Vd. emplea, con el tiempo, mudará de color?

Neće li lak, koji vi upotrebljavate, vremenom promijeniti boju?

| English | Italiano | Français |
|---|---|---|
| It's the same type as the makers use. | E' dello stesso tipo usato dalla casa costruttrice. | C'est la même qualité de peinture qu'utilise le constructeur. |
| The paintwork will be like new again after a coat of polishing paste and wax. | La verniciatura può tornare come nuova con una mano di pasta abrasiva e con cera lucidante. | Avec une couche d'abrasif et un peu de cire lustrante, la peinture sera comme neuve. |
| I should like to have the radiator shield hammered out. | Vorrei far ribattere lo scudo del radiatore. | Je voudrais faire redresser l'écusson du radiateur. |
| Very well. But it will have to be replated as well. | D'accordo. Però bisognerà anche cromarlo di nuovo. | Bien Monsieur, mais il faudra aussi le rechromer. |
| Is it possible to hammer out and replate the rear bumper? | E' possibile ribattere e cromare il paraurti anteriore? | Peut-on marteler et chromer le pare-chocs avant? |
| It isn't advisable. I advise you to have a new bumper. | Non le conviene, le consiglio di far montare un paraurti nuovo. | Je ne vous le conseille pas, faites plutôt monter un pare-chocs neuf. |
| Can you repair this lock? I can't close the door. | Può riparare questa serratura? Non riesco a chiudere la portiera. | Pourriez-vous me réparer cette serrure? Je n'arrive pas à fermer la portière. |
| The hinges must be replaced. They are badly warped. | E' necessario sostituire le cerniere. Si sono molto deformate. | Il faudrait remplacer les charnières, elles sont très déformées. |
| Is it possible to repair the window winding mechanism? | E' possibile riparare la macchinetta alzavetro? | Pouvez-vous réparer le mécanisme du lève-glaces? |
| Is it possible to find a windscreen the right size? | E' possibile trovare un parabrezza a misura? | Peut-on trouver un pare-brise de la mesure exacte? |
| Could you mount a pair of fog lamps? | Potrebbe montare un paio di fari antinebbia? | Pourriez-vous m'installer une paire de phares anti-brouillard? |
| The driving seat keeps on shifting. Can you fix it? | Il sedile di guida si sposta continuamente. Può sistemarlo? | Le siège du conducteur se déplace continuellement, pouvez-vous le fixer? |
| Yes. One of the holding screws has simply come unscrewed. | Sí. Si è semplicemente sfilata una delle viti di ritegno. | Oui, c'est seulement une vis de fixation qui s'est desserrée. |
| The lock of the boot / of the bonnet / of the petrol cap is broken. | Si è rotta la serratura del portabagagli / del cofano / del tappo benzina. | La serrure du porte-bagages / du coffre / du bouchon de l'essence est cassée. |
| Can you replace the rubber strip on the window? | Può sostituire la guarnizione di gomma del finestrino? | Pourriez-vous remplacer la garniture de caoutchouc de la fenêtre? |
| The pull wire that opens the bonnet has snapped. Have you got another that's suitable? | Si è spezzato il tirante che apre il cofano. Non ne ha un altro adatto? | La tirette qui ouvre le coffre est cassée, en auriez-vous une autre? |

**I Exterior** 1. front / rear / right / left door 2. handle 3. lock 4. key 5. duplicate key 6. hinge 7. window panes 8. air-deflectors 9. rubber strips 10. frame 11. windscreen 12. safety glass 13. laminated glass 14. bonnet 15. bonnet hood 16. radiator 17. mask 18. front / rear wing 19. front / rear bumper 20. protuberance 21. rubber-covered protuberance 22. boot lid 23. pull-wire 24. number plate 25. roof 26. hood 27. hard top 28. rear window 29. petrol cap 30. rear mirror 31. mouldings 32. hub-cap. **II Interior**

**I Parti esterne** 1. porta anteriore / posteriore / destra / sinistra 2. maniglia 3. serratura 4. chiave 5. duplicato della chiave 6. cerniera 7. cristalli 8. deflettori 9. guarnizioni 10. cornice 11. parabrezza 12. vetro di sicurezza 13. vetro accoppiato 14. cofano 15. coperchio del cofano 16. radiatore 17. mascherina 18. parafango anteriore / posteriore 19. paraurti anteriore / posteriore 20. rostro 21. rostro gommato 22. coperchio portabagagli 23. tirante 24. targa 25. tetto 26. cappotta 27. tetto

**I Parties extérieures** 1. portière antérieure / postérieure / droite / gauche 2. poignée 3. serrure 4. clef 5. double de la clef 6. charnière 7. vitres 8. déflecteurs 9. garnitures 10. entourage de glaces 11. pare-brise 12. glaces de sécurité 13. verres doubles 14. coffre 15. porte du coffre 16. radiateur 17. calandre 18. garde-boue antérieur / postérieur 19. pare-chocs antérieur / postérieur 20. butoir de pare-choc 21. butoir caoutchouté 22. couvercle du porte-bagages 23. tirette 24. plaque 25. toit 26. capote

| Deutsch | Español | Srpsko-hrvatski |
|---|---|---|
| Es ist der gleiche Lack, den die Baufirma benutzt. | Es del mismo tipo empleado por la Casa constructora. | To je isti lak, koji upotrebljava tvornica automobila. |
| Mit etwas Schleifpaste und einem Poliermittel kann die Lackierung wieder wie neu werden. | La pintura puede quedar como nueva, dándole una mano de pasta abrasiva y de cera brillante. | Lak može postati kao nov, upotrebivši brusnu pastu i vosak za poliranje. |
| Ich möchte die Kühlerverkleidung richten lassen. | Quisiera enderezar la máscara del radiador. | Želio bih ispraviti zaštitnik hladnjaka. |
| Gern, aber dann müsste sie auch neu verchromt werden. | De acuerdo, pero habrá que cromarlo de nuevo. | U redu. No, treba ga takodjer nanovo kromirati. |
| Wäre es möglich, die vordere Stossstange zu richten und zu verchromen? | ¿Puede enderezar y cromar el parachoques delantero? | Da li je moguće ispraviti i kromirati prednji odbojnik? |
| Das lohnt sich nicht. Ich würde Ihnen raten, eine neue Stosstange montieren zu lassen. | No le conviene, le aconsejo montar un parachoques nuevo. | Ne isplati se; preporučam vam, da montirate jedan novi odbojnik. |
| Könnten Sie bitte dieses Schloss reparieren? Die Tür schliesst nicht mehr. | ¿Puede arreglar esta cerradura? No logro cerrar la portezuela. | Možete li popraviti ovu bravu? Ne mogu zatvoriti vrata. |
| Die Scharniere müssen ausgewechselt werden, denn sie sind stark verzogen. | Es necesario cambiar las bisagras. Están muy defectuosas. | Potrebno je zamijeniti šarke. Jako su deformirane. |
| Wäre es möglich, den Fensterheber zu reparieren? | ¿Es posible arreglar el dispositivo de bajar y subir los cristales? | Da li je moguće popraviti uredjaj za podizanje stakla? |
| Könnten Sie mir eine passende Windschutzscheibe besorgen? | ¿Es posible encontrar un parabrisas de este tamaño? | Da li je moguće naći jedno prednje staklo po mjeri? |
| Könnten Sie bitte zwei Nebelscheinwerfer montieren? | ¿Puede montar un par de faros contra la niebla? | Možete li mi montirati dva fara protiv magle? |
| Der Fahrersitz verschiebt sich ständig. Könnten Sie ihn bitte in Ordnung bringen? | El asiento de guía se desplaza continuamente. ¿Puede arreglarlo? | Vozačevo sjedalo se stalno pomiče. Možete li ga popraviti? |
| Ja, es hat sich lediglich eine der Nocken für die Sitzverstellung gelöst. | Sí. Simplemente se ha destornillado uno de los tornillos de retención. | Da. Odvrnuo se je samo vijak za pritezanje |
| Das Kofferraumschloss / Motorhaubenschloss / der Tankverschluss ist schadhaft. | Se ha roto la cerradura del departamento equipajes / del departamento del motor / del tapón del depósito del carburante. | Pokvarila se je brava prtljažnog prostora / motornog prostora / poklopca za benzin. |
| Könnten Sie bitte die Gummidichtung des Fensters erneuern? | ¿Puede cambiar la guarnición de goma de la ventanilla? | Možete li mi zamijeniti gumenu brtvu prozora? |
| Die Betätigungsstange, die zur Öffnung der Motorhaube dient, ist gebrochen. Haben Sie eine neue, die geeignet wäre? | El tirante de mando de la apertura del capó se ha roto. ¿Tiene Vd. otro nuevo? | Polomio se je vučni elemenat za otvaranje motornog prostora. Imate li jedan odgovarajući? |

**I. Aussenteile** 1. vordere / hintere / rechte / linke Tür 2. Türgriff 3. Türschloss 4. Schlüssel 5. Reserveschlüssel 6. Scharnier 7. Fensterscheiben 8. Ausstellfenster 9. Fensterdichtungen 10. Scheibenfassung 11. Windschutzscheibe 12. Sicherheitsglas 13. Verbundglas 14. Motorabdeckung 15. Motorhaube 16. Kühler 17. Kühlermaske 18. vorderer / hinterer Kotflügel 19. vordere / hintere Stosstange 20. Stosstangenhorn 21. Stosstangenhorn mit Gummipuffer 22. Kofferraumdeckel 23. Betätigungsstange

**I Partes externas** 1. puerta anterior / posterior / derecha / izquierda 2. manillas 3. cerradura 4. llave 5. llave de reserva 6. bisagra 7. cristales 8. deflectores 9. guarniciones 10. marco 11. parabrisas 12. cristal de seguridad 13. cristal acoplado 14. capó 15. funda del capó 16. radiador 17. máscara 18. parabarros anterior / posterior 19. parachoques anterior / posterior 20. espolón 21. espolones de goma 22 tapa del portaequipajes 23. tirante 24. matrícula 25. techo 26. capota 27. techo fijo 28. luneta

**I Vanjska vrata** 1. prednja vrata / stražnja / desna / lijeva 2. ručka 3. brava 4. ključ 5. duplikat ključa 6. šarka 7. stakla 8. prednja mala stakla 9. brtve 10. okvir 11. prednje staklo 12. sigurnosno staklo 13. udvojena stakla 14. motorni prostor 15. poklopac motornog prostora 16. hladnjak 17. maska 18. blatobran prednji / stražnji 19. odbojnik prednji / stražnji 20. brk odbojnoka 21. gumeni brk odbojnika 22. poklopac prtljažnog prostora 23. vučni elemenat 24. registarska tabla 25. krov 26. platneni krov

**English** | **Italiano** | **Français**

1. right / left front seat 2. reclinable / adjustable squabs 3. front / rear seat 4. control for distance of / tilt of seats 5. arm 6. rubber mats 7. window handle 8. door handle 9. air-deflector lock 10. safety lock 11. facia 12. ashtray 13. locker 14. locker lock 15. sun visor 16. rear mirror 17. safety belts 18. fittings. **III Repairs** 1. hammering out 2. stopping 3. spraying 4. polishing 5. touching up 6. polishing paste 7. paint 8. polishing wax 9. chromium plating 10. nickle plating. **IV Colours** 1. beige 2. sand 3. white 4. yellow 5. orange 6. rust 7. red 8. magenta 9. black 10. light / dark grey 11. charcoal 12. sky-blue 13. dark blue 14. gun-metal 15. green.

rigido 28. lunotto posteriore 29. tappo benzina 30. specchio retrovisore 31. fregi 32. copriruota. **II Parti interne** 1. sedile anteriore destro / sinistro 2. schienale ribaltabile / regolabile 3. divano anteriore / posteriore 4. comando distanza / inclinazione sedili 5. bracciolo 6. tappetini di gomma 7. manovella alzavetro 8. maniglia 9. fermo del deflettore 10. sicura delle porte 11. cruscotto 12. portacenere 13. portaoggetti 14. serratura vano portaoggetti 15. parasole 16. specchio retrovisore 17. cinture di sicurezza 18. attacco. **III Riparazioni** 1. ribattitura 2. stuccatura 3. verniciatura 4. lucidatura 5. ritocco 6. pasta abrasiva 7. vernice 8. cera lucidante 9. cromatura 10. nichelatura. **IV Colori** 1. beige 2. sabbia 3. bianco 4. giallo 5. arancione 6. ruggine 7. rosso 8. amaranto 9. nero 10. grigio chiaro / scuro 11. antracite 12. celeste 13. blu 14. metallizzato argento 15. verde.

27. hard-top 28. lunette arrière 29. bouchon d'essence 30. rétroviseur 31. ornement 32. enjoliveur de roue. **II Parties intérieures** 1. siège antérieur droit / gauche. 2. dossier abaissable / réglable 3. banquette avant / arrière 4. commande de l'éloignement / de l'inclination des sièges 5. accoudoir 6. tapis de caoutchouc 7. manivelle lève-glaces 8. poignée 9. arrêtoir du déflecteur 10. cran de sûreté des portières 11. tableau de bord 12. cendrier 13. vide-poches 14. serrure du vide-poches 15. pare-soleil 16. rétroviseur 17. ceintures de sûreté 18. attache. **III Réparations** 1. martelage 2. mastiquage 3. vernissage 4. lustrage 5. retouche 6. pâte abrasive 7. peinture 8. cire de lustrage 9. chromage 10. nickelage. **IV Couleurs** 1. beige 2. sable 3. blanc 4. jaune 5. orange 6. rouille 7. rouge 8. amarante 9. noir 10. gris clair / foncé 11. anthracite 12. bleu ciel 13. bleu 14. argent métallisé 15. vert.

## TYRES | GOMME | PNEUS

| English | Italiano | Français |
|---|---|---|
| I have a flat tyre. | Ho una gomma bucata. | J'ai un pneu crevé. |
| Shall we repair it or give you a new inner tube? | La vulcanizziamo o sostituiamo la camera d'aria? | Voulez-vous le faire vulcaniser ou changer la chambre à air? |
| This is a tubeless tyre. To repair it you only need to put a rubber plug in where it's punctured. | Questo pneumatico è del tipo senza camera d'aria. Per ripararlo basta applicare un tappo di gomma nel punto della foratura. | C'est un pneu du type sans chambre à air. Il suffit, pour le réparer, de mettre un bouchon de caoutchouc à l'endroit du trou. |
| I need a new tyre. | Ho bisogno di una gomma nuova. | J'ai besoin d'un pneu neuf. |
| What type, would you like? What ply? Four or six? | Che tipo desidera? A quante tele? A quattro o a sei? | Quel type de pneu désirez-vous? A combien de toiles, quatre ou six? |
| Please change round the position of the wheels. Put the spare wheel in the place of the one at the left in front. | Inverta, per favore, la posizione delle ruote. Monti la ruoti di scorta al posto di quella anteriore sinistra. | Voudriez-vous, s'il vous plaît, intervertir la position des roues, en montant la roue de secours à la place de la roue antérieure gauche. |
| These tyres have been kept too hard. They are worn at the centre. | Queste gomme sono state tenute troppo gonfie. Sono consumate al centro. | Ces pneus ont roulé à une pression élevée, ils sont usés au centre. |
| These tyres have been kept too slack. They are worn at the sides. | Queste gomme sono state tenute poco gonfie. Sono consumate ai lati. | Ces pneus ont roulé à basse pression, ils sont usés sur les côtés. |
| The tyre has a ply cut. It is cut on the sidewall. | Il copertone ha la tela rotta. E' tagliato sul fianco. | La toile est détériorée et coupée sur les côtés. |
| Until you change it, I advise you to drive slowly. | Finché non lo cambia le consiglio di andare piano. | Tant que vous ne l'aurez pas changé, je vous conseille d'aller doucement. |
| Can you do something for it until I find another? | Ma si può fare qualche cosa prima che ne trovi un altro? | Y a-t-il quelque chose à faire en attendant d'en trouver un autre? |
| Yes. I will stick a re-inforcement over the cut | Sí. Applicherò un rinforzo in corrispondenza del taglio. | Oui, je mettrai un emplâtre sur la coupure. |

**Deutsch**

24. Kennzeichenschild 25. Dach 26. Klappverdeck 27. Hardtop 28. Heckscheibe 29. Kraftstoffbehälterverschluss 30. Aussenspiegel 31. Zierleiste 32. Radkappe. **II. Innenteile** 1. rechter / linker Vordersitz 2. umlegbare / verstellbare Lehne 3. vordere / hintere Sitzbank 4. Sitzverstellung / Lehnenverstellung 5. Armlehne 6. Gummimatten 7. Fensterkurbel 8. Griff 9. Sperrhacken des Ausstellfensters 10. Türsicherungsstift 11. Armaturenbrett 12. Aschenbecher 13. Handschuhkasten 14. Handschuhkastenschloss 15. Sonnenblende 16. Rückspiegel 17. Sicherheitsgurt 18. Befestigungsvorrichtung. **III. Reparaturen** 1. richten 2. spachteln 3. lackieren 4 polieren 5. retuschieren 6. Schleifpaste 7. Lack 8. Poliermittel 9. Verchromung 10. Vernickelung. **IV. Farben** 1. beige 2. sandfarben 3. weiss 4. gelb 5. orangefarben 6. rostbraun 7. rot 8. amarantrot 9. schwarz 10. hellgrau / dunkelgrau 11. anthrazit 12. hellblau 13. dunkelblau 14. metallic-silbergrau 15. grün.

**Español**

posterior 29. tapón depósito gasolina 30. espejo retrovisor 31. adornos 32. cubreruedas. **II Partes internas** 1. asiento anterior derecho / izquierdo 2. respaldo basculante / regulable 3. diván anterior / posterior 4. mando distancia / inclinación asientos 5. apoyabrazos 6. alfombrillas de goma 7. manivela de subir y bajar los cristales 8. manilla 9. retén del deflector 10. seguro de las portezuelas 11. tablero 12. cenicero 13. cajoncito 14. cerradura del cajoncito 15. quitasol 16. retrovisor 17. cinturón de seguridad 18. anclajes. **III Reparaciones** 1. enderezado 2. estucado 3. pintado 4. pulimento 5. retoque 6. pasta abrasiva 7. pintura 8. cera de pulimento 9. pintura al cromo 10. niquelado. **IV Colores** 1. beige 2. arena 3. blanco 4. amarillo 5. anaranjado 6. ocín 7. rojo 8. amaranto 9. negro 10. gris claro / obscuro 11. antracita 12. celeste 13. azul 14. plata metalizada 15. verde.

**Srpsko-hrvatski**

27. kruti montažni krov 28. stražnja svjetiljka 29. poklopac spremnika 30. ogledalo 31. ukrasni elementi 32. ukrasni poklopac kotača. **II Unutrašnji dijelovi** 1. prednje sjedalo desno / lijevo 2. naslon sa promjenljivim nagibom / regulirajući 3. klupa prednja / stražnja 4. ručica za horizontalni posmak / za nagib sjedala 5. naslon za ruku 6. gumeni prostirači 7. ručica podizača stakla 8. ručka 9. brava prednjeg malog prozorčića 10. osigurač vrata 11. tabla s instrumentima 12. pepeljara 13. prostor za rukavice 14. brava prostora za rukavice 15. sunčani štitnik 16. ogledalo 17. sigurnosni remeni 18. spoj. **III Popravci** 1. ispravljanje lima 2. štukanje 3. lakiranje 4. poliranje 5. dotjerivanje 6. brusna pasta 7. lak 8. vosak za poliranje 9. kromiranje 10. niklanje. **IV Boje** 1. bež 2. pješćana 3. bijela 4. žuta 5. narančasta 6. rdja 7. crvena 8. 9. crna 10. siva svijetla / tamna 11. antracit 12. nebesko plava 13. plava 14. srebreno metalizirana 15. zelena.

| BEREIFUNG | NEUMATICOS | GUME |
|---|---|---|
| Ich habe eine Reifenpanne. | Tengo un neumático pinchado. | Imam jednu izbušenu **gumu.** |
| Sollen wir den Reifen vulkanisieren oder den Schlauch erneuern? | ¿Lo vulcanizamos o prefiere cambiar la cámara de aire? | Hoćemo li je vulkanizirati ili ćemo zamijeniti zračnicu? |
| Es ist ein schlauchloser Luftreifen. Er kann durch Einführung eines Gummi-Pilzes an der schadhaften Stelle ausgebessert werden. | Este neumático es de tipo sin cámara. Para arreglarlo es suficient aplicar un tapón de goma en el agujero. | Ovo je vrsta gume bez zračnice. Za popravak je dovoljno namjestiti jedan gumeni ćep na mjesto gdje je probušena. |
| Ich brauche einen neuen Reifen. | Necesito un neumático nuevo. | Želim jednu novu gumu. |
| Welche Art von Reifen wünschen Sie? Mit wieviel Leinwandeinlagen? Vier oder sechs? | ¿Qué tipo prefiere? ¿De cuántas telas? ¿De cuatro o de seis? | Koji tip želite? Sa koliko slojeva platna? Sa četiri ili sa šest? |
| Tauschen Sie bitte die Räder aus. Montieren Sie das Reserverad an die Stelle des linken Vorderrades. | Invierta por favor la posición de las ruedas. Monte la rueda de recambio en lugar de la anterior izquierda. | Izmijenite mi položaj kotača. Montirajte rezervni kotač na mjesto prednjeg lijevog. |
| Diese Reifen sind mit Überdruck gelaufen. Sie sind in der Mitte abgenutzt. | Estos neumaticos han trabajado a presión alta; están gastados en la parte central. | Ove gume su bile pod previsokim pritiskom. Istrošene su u centru. |
| Diese Reifen sind mit zu niedrigem Druck gelaufen. Sie sind an den Wänden abgenutzt. | Estos neumáticos han trabajado a presión baja. Están gastados por los lados. | Ove gume su bile pod preniskim pritiskom. Istrošene su na bokovima. |
| Die Lauffläche ist rissig. Die Wand hat einen Einschnitt. | La cubierta tiene la tela rota. Tiene un corte en un lado. | Vanjska guma ima pokidano platno. Prerezano je na boku. |
| Solange Sie den Reifen nicht auswechseln, würde ich Ihnen raten, langsam zu fahren. | Mientras no la cambie, le aconsejo que vaya despacio. | Dok je ne izmijenite, preporučam vam da vozite polako. |
| Aber kann man nicht irgendetwas unternehmen, bis ich einen neuen gefunden habe? | ¿Puede hacer algún arreglo, mientras compro otra? | Da li se može učiniti nešto, prije nego nadjem jednu novu? |
| Doch. Ich werde an der schadhaften Stelle eine Verstärkung unterlegen. | Sí. Le aplicaré un parche coincidiendo con el corte. | Da. Namjestiti ću jedno pojačanje na mjestu reza. |

## English

I should like to check the tyre pressure.

Can you help me to put the chains on?

I need two ice-tyres, the ones with spikes.

The rim is dented. Can you straighten it?

I have lost a hub cap. Have you got one of the same type?

**I Parts and characteristics** 1. tread 2. sidewall 3. shoulder 4. carcass 5. inner tube 6. valve 7. valve cap 8. four / six-ply tyres 9. cintured tyres 10. tubeless tyres 11. snow / mud / ice tyres 12. spiked tyres 13. hub cap. **II Controls and repairs** 1. tyre pressure check 2. gauge 3. air cylinder 4. tyre repair 5. retreading 6. application of re-inforcement.

## Italiano

Vorrei far controllare la pressione delle gomme.

Può aiutarmi a montare le catene?

Mi occorrono due gomme da ghiaccio, quelle con i chiodi.

Il cerchione è ammaccato. Lo può raddrizzare?

Ho perso il copriruota. Ne ha uno dello stesso tipo?

**I Parti e caratteristiche** 1. battistrada 2. fianco 3. spalla 4. carcassa 5. camera d'aria 6. valvola 7. cappuccio delle valvole 8. gomme a quattro / sei tele 9. gomme cinturate 10. pneumatico senza camera d'aria 11. pneumatici da neve / fango / ghiaccio 12. pneumatici con chiodi 13. copriruota. **II Controlli e riparazioni** 1. controllo della pressione 2. manometro 3. bombola di gonfiaggio 4. vulcanizzazione 5. rigenerazione dei pneumatici 6. applicazione di un rinforzo.

## Français

Je voudrais faire contrôler la pression des pneus.

Pourriez-vous m'aider à mettre les chaînes?

Je voudrais deux pneus cloutés pour le verglas.

La jante est bosselée, pourriez-vous la redresser?

J'ai perdu en enjoliveur, en auriez-vous un autre du même type?

**I Eléments et caractéristiques** 1. bande de roulement 2. flanc 3. épaule 4. carcasse 5. chambre à air 6. valve 7. capuchon de valve 8. pneus à quatre / six toiles 9. pneus ceinturés 10. pneus sans chambre à air 11. pneus pour la neige / la boue / le verglas 12. pneus cloutés 13. enjoliveur de roue. **II Vérifications et réparations** 1. contrôle de la pression 2. manomètre 3. bouteille de gonflage 4. vulcanisation 5. régénération des pneus 6. application d'un emplâtre.

## Deutsch

Ich möchte den Reifendruck prüfen lassen.

Könnten Sie mir helfen, die Ketten zu montieren?

Ich brauche zwei Eisreifen mit Spikes.

Die Felge ist verbeult. Würden Sie sie bitte richten?

Ich habe die Radkappe verloren. Haben Sie eine passende?

**I. Einzelteile und ihre Merkmale** 1. Lauffläche 2. Reifenwand 3. Schulter 4. Karkasse 5. Luftschlauch 6. Ventil 7. Ventilkappe 8. Reifen mit vier / sechs Leinwandeinlagen 9. Gürtelreifen 10. schlauchloser Reifen 11. S-M-Reifen / Eisreifen 12. Reifen mit Spikes 13. Radkappe. **II. Prüfung und Instandsetzung** 1. Reifendruckprüfung 2. Druckmesser 3. Druckflasche 4. Vulkanisierung 5. Runderneuerung 6. Unterlegung einer Verstärkung.

## Español

Quisiera controlar la presión de los neumáticos.

¿Puede ayudarme a montar las cadenas?

Necesito dos gomas contra el hielo, con clavos.

La llanta está abollada. ¿Puede enderezarla?

He perdido el cubrerueda. ¿Tiene otro del mismo tipo?

**I Partes y características** 1. banda de rodamiento 2. lado 3. espalda 4. carcasa 5. cámara de aire 6. valvulita 7. casquillo 8. gomas de cuatro / seis telas 9. gomas cinturadas 10. neumático sin cámara 11. neumático de nieve / de barro / de hielo 12. neumáticos con clavos 13. cubrerueda. **II Controles y reparaciones** 1. control de la presión 2. manómetro 3. bomba de hinchar 4. vulcanización 5. recauchutado de los neumáticos 6. poner un parche.

## Srpsko-hrvatski

Želio zih kontrolirati pritisak u gumama.

Možete li mi pomoći montirati lance?

Potrebne su mi dvije gume za led, one sa čavlima.

Čelični obruč je savijen. Možete li ga ispraviti?

Izgubio sam ukrasni poklopac kotača. Imate li jedan istoga tipa?

**I Dijelovi i karakteristike** 1. vanjski gumeni omotač 2. bok 3. ledja 4. rebra 5. zračnice 6. ventil 7. poklopac ventila 8. gume sa četiri / šest slojeva platna 9. pojačane gume 10. gume bez zračnice 11. gume za snijeg / blato / led 12. gume sa čavlima 13. ukrasni poklopac kotača. **II Kontrola i popravak** 1. kontrola pritiska 2. manometar 3. boca za punjenje 4. vulkanizacija 5. regeneracija guma 6. stavljanje pojačanja.

# APPENDIX

# APPENDICE

# APPENDICE

# ANHANG

# APENDICE

# DODATAK

**CONVERSION OF CAPACITY MEASUREMENTS**
**CONVERSIONE DELLE MISURE DI CAPACITA'**
CONVERSION DES MESURES DE CAPACITE
UMRECHNUNGSTABELLEN DER RAUMMASSE
CORRESPONDENCIA DE LAS MEDIDAS DE CAPACIDAD
USPOREDBA ZAPREMINSKIH MJERA

| L | Imp Gal | USA Gal |
|---|---|---|
| 1 | 0,22 | 0,26 |
| 2 | 0,44 | 0,53 |
| 3 | 0,66 | 0,79 |
| 4 | 0,88 | 1,06 |
| 5 | 1,10 | 1,32 |
| 6 | 1,32 | 1,58 |
| 7 | 1,54 | 1,85 |
| 8 | 1,76 | 2,11 |
| 9 | 1,98 | 2,38 |
| 10 | 2,20 | 2,64 |
| 11 | 2,42 | 2,90 |
| 12 | 2,64 | 3,17 |
| 13 | 2,86 | 3,43 |
| 14 | 3,08 | 3,96 |
| 15 | 3,30 | 3,96 |
| 16 | 3,52 | 4,22 |
| 17 | 3,74 | 4,49 |
| 18 | 3,96 | 4,75 |
| 19 | 4,40 | 5,28 |
| 21 | 4,62 | 5,54 |
| 22 | 4,84 | 5,81 |
| 23 | 5,06 | 6,07 |
| 24 | 5,28 | 6,34 |
| 25 | 5,50 | 6,66 |
| 30 | 6,60 | 7,92 |
| 35 | 7,70 | 9,24 |
| 40 | 8,80 | 10,56 |
| 45 | 9,90 | 11,88 |
| 50 | 11,00 | 13,20 |
| 55 | 12,10 | 14,52 |
| 60 | 13,20 | 15,84 |
| 65 | 14,30 | 17,16 |
| 70 | 15,40 | 18,48 |
| 75 | 16,50 | 19,80 |
| 80 | 17,60 | 21,12 |
| 85 | 18,70 | 22,44 |
| 90 | 19,80 | 23,76 |
| 95 | 20,90 | 25,08 |
| 100 | 22,00 | 26,40 |

**CONVERSION OF CAPACITY MEASUREMENTS**
**CONVERSIONE DELLE MISURE DI CAPACITA'**
CONVERSION DES MESURES DE CAPACITE
UMRECHNUNGSTABELLEN DER RAUMMASSE
CORRESPONDENCIA DE LAS MEDIDAS DE CAPACIDAD
USPOREDBA ZAPREMINSKIH MJERA

| USA Gal | Imp Gal | L |
|---|---|---|
| 1 | 0,83 | 3,78 |
| 2 | 1,67 | 7,57 |
| 3 | 2,50 | 11,35 |
| 4 | 3,33 | 15,14 |
| 5 | 4,16 | 18,92 |
| 6 | 5,00 | 22,71 |
| 7 | 5,83 | 26,49 |
| 8 | 6,66 | 30,28 |
| 9 | 7,50 | 34,06 |
| 10 | 8,33 | 37,85 |
| 11 | 9,16 | 41,63 |
| 12 | 10,00 | 45,42 |
| 13 | 10,83 | 49,20 |
| 14 | 11,66 | 52,99 |
| 15 | 12,49 | 56,77 |
| 16 | 13,33 | 60,56 |
| 17 | 14,16 | 64,34 |
| 18 | 14,99 | 68,13 |
| 19 | 15,83 | 71,91 |
| 20 | 16,66 | 75,70 |
| 21 | 17,49 | 79,48 |
| 22 | 18,33 | 83,27 |
| 23 | 19,16 | 87,05 |
| 24 | 19,99 | 90,84 |
| 25 | 20,82 | 94,62 |

**CONVERSION OF CAPACITY MEASUREMENTS**
**CONVERSIONE DELLE MISURE DI CAPACITA'**
CONVERSION DES MESURES DE CAPACITE
UMRECHNUNGSTABELLEN DER RAUMMASSE
CORRESPONDENCIA DE LAS MEDIDAS DE CAPACIDAD
USPOREDBA ZAPREMINSKIH MJERA

| Imp Gal | USA Gal | L |
|---|---|---|
| 1 | 1,20 | 4,54 |
| 2 | 2,40 | 9,08 |
| 3 | 3,60 | 13,63 |
| 4 | 4,80 | 18,17 |
| 5 | 6,00 | 22,71 |
| 6 | 7,20 | 27,26 |
| 7 | 8,40 | 31,80 |
| 8 | 9,60 | 36,34 |
| 9 | 10,80 | 40,89 |
| 10 | 12,00 | 45,43 |
| 11 | 13,20 | 49,97 |
| 12 | 14,40 | 54,52 |
| 13 | 15,60 | 59,06 |
| 14 | 16,80 | 63,60 |
| 15 | 18,00 | 68,14 |
| 16 | 19,20 | 72,69 |
| 17 | 20,40 | 77,23 |
| 18 | 21,60 | 81,77 |
| 19 | 22,80 | 86,32 |
| 20 | 24,00 | 90,86 |
| 21 | 25,20 | 95,40 |
| 22 | 26,40 | 99,95 |
| 23 | 27,60 | 104,03 |
| 24 | 28,80 | 109,03 |
| 25 | 30,00 | 113,57 |

**CONVERSION OF TYRE PRESSURE MEASUREMENTS**
**CONVERSIONE DELLE MISURE DI PRESSIONE DEI PNEUMATICI**
CONVERSION DES MESURES DE PRESSION DES PNEUS
**REIFENDRUCKTABELLEN**
**CORRESPONDENCIA DE LAS MEDIDAS DE PRESION DE LOS NEUMATICOS**
**USPOREDBA MJERA PRITISAKA U GUMANA**

| atm | psi | atm | psi | atm | psi |
|---|---|---|---|---|---|
| 1 | 14 | 1,7 | 24 | 2,4 | 34 |
| 1,1 | 16 | 1,8 | 26 | 2,5 | 36 |
| 1,2 | 17 | 1,9 | 27 | 2,6 | 37 |
| 1,3 | 18 | 2 | 28 | 2,7 | 38 |
| 1,4 | 20 | 2,1 | 30 | 2,8 | 40 |
| 1,5 | 21 | 2,2 | 31 | 2,9 | 41 |
| 1,6 | 23 | 2,3 | 33 | 3 | 43 |

| | NUMBERS | NUMERALI | NOMBRES | ZAHLEN | NUMERALES | BROJEVI |
|---|---|---|---|---|---|---|
| 1 | one | uno | un | eins | uno | jedan |
| 2 | two | due | deux | zwei | dos | dva |
| 3 | three | tre | trois | drei | tres | tri |
| 4 | four | quattro | quatre | vier | cuatro | četiri |
| 5 | five | cinque | cinq | fünf | cinco | pet |
| 6 | six | sei | six | sechs | seis | šest |
| 7 | seven | sette | sept | sieben | siete | sedam |
| 8 | eight | otto | huit | acht | ocho | osam |
| 9 | nine | nove | neuf | neun | nueve | devet |
| 10 | ten | dieci | dix | zehn | diez | deset |
| 11 | eleven | undici | onze | elf | once | jedanaest |
| 12 | twelve | dodici | douze | zwölf | doce | dvanaest |
| 13 | thirteen | tredici | treize | dreizehn | trece | trinaest |
| 14 | fourteen | quattordici | quatorze | vierzehn | catorce | četrnaest |
| 15 | fifteen | quindici | quinze | fünfzehn | quince | petnaest |
| 16 | sixteen | sedici | seize | sechzehn | diez y seis | šesnaest |
| 17 | seventeen | diciassette | dix-sept | siebzehn | diez y siete | sedamnaest |
| 18 | eighteen | diciotto | dix-huit | achtzehn | diez y ocho | osamnaest |
| 19 | nineteen | diciannove | dix-neuf | neunzehn | diez y nueve | devetnaest |
| 20 | twenty | venti | vingt | zwanzig | veinte | dvadest |
| 21 | twenty-one | ventuno | vingt-et-un | einundzwanzig | veinte y uno | dvadeset jedan |
| 22 | twenty-two | ventidue | vingt-deux | zweiundzwanzig | veinte y dos | dvadeset dva |
| 23 | twenty-three | ventitré | vingt-trois | dreiundzwanzig | veinte y tres | dvadeset tri |
| 24 | twenty-four | ventiquattro | vingt-quatre | vierundzwanzig | veinte y cuatro | dvadeset četiri |
| 25 | twenty-five | venticinque | vingt-cinq | fünfundzwanzig | veinte y cinco | dvadeset pet |
| 26 | twenty-six | ventisei | vingt-six | sechsundzwanzig | veinte y seis | dvadeset šest |
| 27 | twenty-seven | ventisette | vingt-sept | siebenundzwanzig | veinte y siete | dvadeset sedam |
| 28 | twenty-eight | ventotto | vingt-huit | achtundzwanzig | veinte y ocho | dvadeset osam |
| 29 | twenty-nine | ventinove | vingt-neuf | neunundzwanzig | veinte y nueve | dvadeset devet |
| 30 | thirty | trenta | trente | dreissig | treinta | trideset |
| 40 | forty | quaranta | quarante | vierzig | cuarenta | četrdeset |
| 50 | fifty | cinquanta | cinquante | fünfzig | cincuenta | pedeset |
| 60 | sixty | sessanta | soixante | sechzig | sesenta | šezdeset |
| 70 | seventy | settanta | soixante-dix | siebzig | setenta | sedamdeset |
| 80 | eighty | ottanta | quatre-vingts | achtzig | ochenta | osamdeset |
| 90 | ninety | novanta | quatre-vingt-dix | neunzig | noventa | devedeset |
| 100 | one hundred | cento | cent | einhundert | cien / ciento | sto |

**Printed by**
**J. H. HAYNES & Co. Ltd**
**Sparkford Yeovil Somerset**
**ENGLAND**